Aspects
of
Fantasy

Aspects
of
Fantasy

Selected Essays
from the
Second International
Conference
on the
Fantastic in Literature
and Film

Edited by WILLIAM COYLE

Contributions to the Study of Science Fiction and Fantasy, Number 19

GREENWOOD PRESS
Westport, Connecticut • London, England

809.3876
Im8a

Library of Congress Cataloging in Publication Data

International Conference on the Fantastic in Litera-
  ture and Film (2nd : 1981 : Florida Atlantic
  University)
  Aspects of fantasy.

  (Contributions to the study of science fiction and
fantasy, ISSN 0193–6875 ; no. 19)
  Includes bibliographies and index.
  1. Fantasy in mass media—Congresses. I. Coyle,
William. II. Title. III. Series.
P 96.F36I57   1986   809.3'876   84–12787
ISBN 0–313–24608–4 (lib. bdg.)

Library of Congress Catalog Card Number: 84–12787
ISBN: 0–313–24608–4
ISSN: 0193–6875

First published in 1986

Greenwood Press
A division of Congressional Information Service, Inc.
88 Post Road West
Westport, Connecticut 06881

Printed in the United States of America

The paper used in this book complies with the
Permanent Paper Standard issued by the National
Information Standards Organization (Z39.48–1984).

10 9 8 7 6 5 4 3 2 1

Contents

Contents   ix

Aspects
of
Fantasy

Introduction: The Nature of Fantasy

William Coyle

This volume contains twenty-five (about 10 percent) of the papers presented during the second International Conference on the Fantastic in the Arts, held at Florida Atlantic University 18–21 March 1981. Essays were selected for their intrinsic merits and as examples of the heterogeneity of the fantastic mode. Though widely diverse in technique and content, they have been arranged in five groups according to their major emphasis: the creators of fantasy, fantastic creatures, the media, the relationship of fantasy to literary tradition, and the relevance of fantasy to contemporary concerns such as ecology.

In A.D. 2222 when (or if) historians assess the literature of the late twentieth century, the most obvious trend is certain to be the diminished prestige of realism, which dominated the literary imagination for about seventy-five years. The waning of realism has been due in part to the cyclical nature of all artistic movements but more importantly to its seeming irrelevance in a fragmented culture haunted by threats of economic, ecological, nuclear, and other types of disaster. However grim or angry it may be, realism is fundamentally hopeful. It assumes that cause and effect operate in human affairs, that behavior can be analyzed and understood, that a verifiable record of everyday life is both feasible and useful, and that amelioration of injustice or unreason—however unlikely—is at least possible. The realist looks outward at a world he never made; he observes a looking-glass and objectively records what is reflected there. The fantasist looks inward to a world that never was, the jungle of his own psyche; he passes through the looking-glass into a subjective world of distortion and illusion.

The retreat from realism is too widespread and too varied to be encompassed satisfactorily by a single term or definition. In fiction alone, surrealism, meta-realism, anti-realism, non-novel, fabulation, paranoic fantasy, absurdism, homocentric humanism, and a dozen other captions have been proposed, but all seem inadequate. To signify the creation of an alternative world as opposed to realistic transcription of the observable, the term *fantasy* is perhaps most suitable. Negatively, fantasy rejects the empirical, logical world of appearance; positively, it accepts the magical, non-rational, impossible world of imagination. The realist, of course, also uses imagination, but he uses it to create a credible model of what he considers reality; the fantasist imaginatively projects the incredible. It should be stressed that fantasy is not a genre; its literary expression includes science fiction, utopias and dystopias, lampoon and parody, fairy tales, folk legend, allegory, myth, fable, nonsense verse, dream literature, absurdist drama, and numerous other forms. Infinitely adaptable, it lends itself to satire, farce, enchantment, horror, and a wide range of effects. To extend the term beyond limits of usefulness, fantastic qualities can, in fact, be discerned in film, flower arrangement, architecture, music, costume, painting, or any other human activity in which imaginative creativity takes precedence over scientific observation. Fantasy is not a genre but a mode, a way of perceiving human experience.

It requires the suspension of conventional expectations regarding causation, chronology, identity, appearance, and similar matters. To the distortions of subjective perception, it usually adds the illogic of dream and often the terror of nightmare.

Many serious students of fantasy are annoyed by three simplistic generalizations, two of which have been perpetrated in the preceding paragraphs: considering fantasy as merely an alternative to realism, using fantasy as an omnibus term for any expression of the individualized imagination, and regarding fantasy as a byproduct of romanticism. Like most simplifications, each of these contains a kernel of truth. In its openness, its diversity, its subjectivity, and its concern with psychological aberration, fantasy does seem to derive from the romantic impulse. In its infinite variety, it can comfort or appall. Some fantasies afford escape to a remote and secure Shangri-la; more often fantasy presents a cautionary vision of future society extrapolated from Skinner Boxes, clones, ecocide, exploding population, space walks, nuclear stockpiles, and other manifestations of our apocalyptic culture. Similarly, fantasy may offer a pleasant Arcadian reverie or a terrifying journey through the landscape of nightmare. Fantasy lends itself to hallucinations, phobias, and terrors of all kinds; and in its adaptability to delusive projection it is especially suitable to rendition of the characteristic sickness of our age—paranoia. The world of fantasy is inhabited by elves, fairies, nixies, unicorns, and fauns but also by ghouls, witches, vampires, phantoms, doppelgängers, demons, mutants, and monsters. Except for science fiction, which is essentially rationalistic, most fantasy, like other products of the romantic imagination, resists formalization, so that attempts like this one to confine it within definitions and categories are generally futile and ironic exercises in self-defeat.

Both the diversity and the wide appeal of fantasy are demonstrated by the success of the annual conferences held at Florida Atlantic University from 1980 to 1984. In 1979, a conference for teachers of science fiction, organized on a rather modest scale by Professor Robert A. Collins of the English Department, generated enthusiasm and support that burgeoned into a three-day Conference on the Fantastic in the Arts the following year. More than 200 papers were presented by scholars from all parts of the United States and Canada and from a half-dozen European countries; Eric Rabkin and Isaac B. Singer were featured speakers. In 1981, attendance and the number of papers increased; Brian W. Aldiss, Hetty Clews, and John Barth were featured speakers. In 1982, a full program of papers, music, and film was again presented; Samuel R. Delaney, Richard Ellman, and Tom Stoppard were featured speakers on successive evenings. At the 1982 conference, groundwork was laid for a national organization to assure continuation of the annual meetings. Harlan Ellison was guest of honor and a featured speaker in 1983. Leslie Fiedler and Stephen King were guests of honor at the 1984 conference.

The conferences have been subsidized in part by the Thomas Burnett Swann Fund, established by Margaret Gaines Swann in memory of her son, Tom Swann (1928–1976), who taught in the English Department of Florida Atlantic University before his untimely death. He wrote more than twenty novels and many short stories—most of them fantasy adapted from myth and legend, written in a unique and delightful style that has endeared him to a steadily increasing cult of admirers. As Theodore Sturgeon described him, Tom Swann wrote "blissfully and beautifully separated from trend and fashion . . . his own golden thing his own way." A shy and gentle man, Tom Swann would undoubtedly be embarrassed by the uproar committed annually in his name; but he would also, it seems certain, rejoice in the vitality of the fantastic mode in which he worked so effectively.

In compiling this collection of essays, I have received valuable editorial advice and assistance from Marshall B. Tymn, series editor, Eastern Michigan University; Robert A. Collins and Howard D. Pearce, Florida Atlantic University; and, most particularly, the board of advisory editors: Robert Crossley, University of Massachusetts; George P. Landow, Brown University; Roger C. Schlobin, Purdue University; Mark Siegel, University of Wyoming; C. W. Sullivan III, East Carolina University; Raymond H. Thompson, Acadia University; Carl B. Yoke, Kent State University; and Jules Zanger, Southern Illinois University. Dean Jack Suberman of Florida Atlantic University provided released time and secretarial aid. The assistance of Phyllis Surbaugh and Ann M. Hitt in the preparation of the final manuscript has been invaluable. I am most grateful for the help of all these persons and wish to exonerate them from culpability in my errors of omission and commission and in my egregious violation of the three major taboos of fantasy criticism.

I. CREATORS OF FANTASY

Essays in this section focus on authors: their motivation and techniques in the creation of fantasy and the relationship of fantasy to the totality of their work. Alice Parker analyzes feminocentric elements in the poetry and prose of Renée Vivien; Ruth B. Antosh finds camouflaged social protest in the often-ignored short stories of Michel Tremblay; Robert A. Collins examines both literary and psychological functions of fantasy for Thomas B. Swann; and Janet Pérez finds two novels by Gonzalo Torrente Ballester a refutation of the notion that the fantastic is alien to the Spanish temperament. The universality of fantasy is suggested by the cosmopolitan backgrounds of the subjects: British-French, French Canadian, American, and Spanish.

Renée Vivien in the Night Garden of the Spirit

Alice Parker

Dusk and finally nightfall provide a welcome relief from the vulgar spectacle and clamor of daylight reality. Only then can the spirit awaken. The light, if there is any, comes from the last rays of the sun, the moon, a few candles. The garden is often enclosed. It can be a labyrinth, an abandoned and overgrown temple, a somber pagoda, an endless path between the cypresses of purgatory, a palace at the bottom of the sea, a winter landscape frozen in white, magical shapes. The flowers range from the pure violets of the soul and the lilies of death to the dangerous and intoxicating belladonna and other poisonous blooms. The season is most often autumn or winter, when life's forces have slowed their bothersome struggle and the brilliant colors of fallen leaves signal that Persephone can at last return to the underworld. Music and the incantations of women's voices create structures of formal harmony. But under the eyes of the all-seeing goddess the winds of destruction threaten.

Fantastic elements in the poetry and prose of Renée Vivien indicate a desire to construct a discourse from mythic and imaginary sources which goes far beyond the Hellenism and decadence of her circle and of the Parisian literary scene around 1900. Her work is difficult to classify, falling somewhere between symbolism and surrealism. To the characteristics of these systems must be added her cult of Psappha (Sappho), Lesbos, and paganism, as well as her ambivalent but keenly felt relationship to Roman Catholicism. Vivien likewise encoded the communal fantasies of men and women who revolved, like so many satellites, about the charismatic figure of Natalie Barney.[1] In particular this group rejected the "natural," not as a humanistic myth but as an element of humdrum reality; Vivien further associated the phenomenological world of everyday experience negatively with androcentric motifs and the burgeoning energy of the machine age.

In comparison with androcentric literary models, especially Baudelaire, Vivien's language seems precious and hermetic. She was attempting to create a system that was feminocentric in typology, to invent signs that would permit women to live and to write with their bodies, using the rediscovered energy of a repressed libido in the sense that contemporary French feminists explain the concept.[2] Clearly sensing her difference from her family, who wanted her to fulfill the social obligations of a proper daughter of the upper class, from her peers, and later even from her close associates, Vivien explored in her writing the many modulations of a deviant and at times morbid sensibility.[3] As she became obsessed with death, the line between literature and everyday existence blurred. While heroically struggling to preserve her lucidity and her fidelity to her poetic gift, she constructed a language to record an inner journey that took her so far into the twilight world of dreams and visions that finally she could not, or would not, reemerge.

Literary history has been unkind to the work of Renée Vivien and, indeed, often has suppressed it completely for its explicit cult of women. In the estimation of her contemporaries and a number of later writers, Vivien wrote some of the most perfect poetry in the French language, all the more surprising in that it was not her native tongue.[4] When the poet, whose original name was Pauline Mary Tarn, chose the name Renée Vivien around 1900, it was to ally herself with the new century in a symbolic rebirth and to celebrate her escape from her family and the puritanical constraints of British society. There are many ironies in her work and in her personal history. It is regrettable that this woman, who was to travel roads untaken since preclassical Greece for the sake of sisters yet unborn, should have shared her personal and esthetic vision with so few of us, precisely because of her outspoken feminism and lesbianism.[5] Her twenty-odd volumes of poetry and prose, with their unmistakable eroticism and sensuality, continually revert to themes of death and despair. She saw the cults of early Greece, beauty, and women as "serving . . . abandoned altars, reviving the sacred fires of ruined temples, and wreathing broken statues with roses" (Vivien, *Woman*, p. 6). Two verse plays dealing with Sappho portray the poet at the last desperate ebb of her life, before, during, and after her ritually enacted suicide.[6] This involved more than a decadent taste for morbidity and paradox. Vivien was not at all the sensual pagan she claimed to be. Spiritually she was closer to the martyred women of early Christendom like her childhood friend, Violet Shilleto, the "snow-white sister" to whom she confided her "most intimate dreams" (Vivien, *Woman*, p. 13); to the mysteries of the Pagoda, a recurrent figure in her late poetry; and to the Oriental women of the Old Testament (Vivien, *Woman*, p. 68).

Although Vivien decided quite young to become a poet, it was Natalie Barney, the great passion of her life, who introduced her to Sappho and to Greek, who was the indispensable muse. Vivien translated some 250 lines of Sappho's extant work into French and published another volume of translations and adaptations of Greek poems by and about women.[7] The mythological sources she tapped— early Mediterranean, Old Testament, Christian, folk and fairy tales—were complemented by a personal cosmogony. Vivien preferred autumn and winter to spring and summer, night to day, dusk to dawn, and she developed a symbology of flowers, scents, and landscapes. Feeling that new art forms were about to be born in the twentieth century, Vivien used esthetic insights articulated by an avant-garde tradition from the symbolists to the decadents. In paintings she admired "only imaginary landscapes, dream flowers, faces one will never see in life" (Vivien, *Woman*, p. 19). True creation, she felt, is innovative rather than mimetic. Vivien, the mystic, the inveterate wanderer for whom sights and sounds of the Orient became familiar enough to reconstruct with imaginative ease, tempted by and finally succumbing to drugs, explored those parts of the psyche that Freud and surrealism were soon to validate.

The autobiographical narrative *A Woman Appeared to Me* is at once a symbolist re/vision of the Vivien-Barney affair and a bringing into language previously uncharted spaces of women's relationships. Attempting to locate herself with regard to what Freud was to call the "dark continent" of female desire, the narrator says to her alter ego, the androgyne San Giovanni: "You yourself are the bizarre flower of some unknown dream. I try with deliberate sharpness to clarify the obscure causes of which you are so paradoxical a product" (Vivien, *Woman*, p. 19). The poet mystified many of her contemporaries by the roles and the decor she created for herself. A vivid though admittedly biased description was left by a later lover of Natalie Barney, the painter Romaine Brooks:

There comes before me the dark heavily curtained room, overreaching itself in lugubrious effects: grim lifesized Oriental figures sitting propped up in chairs, phosphorescent Buddhas glowing dimly in the folds of black draperies. The air is heavy with perfumed incense. A curtain draws aside and Renée Vivien stands before us attired in Louis XVI male costume. Her straight blond hair falls to her shoulders, her flower-like face is bent down; she does not lift it even to greet us. . . . We lunch seated on the floor Oriental fashion and scant food is served on ancient Damascus ware, cracked and stained. During the meal Renée Vivien leaves us to bring in from the garden her pet frogs and a serpent which she twists round her wrist.[8]

In his biographical study, Paul Lorenz speculates that the early death of her father may have been a significant trauma in Vivien's development (Lorenz, *Sappho*, p. 30). Two other elements may have been of far greater significance. The first was the absence of a strong and supportive mother, a mother like Alice Pike Barney or Sidonie Colette. Evidence is scanty since Vivien's papers have not emerged from obscurity, but we know that when Renée was in England she appeared to avoid her mother, spending time instead with relatives in London or with her sister and brother-in-law in Scotland. The second was a literary and cultural tradition which, since the publication of Diderot's *The Nun* in the 1760s, had relegated women-identified women to the ranks of the "damned." Vivien likewise was ambivalent toward her chosen vocation, or avocation, influenced by a tradition that treated "lady" poets with condescension (Vivien, *Woman*, p. 48).

In her work Vivien constructs two opposing forces, the spiritual and the erotic, both of which act on the personae from without. Through an elaborate system of correspondence, the forces are color-coded, assigned certain flowers, perfumes, times of the day, and seasons of the year. They are activated in a series of interiors and gardens. The original garden, to which we try to return and which may represent early childhood or paradise (from which the poet may have been prematurely excluded), becomes the real and mythic landscape of Mytilene on the island of Lesbos. To this homeland Renée and Natalie had journeyed as prodigals, but real life intervened in the form of a possessive new lover of Renée's. They were unable to realize their dream of a perfect love, which for each had assumed such different forms, or their dreams of a school for beautiful young poets, which the ascetic Renée decided was Natalie's excuse for a harem. The shifting scenes of her poetry and prose represent symbolically Renée Vivien's real and imaginary travels and her seeming inability to become rooted. At the close of *A Woman Appeared to Me*, the garden has become the walled enclosure extending from a reassuringly mundane English-style apartment. It is, however, a dangerous area that now represents for the poet the garden of earthly delights in the medieval sense of carnal temptation. Imagining herself in exile like another Dante, clinging without much hope to an unlikely Beatrice, the poet creates a palace in her late poems that is the landscape of Purgatory, a strange and somber land that more and more seems like home.[9]

The land of the blessed, which appears in Vivien's work only once, is her projection of a future of "Eternal Music," representing the "Infinite" or pure form, harmony, and beauty (Vivien, *Woman*, p. 24). Hell is represented by the discord of the machine age, the screaming of children, howling sirens, and the "pounding of inexpert pianists" (Vivien, *Woman*, p. 27). Vivien was a talented musician who considered her poems lyrical in a generic sense and set her autobiographical novel in a context of musical referents. Music, poetry, and love were the means to ascend to higher planes of existence. The problem with the latter was that Natalie Barney could scarcely breathe the rarefied air that Vivien required. But her contemporaries were wrong to accuse Vivien of "being in love with love" (Lorenz, *Sappho*, pp. 73–74). There is a mystical strain in her work that becomes more and more pronounced. In *A Woman Appeared to Me*, the poet is led to commit a symbolic murder in order to free her inner vision from the phenomenological restrictions of real life: "I have killed her! Then she would remain forever my virgin Priestess. She would be the pure whiteness of my dreams, the Inaccessible, the Untarnishable" (Vivien, *Woman*, p. 36).

Barney and Vivien were of one mind about the political significance of their feminism and the cult of Sappho. The reason there were so few women writers, Vivien felt, was that women were obliged by literary convention to write about men. This was "enough to paralyze any effort toward Beauty" (Vivien, *Woman*, p. 48). However, neither writer betrays any consciousness that women can be oppressed by other categories such as race or class. It was as a woman writing to women that Vivien set herself the task of recreating for her time the lyrical discourse of Sappho's verses. With incredible persistence she examined the slightest variations of her inner thoughts, feelings, and perceptions, not as Narcissus but as an analyst, translating the life within into an elaborate grid of signs and symbols. Spatializing metaphors relate inner and outer geography. The desolate city of Toledo, with the church dedicated to Our Lady of Fevers, welcomes the narrator of *A Woman Appeared to Me* when her personal life is most painful. The "cruel pallor" of the Madonna of lepers, plagues, and death, her distorted face, and stagnant eyes convey an "Image of Mortality" that is likened to Vivien's beloved Vally (Vivien, *Woman*, pp. 58–59). This is one of her most haunting and disturbing poems, transferred in its entirety to her prose narrative in a good example of the self-reflection evident in her work.

In the inner environment of her grief stemming from the double loss of Violet, her friend of the spirit, and Natalie, her great love, Renée is struck by the sterility of her writing—"useless, helpless, feeble" (Vivien, *Woman*, p. 60). A consistent element in the poetry and prose is an identification with the North; she calls herself a daughter of the North and the snow who often dreams of sleeping beneath "a shroud of ice" ("La Fourrure," *Poèmes*, I, 185). In a short dramatic narrative Svanhild, the principal persona, imagines one evening that the wild swans she has been awaiting have returned, and she disappears into the fog on a mountain path above the fjord in pursuit of them.[10] The North may represent clarity and the finality of death or the mists that veil reality in mystery (Vivien, *Woman*, p. 60). While it may signify inspiration and deliverance from eros, the North also signifies ultimate purity of form for Vivien.

Because of her very personal cosmogony and symbology which make her writing difficult to decipher and because of an unpopular literary canon, readers have been overly hasty in attaching derivative labels to Vivien's poetic vision.[11] It is more productive to see Vivien as an early practitioner of "ecriture feminine," female inscription in writing.[12] She knew that her writing, insofar as it brought herself and other women into being, was a subversive activity. Catherine Stimpson points out: "Literary texts do have the strength to subvert ordinary modes of consciousness. Naming the strange, unfamiliar, unpalatable, and alarming, they can, potentially, rearrange habitual modes of thought and feeling.[13] Critics like Hélène Cixous go further and prescribe a program of psychic regression to the sources of preconscious existence that have been repressed in the process of phallologocentric cultural development.[14] Vivien tries to name aspects of the female libidinal economy that have been repressed. Certainly she dares to name the multiple circumstances of women loving women and defines with discretion the paneroticism of the female body. She also knows that she is not free; her androgyne, San Giovanni, is more asexual than bisexual in the sense that contemporary feminists use the term "bisexual."

Vivien is not afraid to name the violence that can be an element of sexual attraction: "I felt a sudden burning tenderness for this creature so like fruit and roses. I desired her like blue water at dawn. And then the cruel need to bite those lips naively offered for a kiss, to bruise that flesh like rosy eglantines,

became so violent that I abruptly took my leave" (Vivien, *Woman*, p. 66). The
young love that arouses such conflicting desires represents spring, opals, and
lilacs. But in spring, continues the narrator, "the defiance of young sprouts
against inevitable death, the useless striving of life, weighed me down with
suffering" (Vivien, *Woman*, p. 63), making the reader think more of Eliot's
Wasteland than of Botticelli's *Primavera*. In rejecting this hopeful new love, a
reincarnation of eros and life, the narrator identifies with the race of self-willed
exiles represented by the Oriental women of the Old Testament.

Poetry and passion are, however, interdependent. The poet is condemned to
suffer, to find her old love reborn like the phoenix and with it her poetic inspiration, her power to name. It does not matter whether the love was real, because
everything is in the power of words. In this sense everything and nothing are
autobiographical. Like the surrealists Vivien believed in the power of images,
in the consonance of inner and outer reality as in the conclusion of *A Woman
Appeared to Me*:

The sky was now a marvelous roof of cedar, ivory, and mother-of-pearl. The night
seemed a mystic palace of Boabdil. . . . A dead serpent was lying at our feet. . . . A slanting
last ray of moonlight struck a strange light from the tarnished gold of its green scales
which seemed to quiver in slow waves. And I remembered San Giovanni's enigmatic
phrases: "Dead serpents come to life beneath the gaze of those who love them. The
magic eyes of Lilith revive them as moonlight moves stagnant water."

Our Lady of Fevers suddenly corrupted the garden with her fatal breath. Digitalis and
belladonna offered her their perfumes and their poisons. . . . A leprous moon wasted the
trees, and the red roses bled like new wounds. (Vivien, *Woman*, p. 88)

The narrative ends on an ambiguous note with the poet caught between conflicting
impulses. The later poetry expresses the poet's need to free herself from the
snares of love and language and life in an unending series of invocations to
death.

In her earliest books of poetry, published in 1901, Vivien had evoked mournful
landscapes ("Les Yeux gris"), frightful voices weeping horribly from the depths
of silence ("Sonnet"), and tortuous, anguished flights of bats with bruised wings
("Chanson"). By 1903 there are continuous images of drowning (*Evocations*)
and in "Velleda," a poem about a Druid priestess and prophet, murders, broken
empires, temples without hope, and mourning veils of exiled women (*Poèmes*,
I, 112). A new political energy animates a volume called *The Venus of the Blind*
(1903) as in "Litany of Hatred," where the poet writes of hatred for the crowd
and laws and society, inspired, she claims, by the "dark breath of Lilith"
(*Poèmes*, I, 217). Although the temple has been abandoned, the goddess still
watches over the earth with her "eternal eyes" (*Venus of the Blind*, p. 201).
However, the title poem celebrates the black goddess whom nothing living can
approach and whose space is the eternal night (*Venus of the Blind*, p. 183).

At the Hour of the Joined Hands (1906) recalls familiar iconography of ruined
temples and gardens in decay. In "Je connais un étang" the poet refers to the

water of a pond, mirroring illusions, where women will die like ephemeral insects (*Poèmes*, II, 69–70). Comparing herself to Dante and Lear, beaten by the storm, she complains that her family and friends have repulsed her, vomiting outrageous insults ("Sous la rafale," *Poèmes*, II, 79–80). "Le Pilori" gives us strong images of the poet's sense of personal martyrdom (*Poèmes*, II, 112). The fairy-tale decor with "fruits of precious stones" in a poem about destiny, "Ermine," is an ironic attempt to write her own scenario (*Poèmes*, II, 84–85). Certain that no one will ever read her poems ("Vaincue," *Poèmes*, II, 113), that she must perpetually confront an illness that is negligible but deep, that she has lost her strength, her dreams, and her faith pursuing an elusive glory (*Poèmes*, II, 117), the poet creates a land of mystery where a guide will lead her, pale as Aladdin, into a terrible garden ("Ermine," *Poèmes*, II, 84–85). Finally, in the garden of the world everything dies (*Poèmes*, II, 114), and the poet, like the leper, is an alien and an exile.

In *Sillages* (Furrows), published in 1908, Vivien writes that she has looked with her eyes blindly open on the terrible, incomprehensible universe. Images of inconstancy (April, rainbows, the moon) reinforce her identity as "daughter of the night," which now signals the dangerous inward journey the poet embarked on in her last years and from which she was not to reemerge. "Nighttime Beings" with whom she classifies herself now exclusively (*Extinguished Torches*, II, 197) are deceptive, fearful, intangible. The nocturnal landscape persists in three volumes published after Renée Vivien's death in 1909 at the age of thirty-two. No longer is her destiny merely mysterious, symbolized by the dark cypress and ebony cathedrals of death. No longer can she fly north with the seagulls to the mythical land of the dead. Her wings are broken and her fate is with despised things (*Poèmes*, II, 229–30). The poet feels that she has lost control, perhaps is possessed (*Poèmes*, II, 231, 234, 237), but never completely loses her faith in posterity. The most disturbing of the posthumous books is *Haillons* (Rags), where the meditations on time and death take the form of terrifying visions. In her epitaph Renée Vivien declared that she had found peace and joy, having "for the love of Death pardoned the crime Life" (*Poèmes*, II, 256).

The Muse of the Violets, as she was called, whom her fellow poets "admired, as connoisseurs, for the perfection of classical form in her verse, its harmonious rhythm, the purity of her French," inscribed her texts with a host of known and unknown female spirits.[15] She wove her words in and out of women's bodies and psyches, anticipating the project of feminists in future evenings "of roses and flames" as mysterious as Hindu temples to name what phallocentric discourse could never know or say (*The Muse of the Violets*, p. 72). At the end of "the terrible and long pilgrimage," Vivien wrote just before her death that she sometimes felt someone lifting her up, a woman reaching out her hand so that together they might beseech the "tranquil Divine Night" (*Muse of the Violets*, p. 78). She whose dreams were conditioned by hearing the bird's song anticipated the disdain future generations would have for her work (*Muse of the Violets*, pp. 72, 77). We for whom she sang are beginning to rediscover in her poetry and fiction links to Sappho and Lilith and the rebellious women of the Old Testament like Queen Vashti, who defied King Ahasuerus in a gesture that she felt would free all women who heard of it, choosing the freedom of the desert where she would take her chances with other wild things, where "dead serpents revive under the rays of the moon."[16]

NOTES

1. The best work on the Barney circle is George Wickes, *The Amazon of Letters* (New York: Popular Library, 1978). Natalie Barney did not establish her famous salon at 20 rue Jacob until after the death of Renée Vivien.

2. See the excellent review-essay by Elaine Marks, "Women and Literature in France," *Signs* 3 (Summer, 1978), pp. 832–42.

3. The best biography of Renée Vivien is Paul Lorenz, *Sappho 1900: Renée Vivien* (Paris: Julliard, 1977); hereafter cited in the text. It remains incomplete and is often speculative; it will have to be redone when Vivien's papers come to light.

4. Renée Vivien, *A Woman Appeared to Me* (*Une Femme m'apparut*), trans. Jeanette Foster, introduction by Gayle Rubin (Bates City, Mo.: Naiad Press, 1976); hereafter cited in the text. The excellent introductory essay provides accurate information from a radical feminist perspective.

5. It is particularly surprising and disappointing that Monique Wittig, in *The Lesbian Body* (New York: Morrow, 1975), ignores Vivien both as a foremother and as a model.

6. *Poèmes de Renée Vivien* (New York: Arno Press, 1975). This edition is a reprint of *Poésies completes*, 2 tomes (Paris: Lemerre, 1934). Translations from this edition are my own. The suicide plays involving Sappho are "La Mort de Psappha," I, 88–93, and "Dans un verger," II, 129–44.

7. "Sappho" in *Poèmes*, I, 143–78; "Les Kitharedes" in *Poèmes*, II, 4–45.

8. Reprinted in *Paris Review* 61 (Spring, 1975), 102.

9. See especially "Le Palais du poete," *Poèmes*, II, 227, and "Cypres du Purgatoire," *Poèmes*, II, 225.

10. Renée Vivien, *La Dame à la louve* (Paris: Régine Desforges, 1977), pp. 199–202.

11. In "Lesbian Intertextuality," a recent attempt at reevaluation, Elaine Marks leaves the reader poised between a judgment she ascribes to Colette without citing a source that Vivien wrote "sentimental imitative poetry," and the desire to reintegrate Vivien into the canon with the timorous opinion that her work represents "interesting attempts by a lesbian to write as a lesbian about lesbianism." *Homosexualities and French Literature* (Ithaca: Cornell University Press, 1979), pp. 367–77.

12. For an explanation of this concept see Hélène Cixous, "The Laugh of the Medusa," *Signs* 1 (1976), 875–93.

13. Catharine R. Stimpson, "The Power to Name" in *The Prism of Sex: Essays in the Sociology of Knowledge*, ed. Julia A. Sherman and Evelyn Tordon Bock (Madison: University of Wisconsin Press, 1979), p. 56.

14. Hélène Cixous, *La Venue à l'écriture* (Paris: Union Generale d'Editions, 1977), pp. 20–24.

15. Renée Vivien, *The Muse of the Violets*, trans. Margaret Porter and Catharine

Kroger, introduction by Louise Faure-Favier (Bates City, Mo.: Naiad Press, 1977), p. 14; hereafter cited in the text.

16. "Le Voile de Vashti" in *La Dame à la louve*, p. 144. When Vashti refuses the king, she declares, "I will not unveil my sacred forehead in front of the crowd of drunken courtesans. The impure eyes of men must not profane the mystery of my face. The order of King Ahasuerus is an outrage to my woman's and queen's pride" (p. 139).

Michel Tremblay and the Fantastic of Violence

Ruth B. Antosh

The controversial Quebec playwright Michel Tremblay is best known for his visceral dramas depicting the bleakness of life in the québecois "ghetto" of Montreal. His use of *joual*, the earthy, harshly vocalic dialect of French Canada, has been hailed by some critics as realistic and supremely suited to his theme of the isolation and hopelessness of lower-class French Canadians. Others have deplored what they see as the excessive profanity and vulgarity of his writing. Such plays as *Les Belles Soeurs* (1968), a portrait of the empty lives of working-class housewives in Montreal's grim Plateau Mont-Royal district; *Bonjour, Là, Bonjour* (1974), a study of a large Quebec family and the impossible demands it makes on its members; and *A toi pour toujours, ta Marie-Lou* (1971), a story of an unhappy marriage which ends in a double suicide, are examples of this playwrights's stark view of the predicament not only of the poverty-stricken Québecois, but by extension of all victims of social inequities. Concerning his goals as a playwright, Tremblay himself has declared: "I am here to denounce injustice, and I have a feeling that's what I am going to be doing for the rest of my days."[1]

Given this "socially conscious" approach to the theater, which seeks to jar the audience into an awareness of the hell the characters live in, it seems surprising that Tremblay's first published work was a collection of Gothic short stories in which the real world is eclipsed by the Otherworld: vampires, witches, monsters, and madmen fill this work, entitled *Stories for Late Night Drinkers* (*Contes pour Buveurs Attardés*), published in 1966. Why, one wonders, did Tremblay, an author known for his dual obsessions with theater and with social/political subject matter, begin his literary career with this flight into the fantastic? Little critical attention has been given to this remarkable first work, and the question of his reasons for writing it has not been satisfactorily resolved. Is *Stories for Late Night Drinkers*, as Tremblay's admirers among the Quebec literary avant-garde doubtless believe, a youthful caprice, a frivolous deviation from his other, more purposeful work? Or is there, in fact, some essential link between the work and his theater? A cursory reading of the collection, which includes stories with familiar Gothic-sounding titles like "The Vampire Moon," "The Hanged Man," "The Ghost of Don Carlos," and "The Eye of the Idol," reveals no apparent connection between this work and the plays for which Tremblay is famous. One is tempted to subscribe to the time-honored theory that realistic writers need to turn to fantasy from time to time to renew their creative energies and to escape the real world that normally provides the basis for their writing. Robert Irwin's observation that "one mark of a lively mind is its desire to depart from the familiar and the conventional"[2] would seem to apply to Tremblay.

This theory that Tremblay is seeking escape from here-and-now by writing about ghosts and vampires seems to be supported not only by his choice of subject matter but also by his decision to situate his stories outside the normal confines of culture, geography, and time. While Tremblay sets most of his plays in the same seedy district of Montreal, he places his Gothic stories in nameless countries with few identifiable cultural characteristics, or in imaginary kingdoms with exotic-sounding names like Paganka, the land of the Mountain with no Summit, and the Island of Birds, where the flowers, trees, and stones are pink. Quebec is never even mentioned in these stories, and it seems clear that Tremblay is striving for the timeless universality of fairy tale and myth.

Despite these indications that in *Stories for Late Night Drinkers* Tremblay is searching for escape from the drabness and misery of the real world, a careful reading of his stories reveals that, in fact, Tremblay is working with some of the same obsessive themes around which his best-known plays are written, themes that are related to man's unhappy, earthbound condition. Tremblay's major obsession in his theater is with the subtle violence done to the Québecois during centuries of poverty and oppression. It is surely no accident, then, that the most striking aspect of his Gothic stories is the tremendous violence which pervades them, lending cohesiveness to an otherwise disparate group of tales. This violence is not the psychological anguish of a Poe but physical violence that is usually swift, remorseless, and unprovoked; more than half the stories end in death. Tremblay's preoccupation with violence in *Stories for Late Night Drinkers* can be illustrated by a partial listing of the means by which his characters are dispatched; they are variously strangled, trampled, stabbed, pushed off a ladder, torn to pieces by invisible monsters, beaten to death with a stone, and, in perhaps Tremblay's most memorable story, roasted alive and eaten for dinner.

Since no murders occur on stage in Tremblay's plays, it is natural at this point to ask what relationship, if any, exists between the lurid, ghastly violence found in his Gothic stories and the subtle political and psychological violence that occurs in his plays.[3] I suggest that the link may be found, not in the type or degree of violence but rather in the nature of the relationship between the aggressors and their victims. I have noted that similar patterns or types of relationships between aggressors and victims may be discerned throughout his writings. These patterns reveal Tremblay's deepest obsessions and can be divided into three categories: violence against a member of the opposite sex, violence against one's own kin, and violence against God. Let us examine each of these categories in greater detail. In our analysis we shall focus on *Stories for Late Night Drinkers*, with brief references to the plays.

The first of these categories is violence with distinctly erotic overtones, involving the victimization of one sex by the other. In one story, a variation of the Bluebeard tale entitled "The 13th Wife of Baron Klugg," a husband terrifies his wife by showing her the bodies of her predecessors and then strangles her to death. A new twist to Tremblay's version of this old folktale is that the wife knows in advance that her husband intends to kill her, yet she does little to save her own life. It is also interesting to note that in Tremblay's story the taboo motif of the original folktale is missing: the wife has not gone into a forbidden room or disobeyed her husband in any way. She is innocent of all wrongdoing, and the husband's act of violence seems completely gratuitous. In another story, "The Ghost of Don Carlos," a ghost is conjured up at a seance, and a lovely young woman approaches him, drawn by some erotic impulse. The ghost puts out his hand as if to caress her cheek; as she stands transfixed, he claws her face to shreds. Again, the violence seems unprovoked and the victim does not resist.

Tremblay's most grimly refined tale of erotic violence is "Gentle Warmth." In this story, a wealthy, middle-aged nobleman lures a young peasant girl into his castle, promising her trinkets in return for sexual favors. Overjoyed at the prospect of spending a night in a real bed and intrigued by the elegant manners of the mysterious aristocrat, the girl accepts. Upon entering the castle, she notices a magnificent brass dress encrusted with gems beside the fireplace. She begs to be allowed to try on the dress; her host acquiesces, and she discovers too late that she is trapped inside an instrument of torture that is actually an oven. The story ends as the fiendish villain exclaims, "Mademoiselle, I am happy to have you for dinner."[4] This tale, with its overtones of ritualistic blood rites and medieval tortures, is all the more appalling in that the unwitting victim is tricked into asking for her own death (it is her idea to try on the dress, and her willingness seems to be a necessary part of the ritualistic killing). The act of cannibalism with which the story presumably concludes seems to be a superb metaphor for victimization of all types, for it involves not only the death of the victim but also his/her total absorption by the aggressor. One is reminded of the belief among primitive peoples that when a man devours his enemy, the soul of the person consumed becomes bound to the consumer and thus forever subservient to him. It is of interest to note that the story can be read on the level of political allegory as the depiction of the exploitation of a trusting peasant by a devious member of the ruling class. In any case, it is important that in all three stories discussed so far, the victim submits meekly with no attempts at resistance.

Although Tremblay has written two very brief stories in which the woman is the aggressor who kills or abuses her passive lovers, I feel that his stories of violence done to women by men are more inspired. Tremblay has often stated that he feels a particular sympathy for women; and two of his best-known plays, *Les Belles Soeurs* and *A toi pour toujours, ta Marie-Lou*, deal with the unhappiness of wives neglected or misunderstood by their husbands. It should be apparent from these brief sketches that Tremblay is bent on exposing the hostility that he sees as innate in male/female relationships.

If associations between the sexes are fraught with violence in Tremblay's stories, so are actual blood relationships. The second of the three patterns of violence in his works involves hostile and unhealthy dealings between members of the same family. In his plays, Tremblay portrays the family as a sort of trap or prison which stifles its members and inhibits their growth as individuals. The same negativity in regard to family ties can be seen in *Stories for Late Night Drinkers*, but to a more extreme degree. In this work, Tremblay does not aim at criticizing family ties as impediments to personal freedom; rather, he seems intent on totally destroying all sense of the inviolability of blood relationships. Kinship ties are portrayed as tainted by blood, perversion, and violence. The two categories of violence mentioned so far might be said to meet in the story "Amenachem," which tells of a lecherous king's incestuous desire for his daughter. In order to gain his daughter's love, he sells his soul to a sorceress and brings disaster to himself, his innocent daughter, and his kingdom. In another story, "Wolfgang, on His Return," a father discovers that his young son is possessed by a demon. The reader versed in Gothic lore expects the man at least to attempt to save his son from the forces of evil which inhabit him, perhaps by thrusting a crucifix at him or by enlisting the aid of a priest; instead, the father promptly and remorselessly beats the unresisting boy to death with a stone. Where are paternal love and devotion, one wonders? The ultimate story of violence between kinsmen is surely "Erika's Steps," the description of a hostile relationship between fraternal twins. The twins' mutual hatred leads to an ingenious double murder in which each twin kills the other: the brother kills his sister by pushing her off a stepladder, and she retaliates by returning from the grave to push him off the same fatal ladder. Thus, in this story, each twin is both victim and aggressor, and violence may be said to have canceled itself out, at least in this particular family; the reader can only wonder why either was foolish enough to climb the ladder in the first place. Once again, there seems to be an almost masochistic cooperation on the part of the victims in this story. In the three tales discussed, Tremblay manages to attack and demystify such basic blood relationships as those between father and son, brother and sister, and father and daughter.

We have seen how Tremblay exposes the hostility in human relationships. This sense of all-pervasive violence is extended to a cosmic dimension in a pair of stories dealing with violence between man and his gods. The deities in Tremblay's tales are imaginary pagan ones, but the absence of the Christian God from this work does not necessarily exclude the possibility that he is commenting indirectly on the failing relationship between man and God within the Christian context.

Tremblay has written two stories dealing with hostility between man and his gods (or, to be more exact, between man and his goddesses, for in both stories the deity is feminine). In each case, it is man who is the aggressor, and neither goddess initially offers any show of resistance when attacked. Both tales might in this sense be said to illustrate the tendency which we have already remarked for victims to submit passively to their assailants. Maouna, the goddess in the story by the same name, allows her human attackers to burn her to death, and the goddess in the second story, entitled "Lady Barbara's Last Outing," calmly submits as her assailant stabs her in the neck. However, unlike all the other victims thus far discussed, these female deities have cosmic powers which are only strengthened when their souls are released from their bodies. The futility of man's attempts to destroy his gods and gain control over the universe becomes clear when Maouna rises from her own ashes and vows to take revenge on mankind by reducing the world to chaos: "Your universe will be seething with worms and grasshoppers and madmen will be the most rational among you; and clouds will fall from the thornbushes; and woman will suckle leeches; and the churches will be full of vermin; and roads will no longer cross" (Tremblay, *Stories*, p. 54).

In similar fashion, the goddess in "Lady Barbara's Last Outing" promptly turns into a strange bird after she is killed and flies away, crying to her attacker: "Did you dare to think that such a vile and stupid being as you could ever vanquish me?... Know that everlasting war has been declared between the Universe and Me!" (Tremblay, *Stories*, pp. 45–56). Thus, although in each case the goddess's body is destroyed, her soul remains and her powers seem in some mysterious way increased. In each story it is clear that the seemingly passive, victimized deities are about to turn the tables and demolish their attackers. In the end, then, it seems apparent that even the aggressors among mankind, who in Tremblay's other stories meet with no resistance from their victims and are seemingly taking over the earth, will be destroyed by the gods. The violent will not take over the earth because it is about to be laid in ruins by the cosmic powers which control it; thus, there is a kind of Old Testament justice in Tremblay's *Stories for Late Night Drinkers*. Those who live by brutality will die by it, and if in Tremblay's tales the meek do not inherit the earth, neither do the strong and the violent. We are left with a sense that he believes a solution to man's ills can come only after the complete destruction of the world as it now exists.

By now it should be apparent that Tremblay did not write *Stories for Late Night Drinkers* as an escape from his concerns with injustice and oppression. His aim seems to be a subtle form of subversion of the existing social order; for using the seemingly innocuous vehicle of a collection of Gothic tales, he has managed to attack the "sacredness" of the relationships on which society is based—those between man and woman, between family members, and between man and God—by showing that they all involve violence and victimization. Tremblay seems particularly obsessed by the victim who is submissive and even willing, and I would suggest that by examining victimization from so many different angles in *Stories for Late Night Drinkers*, he is venting his personal frustrations over the general passiveness of oppressed peoples the world over in an attempt to exorcise his own demons. In so doing, he has created a collection of what might be termed adult fairy tales whose ultimate effect is to provoke indignation, outrage, and rebellion.

NOTES

1. Michel Tremblay, interview in *Canadian Theater Review*, no. 5 (1979), p. 37.
2. Robert Irwin, *The Game of the Impossible: A Rhetoric of Fantasy* (Urbana: University of Illinois Press, 1976), p. 182.
3. There are only two plays by Tremblay in which a violent death occurs: *Sainte Carmen de la Main*, in which the heroine is shot down by gangsters, and *A toi pour toujours, ta Marie-Lou*, in which the husband kills himself, his consenting wife, and their young son by driving his car into a highway bridge. In both cases, however, the deaths occur offstage and are announced after the fact in the tradition of classical French theater.
4. Michel Tremblay, *Stories for Late Night Drinkers*, trans. Michael Bullock (Vancouver: Intermedia Press, 1977), p. 96; hereafter cited in the text.

Swann on Swann: The Conscious Uses of Fantasy

Robert A. Collins

Myth—classical, Celtic, Hebrew, Egyptian, Zoroastrian—was a lifelong obsession with Thomas Burnett Swann. His careful research notes, some of which survive among his papers, indicate both the wide range of his reading and his deep and abiding interest. Mythography as an influence on his work has not gone unnoticed, of course; the most basic sources from *Who's Who in America* to the *Science Fiction Encyclopedia* remark on it. Two of the papers presented in this forum last year (1980) explored it: Jerry Holt's analysis of the Zoroastrianism in "Vashti" and Casey Frederick's study of what he called "the pastoral inversion of classical heroic myth" in several of the Mediterranean novels.[1] In both interviews and letters, Swann freely identified his mythic sources as well as his classical models, from Vergil to Mary Renault.

One can safely predict neither theme nor character from a knowledge of the classical models, however. The author's use of the traditional materials is highly idiosyncratic. As Fredericks observed, Swann cannot be said to "re-tell" classic legends at all; rather, he reshapes, recreates to reflect the "inner landscape" of his own vision of a world. That "growing sense of unease about Man's continuing violation of the natural order on this planet," an attitude identified by Peter Nichols as characteristic of Swann's audience, serves to link modern sensibilities with Swann's treatment of the legendary material. The "counter-narrative" (Nichols's term) focused on the doomed encounter between the creatures of legend and "insensitive, triumphant Mankind" appeals to the sensibilities of the ecologically aware. Thus, though Swann's settings are recognizably ancient and historically accurate, he did not write historical novels in the sense that Mary Renault does: the focus on the legendary beings themselves contradicts the expectations fostered by the modern concept of history. Rather, the materials of ancient myth and legend are endowed with the remoteness and glamour of fantasy romance, while the themes, as they emerge, appeal covertly to the contemporary mind.

As his letters and interviews make plain, Swann's approach to his materials was neither naive nor merely intuitive; he knew what he was doing. I wish to explore here, briefly and in a preliminary way, Swann's own comments about his work in order to sketch a portrait of the artist consciously involved in the reinterpretation of myth—the artist aware of the processes and rewards inherent in the nature of fantasy. His own remarks will demonstrate, I think, that his attraction to the ancient world was partly dictated by a deep distaste for the ugliness, ethical as well as physical, of the modern world and by the possibility of beauty and ethical freedom represented in the pagan cultures of the Mediterranean. On the personal level, he saw fantasy as a method both of exorcism of repressions and of compensation for values missing in the modern world.

The esthetic bent of Swann's mind is already clear in a set of charming letters written to his mother during his first European cruise, when he was nineteen and a student at Duke University. Botticelli's Venus, he writes, is "the loveliest woman in all of painting" despite her "remoteness," which the critics translate as coldness, but which is for Swann an enhancement of her glamour. He prefers the Roman Pantheon, which "seemed by the power of moon-magic to live again," to all those "gilded angels and bovine saints" at St. Peter's Cathedral. "Pre-Christian architecture," he reports, "appeals to me much more." Yet he is entranced by the myth that the beard of Michelangelo's Moses hides a portrait of Victoria Coronna, "the woman Michelangelo loved all his life."

It is, of course, a giant step from these impressions of a European tour to the corn goddesses and pagan lovers of his mythical fantasies, but the drift is clear. Swann's early muse was devoted to poetry—he wrote little fiction until he felt himself exhausted as a poet. Several early novels, as yet unpublished, treated the settings and themes of ancient Crete and the Greek islands in the manner of Mary Renault, focusing on the human personae, with legendary figures either appearing fleetingly in the background or given modern, "rationalized" explanations. He was still concerned about the demands of history in creating his first great success, "Where Is the Bird of Fire?", the novella that established his British reputation in 1962. In a note to Ann Peyton, a colleague at Florida Southern College and later at Florida Atlantic University, he remarked, "I've just finished a novelette about Romulus and Remus, a Faun and a Dryad, for the English fantasy magazine I sometimes contribute to. . . . I wanted to have Remus, not Romulus, survive to build Rome, but legend was against me. I had to kill my Dryad too. . . . It was terribly depressing" (5 July 1961). In the novel Remus represents the wise passivity of nature, Romulus the warlike aggression of the empire-builders. As twins they symbolize the opposing forces in most of Swann's work and by implication a dichotomy in the minds of humankind. Romulus is the male principle, reason, patriarchy, military and industrial progress; Remus and his dryad lover, Mellonia, represent the passive female principle, intuition, nature, magic, the mother. Historically, Romulus won, and in his earliest work Swann feels constrained to represent history, even in a fantasy, but he finds it depressing.

Swann's correspondence with Mary Renault (she did not like Thea in *Day of the Minotaur*; Swann said she told him, "I hoped Thea would fall overboard and drown on the voyage to the Isles of the Blest") tended to reinforce the claims of history for a time. Writing to a friend, Robert A. Roehm, about *Will-o-the-Wisp*, a novella involving the poet Robert Herrick, who served as priest in a rural parish, he remarked: "Mary Renault says that a writer may fill in the gaps of history, but never change a known fact. Do you think I took too great a liberty with history in marrying Robert to Stella according to her own service?"[2] History says that Herrick never married, but Swann's solution was to stage a pagan ceremony unrecognized by the church; in that way Herrick might live in technical adultery (many clerics did, and no one cared) and yet within the moral and emotional fidelity demanded by the couple's own vows.

As his powers grew, however, Swann made fewer and fewer compromises with his ideal vision of the world. Fourteen years later, on his deathbed, approaching the long-delayed story of Dido and Aeneas, he wrote to Roehm:

I'm using very little of Vergil, much of the Carthaginian and Greek legends which he [Vergil] distorted to glorify Rome, and mostly me. My main characters have turned out to be Aeneas' son, Ascanius, at the age of ten, and a super-intelligent elephant named Iarbas. In Vergil, Iarbas is a black African chieftain, but the original legend doesn't say what he was, black or white, human or animal; hence, my elephant. (9 September 1975)

Swann's changes in the legend allowed him to present Dido's suicide nobly and constructively, not as the petulant revenge of a woman scorned but as a sacrifice to preserve the lives of her loved ones, Aeneas and Ascanius, father and son.

Finally, even when he began with figures from written history as his models, Swann could not resist the impulse to shape them in the patterns of myth. According to Robert A. Roehm, the genesis of Swann's most outspoken novel, *The Gods Abide*, stemmed from an imaginative link between the famous elopement of Elizabeth and Robert Browning and two poets Swann admired much more: William Morris and Christina Rossetti. "I have always fantasized their running away together like the Brownings," he wrote to Roehm, "and I can make them do just that if I use fictional names." Part of his reasoning for fantasizing the elopement was sympathy for Morris: "Imagine his hurt when he invited his best friend, Dante Gabriel Rossetti, to come and visit him and his wife, Janey, and then learned the two had been lovers . . . and Rossetti had told her to marry Morris so they could keep on trysting under the guise of simply being Pre-Raphaelites together. It's widely believed that Morris . . . became a ranting Socialist to cover his hurt" (11 March 1974). Metaphorically rewarding Morris with Rossetti's sister was for Swann an amusing use of the power of fantasy.

But the novel did not work out that way, of course. A month later Swann reported that it was developing "into something totally different from what I first envisioned. The Morris character has become a fire daemon in Roman times . . . and the Christina character is now a corn goddess" (8 April 1974). Once again Swann's rage against the repressive, often cruel dogmas of the Christian church intruded.

The first part of the story, laid in an old Etruscan city, concerns the conflict between the old pagan spirits . . . and the newly recognized Christian church. In the second part . . . the pagan spirits will depart for Roman Britain, hoping to escape the Church, but they will find it growing there too. But at the end, they learn how to abide, and there is the implication that they will one day return to their old power. (25 April 1974)

Concerning the character of Nodotus (Nod for short), in the same letter Swann wrote: "He's going to be . . . not unlike Tom Ligon, the boy in *Paint Your Wagon* who gets introduced to Sin and much prefers it to virtue. He will start as a Christian but *ascend* to a pagan, and then discover his true identity as a corn spirit." At the end of the novel, Stella, the mother goddess, sends her freedom-loving fertility spirits into the "Not-World" of Celtic mythology, blaming the destruction of joy and beauty in the physical world upon the jealous ambitions of Hebrew Yahweh:

He must have a bride; if not a goddess, a mortal girl named Mary, a virgin from Bethlehem.
    "She will bear me a son to build my earthly kingdom," he said. But the Christ-child grew to a man and hearkened to me, and his father averted his face and allowed an ignorant mob to seize and crucify his son. And Christ wept from the cross, "My father, why hast thou forsaken me?" And the love he taught was turned into Law by Paul, that hater of women and woman's gentleness, and those who revered the Christ forgot the man. . . . Soon they will rule the earth—conquer her not befriend her—and lose a part of themselves, for they were born of the earth, and of me, the Mother.[3]

Thus Swann, fantasizing an ancient era of freedom and Edenic fruitfulness, communicates his ethical and ecological message through the destruction visited upon that world by history, by the wars and religious persecution familiar to any modern reader. Yet the genesis for this message is personal—resentment against the repressive ethical standards which cause pain among those one loves or admires.

    Let us turn now from the conscious manipulation of myth to express the artist's vision of the world and examine the more personal role of fantasy in the artist's own life. In a letter to Roehm, Swann suggested that fantasy served two purposes for him—compensation for the sense of loss and exorcism of personal fears and evils. In a paragraph about the loneliness of the writer's life, he remarked:

Writing is the best possible antidote for a certain kind of loneliness. If you have something and lose it, then you can write about it and preserve it, at least for a little while. . . . I can pinpoint the precise reason why I so often write about children or adults or aliens like Gloomer so often looking around for brother or sister figures. The reason is much simpler than Lin Carter's Freudian conjectures. I lost a brother when I was a little boy. Actually, he was never born, my mother miscarried in a late stage of pregnancy, but I had been told I was going to have a little brother to play with . . . and he never showed up. . . . I felt cheated in the unreasoning but very real way of a small child. So my writing career has been telling story after story in which Remus has Romulus and Sylvan, Gloomer finds Charlie, the Minotaur adopts or is adopted by Icarus and Thea, etc. Thus writing grows out of loneliness, but the loneliness is positive and productive. . . . It's a gift from the muse, and to me it's one more proof that in the lives of most people, a loss is going to be balanced by a gain, if they just know how to wait. . . . The power of positive thinking doesn't work for me, but the inevitability of balance does. (14 February 1974)

The urge to preserve a memory or to compensate for a loss, real or imagined, is a traditional motive for the artist, yet Swann returns to it again and again in the most personal way. Discussing his maternal grandfather's delight in Edgar Rice Burroughs, Swann remarks: "He had a special way with the young; he was the nicest older man I have ever known, and I think the father-child relationships in my stories reflect him" (9 May 1975). On *Will-o-the-Wisp*, he notes: "Stella . . . is spiritually somebody I once knew and loved, and my fondness for the book is chiefly for the woman, the Pita, now dead. . . . It's a way of holding on to her and, at the same time, sharing her loveliness with other people" (21 September 1974). In response to criticism of the prissy Thea in *Day of the Minotaur*, Swann wrote: "I was never popular with girls in high school and I just don't know much about that age. My sister seemed to me much older, and the greatest influences on me were my mother and her sister, both of whom made maturity seem a splendour, and old age (for my mother—the aunt is dead now) a transfiguration. Hence my Lady Marys and Ahinoams." Concerning the protagonists of his early critical success, "The Manor of Roses," he wrote: "Lady Mary as I've said was patterned after my mother, John was me at the age of twelve, Stephen was the way I wanted to be, Ruth was a brassy but well-intentioned girl I knew back in grammar school, and Miriam, who is in the novel but not [the story] came out of a dream" (18 April 1974). Of *The Not-World*: "The heroine is partly based on Mrs. Browning and Mrs. Radcliffe (and partly on an exquisite, very much alive woman named Helen)" (8 January 1973). The transferences are not literal, of course. "Something mixes these elements in your brain," Swann wrote, "and adds a touch of racial memory, perhaps, and gives forth something which is different from the sum of its parts. In other words, the Muse has a hand in everything, and one can only hope she is in a good mood" (18 April 1974).

If Swann saw many of his characterizations as conscious attempts to enhance and preserve the most memorable figures from his past, he also saw the process of fantasy as an opportunity to exorcise his personal demons. The most significant of these was the fear of death, which Swann dealt with in a major way in two novels. The second, written in 1972 after his initial bout with cancer, involves a fantasy projection: "The anxiety, the operation, and the recuperation culminated in my Biblical novel, *How Are the Mighty Fallen*, much my starkest book but also, at the ending, my happiest,'' Swann wrote (29 December 1972). By imagining himself directly as Jonathan, the hero killed on the battlefield at the height of his powers, Swann was able, as he told an interviewer shortly before his death, to work out the circumstances of his life and death in an esthetically rewarding vision. However, the universal fear of the dark powers already had been faced, metaphorically and indirectly, in Swann's award-winning, popular novel, *Wolfwinter*, published the year before.

"I exorcised two childhood bogeys who used to haunt my dreams," Swann wrote, "a giant spider and a white wolf. I used to dream about them again and again, even when I was mature, and wake up screaming. But at last they are laid to rest" (29 December 1972). Swann clearly recognized these images as figures of death; he recreated them in order to "exorcise" the fear they generated. The theme of *Wolfwinter* is classical *carpe diem* in every sense, drawing upon a series of images of the transience of life and of beauty, some drawn from the poems of Sappho, others inherent in the mythological situation, the love between a mortal and a short-lived faun. Omnipresent, lurking behind these images of vitality, of pathos, of joy and sorrow, are the images of death, threatening yet coldly beautiful. The most striking of these are the white wolves, which excite awe and admiration as well as terror. "The wolves were the white of a corpse awaiting cremation," Swann wrote, "and the very lordliness of their movements, their strength, their grace, seemed a contradiction, a mockery of life."[4] Erinna's dying mate, Goathorn, remarks, "I am winter to your spring," and she responds hastily: " 'No! . . . It may be true that you're in the winter of your life. But you haven't *become* winter. There is a great difference.' (The wolves were winter; Death was winter.)" (p. 144). The wolves are not merely forest predators; they are killers of children in the service of Hades, hunters of souls in the dusk and the darkness, companions of the "white ones," the living dead, who dwell in a marble city stark as a mausoleum. No paraphrase of the plot can capture the bittersweet ambience of this novel. Erinna, a companion of Sappho, conceived a child by a Satyr, and when her subsequent husband exposes the baby in a graveyard, she fights off the white wolves to save him and flees to the forest. There her ripening love for a young faun is interrupted by the necessity to nurse the child's father, now aged (fauns live only fourteen years), through his last illness. Much of the novel's pathos centers on the need to "seize the day" with Skimmer, Erinna's young lover, but she cannot abandon the aged father of her child. At Greathorn's death, marked by mingled grief and joy, the lovers are united, only to be captured by the "white ones" who demand the life of the child. Skimmer raises an army, but Erinna knows that he and his friends will be slaughtered, and to save both lover and child she offers her life to Cerberus, who is presented as an enormous white wolfspider, whose hairy legs have duped others into perceiving him as a two-headed dog. At the moment of Erinna's death, Aphrodite, the goddess of life and love, speaks the theme of the novel: "Do you and your creatures lust for my beloved, she who with Sappho has sung my praises from girlhood? She who has loved twice freely and once truly? Mistress, wife, mother, giver of life, lady of laughter? . . . I know how you stole your bride from the fields of Enna. . . . You shall not steal a second'' (p. 197). Erinna miraculously returns; Skimmer dies in her arms, and she retires to a cave to live the life of a Sybil. The story is framed as a tale told by the now-aged heroine to a grief-stricken young man; its message is transcendence, the victory of life, of love, of vitality, of the mother. The young seeker sums up the theme in the last lines: ''He looked at her hair and thought that white was not always winter, and wondered if he would ever see a face more woundingly beautiful'' (p. 203).

For Swann, then, these were the uses of fantasy: first to communicate, through his vision of the world and its history, an ideal of sentient behavior and a criticism of contemporary life; and second to enhance and preserve the beautiful, while exorcising, for himself, the creatures of the night. His fantasies, like classical sculptures, are the artfully and consciously crafted icons of the mind.

NOTES

1. See Robert A. Collins and Howard D. Pearce, eds., *The Scope of the Fantastic* (Westport, Conn.: Greenwood Press, 1985), 201–5, for Fredericks's essay, ''The Fantastic Pastoral of Thomas Burnett Swann.''

2. Letter to Robert A. Roehm of Clarksville, Indiana, 8 November 1974. Swann corresponded regularly with Roehm from the mid–1960s until his death. All readers interested in Swann's fiction owe Roehm an enormous debt of gratitude for preserving more than 100 of Swann's letters, and I am especially grateful to Robert Roehm and to Mrs. Margaret G. Swann, Literary Executrix of the Thomas B. Swann estate, for permission to quote from them here. All subsequent quotations are from letters to Roehm and are identified by date within the text.

3. Thomas B. Swann, *The Gods Abide* (New York: DAW Books, 1976), p. 156.

4. Thomas B. Swann, *Wolfwinter* (New York: Ballantine Books, 1972), p. 105; hereafter cited in the text.

The Fantastic in Two Recent Works of Gonzalo Torrente Ballester

Janet Pérez

Spanish literature is commonly thought to be poor in fantasy. No important history, survey, or anthology of Spanish literature devotes a chapter or even a page to works of fantasy. If fantasy is mentioned at all, it is in a negative context, usually dismissing the subject with the assertion that Spanish writers are collectively underendowed when it comes to pure imagination. The national spirit is said to be rooted in realism from its earliest manifestations, and the sober, eyewitness documentary nature of Spanish epic poetry is cited, contrasting the decidedly human exploits of El Cid with the supernatural feats of Roland. The picaresque genre, invented in Spain, is usually adduced as the most striking example of the alleged national bent for realism, irony, and satire. Yet Spanish literature is by no means devoid of works of fantasy—indeed, the romances of chivalry with their dragons and enchanters, magical swords and miraculous resuscitations are highly fantastic, and the genre reached unparalleled extremes of popularity in Spain. Fantastic elements occur in subsequent periods as well, especially the Romantic era, although to catalog the instances would be the task of another study.[1]

It is generally true, however, that Spanish literature offers relatively few examples of fantasy in what Todorov would call a pure state, fantasy unmixed with allegory, satire, parody or other elements, fantasy which serves no end but itself.[2] The great flourishing of the romance of fantasy in England and America beginning late in the nineteenth century has been seen by W. R. Irwin as a reaction to the realistic and naturalistic movements.[3] No analogous flowering of fantastic literature occurs in Spain during the period Irwin studies (1880–1950), but writing of a fantastic bent has increased considerably since the decline of the Neo-Realist or Neo-Naturalist (Objectivist) movement which flourished in post-Civil War Spanish writing during the 1950s and 1960s. During the 1970s cultivation of science fiction by serious writers in Spain ceased to be a rarity and began to gain a measure of intellectual respectability. Simultaneously, fantastic elements have become more frequent in the works of certain important novelists, although thus far no first-rate narrator in Spain has devoted himself exclusively or even primarily to cultivation of the fantastic.

An exception to the national stereotype of austere realism is found in the region of Galicia, in the far northwest corner of the peninsula, an area whose strong Celtic background is still reflected in surviving myths and legends, in the local folklore, and (supposedly) in the continuing practice of witchcraft. The great Spanish medieval shrine of Santiago (the Apostle Saint James) is in Galicia, and the peninsula's earliest flowering of lyric poetry was in the Galician language. Whether or not it is true that lyricism and imaginativeness are present in larger doses in the Galician than in works from other parts of Spain, as the collective peninsular stereotypes suggest, Galicia has produced the country's most original and imaginative narrators in modern times, the late Valle-Inclán and the contemporary novelist and critic Gonzalo Torrente Ballester. Although Torrente's earlier works are largely realistic, the fantastic is prominent in those of the last decade.

A thoroughly fantastic event, the levitation of a provincial city in northern Spain, opens and closes Torrente's *La Saga/fuga de J.B.*[4] Although the nature of this happening is not clarified until the closing pages of the novel, the fortified town of Castroforte, its medieval walls and stone streets, and a substantial portion of the earth beneath it simply rise skyward. The author has explained elsewhere that the inspiration came as he contemplated a painting wherein distance was distorted so that the city seemed to be floating. Actually, the event is a version of Celtic legends still current in modern Spain, centered around a city that sinks beneath the water. These are variants of the legend of Atlantis, which Torrente has inverted. The author's purpose in this fantastic episode—actually the final event of the novel, despite presentation of portions of it at the beginning—proves to be satiric. The satire is political, a spoof of Spanish separatism and individualism, as becomes apparent when the cause of the city's levitation is revealed: it happens at the precise and unprecedented moment when all the city's inhabitants share the same concern or preoccupation at the same exact time.

Likewise fantastic, though involving fantasy of a different nature, is the protagonist's experience of the revelation of the serial nature and geometric duplication of his own personality, as he becomes aware that he is but one in an almost endless chain of JBs (persons with the same initials) down through the unending ages: *"Miles [Thousands] y miles y miles de J. B."* (Torrente, *La saga/fuga*, p. 451). In this sophisticated application of fantasy to metaphysical speculation, Torrente parodies popular Western concepts as to the uniqueness of each individual.

It is possible that Torrente's inspiration for the multiple JBs came indirectly from Todorov. In a 1975 interview subsequent to his election to the Real Academic Española, Torrente noted his agreement with an observation by Andres Amoros that *La saga/fuga "habia nacido de un curso sobre Cervantes y una*

*frecuentacion del estructuralismo. Efectivamente, formalmente tiene este ori-
gen"* ("was born from a course about Cervantes and a familiarity with structuralism. Effectively, seriously it has this origin").[5] Torrente's relation to Todorov
would be that of parody to its model—the interview just cited alludes to a satire
of structuralism. If Torrente's point of departure is Todorov, it is almost certainly
his treatment of the theme of metamorphosis, identified as a general characteristic
of the fantastic. Todorov affirms, "We can generalize the phenomenon of metamorphosis and say that a character will be readily multiplied. . . . The multiplication of personality, taken literally, is an immediate consequence of the
possible transition between matter and mind: we are several persons mentally,
we become so physically" (Todorov, *Fantastic*, p. 116). The principal point on
which Irwin and Todorov agree, despite different treatment, is the theme of
metamorphosis. Torrente applies the notion of a character's being multiplied in
La saga/fuga, and that of the transition between matter and mind in his next
novel, *Fragmentos de apocalipsis*.

JB experiences something analogous to a series of reincarnations or, more
precisely, relives in serial simultaneity several of his previous incarnations as
other individuals with the initials JB who share the same personality. This
structures the novel "fugally," with numerous subsections corresponding to the
major historical incarnations of JB—medieval bishop Jerónimo Bermúdez; eighteenth-century necromancer Jacobo Balseyro; nineteenth-century admiral John
Ballantyne; Romantic poet José María Barrantes; and their contemporary counterparts, José Bastida, Joaquín Barallobre, and Jesualdo Bendaña. These three,
while distinct individuals, have the following in common: each is a writer of
strictly local fame, each is past his prime and physically unattractive but is
involved in a love triangle, and each is a falsifier or impersonator. Indeed, all
of the supposedly heroic and charismatic JBs are imposters, their deeds only
infrequently approaching the exceptional.

Five canons, each with the initial A, are adversely involved with the destinies
of the respective JBs and suggest another case of serial personality. Each canon
comes from a distant, exotic diocese; none is a native of Castroforte. Each has
wrongfully appropriated a treasure, betrayed a woman, and negligently caused
her death. Each is a musician of some note, allied with a different generation
of the Bendaña family, nemesis of the Barallobre clan. The myth of the JBs,
pseudo-messianic figures who emerge at critical moments in the history of Castroforte, is a by-product of the rivalry between these two families and their
supporters. Rather than saviors, however, the JBs are protagonists of Castroforte's various defeats—military, religious, cultural, or symbolic—and their legendary transformations constitute an idealized rationalization whereby the natives
convince themselves that each past disaster was somehow a triumph.

Tradition holds that the JBs, like King Arthur, do not die but embark mysteriously in a magical craft and are wafted to eternal sunset isles to await a
glorious return. The myth or legend of the Islas Afortunadas, common in Spain,
is also of Celtic origin and, like its Arthurian counterpart, has been shown to

be related in prehistoric times to the myth of Atlantis by Lewis Spence.[6] There
is, therefore, a logical connection between legends attached to the JBs and the
final fate of Castroforte. Reinforcing the motif of the Fortunate Isles is another,
that of the Round Table, recreated as the mystical basis for a perpetual tertulia
(fellowship) in nineteenth-century Castroforte. With time its function becomes
perverted, but each member of La Table Redonda adopts the name and identity
of an original hero of the Table Round, so that with each recent incarnation of
JB goes a contemporary Merlin, Arthur, Lancelot, and so on, with a corresponding reenactment of the Guinevere episode, entangled with the amorous
fortunes of the JB of the moment.

Torrente's variation on the fantastic theme of metamorphosis, the multiplicity
of personality, is not unique in fantastic fiction. The doctrine of co-inherence,
a unitary principle which proposes, among other things, that individual uniqueness is illusory, or that one person may contain many and the many are ultimately
parts of one, was used by Charles Williams in *War in Heaven*. The doctrine
posits a universal community in which accidents of time, space, language, individual endowment, personal station, and identity are subsumed. Torrente does
not stop with the JBs just mentioned, but the others are not presented in detail.
Even greater complication and bifurcation ensue when the narrator (José Bastida,
the most insignificant and unprepossessing of the JBs) learns that each of the
several JBs is a multiform, multifaceted personality with the potential of rein-
carnating in the others and in various combinations. Thus, JB's possible permutations are not arithmetical but geometrical, with personality projections
reaching almost to infinity. In living parts of the lives of a number of them,
Bastida discovers "facts" whose veracity he is able to test when he returns to
the world of the present.

Not all of the fantastic elements involve a projection of serious doctrines or
even simple mathematical speculation. The purpose and effect of some is humor
pure and simple. Thus, Bastida, in the body and identity of the necromancer
and wizard Jacobo Balseyro, works a minor miracle for the disconsolate widow
of another JB, the nineteenth-century admiral John Ballantyne executed by English pirates. Since the grieving lady is too faithful to her husband's memory to
satisfy her physical yearnings with another man, the wizard revitalizes by supernatural incantation the late husband's male organ. Preserved in a flask of
aguardiente, it is endowed with the capacity to acquire independent existence
and mobility upon pronunciation of a magical phrase, thereby to assuage the
lady's longing upon demand. In addition to the risqué wit of the events themselves, this particular anti-fact burlesques pornography, for the scabrous detail
and salacious narration the reader is led to expect are not forthcoming.[7]

Bastida reincarnates in the bodies of his predecessors from several centuries
in a seeming annihilation of sequential time, allowing for some amusing anach-
ronisms. In fantastic narratives generally, liberties taken with time in relation to
point of view or the narrative's chronological focus function as a "release from
restricted time setting" (Irwin, *Game*, p. 146). Such treatment of time is found

in T. H. White's version of Arthurian legend, *The Once and Future King*, which shares some other elements with Torrente's novel: the blend of medieval and later elements, the secret societies, and the motif of incest (the incestuous relationship of Joaquín Barallobre with his sister Clotilde ends with his killing her). Merlin possesses the ability to live backward in time, while JB moves more or less at will, backward and forward and laterally. His presence and participation in the life of various ages helps to create a kind of fluidity within time. Irwin notes: "In combination with other manifestations of magic and prodigy, fluidity within time seems entirely plausible" (Irwin, *Game*, p. 147). Todorov observes that in narratives of the fantastic, time seems suspended (Todorov, *Fantastic*, p. 116), while Irwin concludes that the fantastic is "suprahistorical," not bound to historical time. There is, thus, essential agreement as to the fundamental modification of time in fantastic literature.

Time in *La saga/fuga* is extraordinarily complex, ranging from remotest prehistory to the present, from the dawn of human evolution—when man is humorously depicted as having only one eye in the base of his skull—to 2000 B.C., legendary beginning of human occupation of the area of Castroforte, to the heyday of the cult of Diana at Ephesus in approximately 1000 B.C., and thence to the Roman conquest of Galicia around the dawn of the Christian era. Especially important is a period in the Middle Ages, around the year 1000, when foundations were laid for the present ecclesiastical and sociological mythology of Castroforte, with the miraculous appearance of the remains of the local saint, the "Santo Cuerpo Iluminado" in circumstances suspiciously similar to those of the legend of Santiago. Narrative attention is not equally divided among these time planes, which by the author's count are twenty; the present and immediate past, encompassing some two months, receive greater emphasis, followed closely by moments from the lives of known antecedents of the contemporary inhabitants of Castroforte, drawn largely from the eighteenth, nineteenth, and early twentieth centuries.

Further variation on the theme of personality duplication or fragmentation is provided by Torrente's next novel, *Fragmentos de apocalipsis*.[8] The protagonist is plagued by having his memory supplanted and replaced by memories belonging to other persons, some of them familiar personalities and others unidentified. Looking backward over his recollections, he finds that his past from the age of twenty-one has been replaced by that of Napoleon: he speaks French with a Corsican accent, and his memories are of intimate and significant events in Napoleon's life. His past prior to that time is contradictory, a patchwork of various lives, but two in particular—Alberto Caiero and Abel Martín—appear as more or less habitual companions to his own personality, a personality more intuited, deduced, or suspected than actually known; it exists as something of a hypothetical construct abstracted from qualities of the others and functions, he says, as a hook on which the others hang, a support. Attempting to impose order on the jumble of conflicting and mysterious memories, he reviews his own life, arriving at his parents, whom he does not recognize and whose names he has forgotten. Nor is he able to recognize siblings, friends, surroundings, or his native language (this suggests a spin-off of the doctrine of co-inherence). The narrator-protagonist's impressions are substantiated as fantasy rather than hallucination, when he has recourse to a doctor who certifies that there exists a hiatus in his consciousness; to a certain point, he *was* Napoleon and, thereafter, someone else. The doctor presumably functions also as a guarantee of the character's sanity.

Convention is here contravened in at least two important ways, for personal experience is held to be untransferable, and the past is supposed to be static, so that memories of it (while subject to forgetfulness, slips, and other minor vicissitudes) are not supposed to change radically or to travel from one psyche to another. Other than simultaneous, multiple reincarnations in a single body, only the doctrine of co-inherence offers a possible explanation, however implausible. Torrente here produces a variation on the theme of metamorphosis in which what is metamorphosed is not the body but the spirit. Todorov in his discussion of "themes of the self," of which metamorphosis is the principal one and multiplication an apparent subcategory, mentions pandeterminism or the notion that everything is causally related and observes that the transition from mind to matter becomes possible (Todorov, *Fantastic*, p. 114). This, in effect, is what happens, in reverse, to the narrator-protagonist of *Fragmentos de apocalipsis*, a novelist. The text the reader has before him is supposedly the novelist's diary, relating aspects of the creative process as such, the genesis of characters and situations, the exploration of alternative narrative paths with rejection of some and abandonment of others, conversations between the narrator-author and his fictional lover, and a burlesque of many literary modes and styles. In a further variation on the theme of metamorphosis, there occurs a bifurcation of the narrative identity, with a "counter-novel"—the work of an unknown secret agent—threatening to swallow the novelist-narrator-protagonist of *Fragmentos* and to imprison him within the fiction of another. Todorov's observation as to the feasibility of transition from mind to matter is reversed, and the supposedly solidly material character finds himself within another's mind, threatened by death and struggling frantically to escape, to find his way out of the mental labyrinth.

Another chain of fantastic episodes involves an unlikely guru or "bonzo" whose soul abandons his body for an extended astral journey. For weeks the body appears to be dead with vital functions suspended, but life-signs resume the day and hour he had predicted his soul would return. The subsequent narration of what was witnessed on the journey among the stars might be viewed by some as impure fantasy, since it could feasibly be explained by the reader as a dream or hallucination experienced while in the coma or trancelike state. However, certain of the guru's revelations are corroborated by events elsewhere in the novel, thereby lending credence to his story.

The bonzo recounts his soul's being transported beyond the solar system, perhaps beyond the galaxy, to a point outside of time from whence he perceives the true essence of history—an endless repetition of events already concluded—

and is able to see that the earth is not one planet but many, an infinite chain of identical planets, each at a different moment in time or a different stage of evolution, but all inevitably condemned to relive the predetermined patterns followed by each and every other one. Once again, Torrente applies fantasy to the realm of metaphysical speculation, burlesquing theories of the creation of the universe and parodying the notion that history repeats itself, while simultaneously satirizing cultists and others who think themselves in possession of ultimate truths. Despite the underlying humor, the theory elaborated is intellectually challenging, and the reader can perceive no internal flaw in the logic. The guru's fantasy compels because, absurd or not, it is logically as probable as several current theories of similar import. Within the structure of the novel, this revelation of the serial nature of time, worlds, and history is analogous to the disclosure of the serial nature of personality in the epiphany of JB in *La saga/fuga*.

While both sequences involve certain scientific principles—and the schema of serial personalities employ geometric and trigonometric constructs—what is involved is not science fiction but fantasy, as is made clear in Kingsley Amis's definition, which points out that the science fiction situation is "hypothesized on the basis of some innovation in science or technology, whether human or extraterrestrial in origin."[9] While science fiction "maintains a respect for fact or presumptive fact, fantasy makes a point of flouting these," according to Amis.[10] Science fiction does not systematically represent what convention holds to be impossible, however improbable certain situations or events may be, but those in *La saga/fuga* and *Fragmentos de apocalipsis* contravene and burlesque convention. As in the earlier novel, the function of certain instances of the fantastic in *Fragmentos* is clearly humorous; for example, the conversations between one of the characters and Felipe II, the Golden Age monarch and inventor of bureaucracy, dead some four centuries. The appearances by Felipe have nothing of the macabre or supernatural, although he has acquired a peg leg. Save for his outdated attire, however, nothing in the king's demeanor suggests deviation from the norm—a probable spoof of Gothic conventions. More humorous still is the subject of the phantasm's conversations, limited almost entirely to off-color jokes. These episodes blend the fantastic with an opposing realistic trend to burlesque official national adulation of the puritanical and fanatic emperor, symbol of the Spanish past idealized by the Nationalists and the Franco regime. His presence in the novel, however, is related thematically to dystopia, the anti-utopian society resulting from the achievement of a seemingly utopian ideal which, however desirable when dreamed of from afar, proves to be ominous. The kind of totalitarian thought-control portrayed in *Brave New World* and *1984* is evoked by Torrente when he attributes to Felipe II the desire to know the minutest details of the lives of the governed, including their innermost thoughts.[11] Irwin identifies utopias and dystopias as a peculiar and specific subgroup of the fantastic.

The idea of a variable past or variation upon the memories of that past underlies another key event of the novel, the return to Villasanta of the Vikings. A thousand years earlier, the Viking King Olaf, defeated in the Galician city by Bishop Sisnando, prophesied his return at the end of a millennium to avenge his defeat with the destruction of the city. Given the fact that history records that their previous defeat was linked with the hazards of maritime approach to the city (and determined to prove that this time history would *not* repeat itself), the Vikings take an overland route, disguised as American Indians to avoid early detection, not only conquering the city but occupying and colonizing it and exploiting it as a market in the best colonial tradition. Their most successful economic venture takes advantage of the indigenous *macho* tendency to convert women into sex objects, purveying a perfect sex object, the inflatable plastic *muñeca erotica*, a sort of mechanized Venus or erotic robot without the imperfections or inconveniences of living females. Devoting themselves to fulfillment of their most personal and exquisite erotic fantasies with their private copy of the *muñeca erotica*, the local males commit inadvertent genocide while the conquerors are free to advance their projected improvement of the conquered race, impregnating the women, who have been forgotten. As with other anti-utopias, the time of this one (about the year 2000) is not far in the future. The prominence of humor in Torrente's work distinguishes it from other dystopias, which are more solemn in their monitory messages. What is portrayed here is not so much "the future as nightmare" as the fulfillment of fantasy as nightmare.[12]

Further deterioration of the utopian ideal is evinced in another piece of science fiction gadgetry, typical of the dystopias, the "*maquina de matar pronto*," which disposes of malcontents and malingerers, liquidating them painlessly and with music at lightning speed and returning their component parts on a conveyor belt, neatly packaged and addressed to the corresponding eye bank, blood bank, or kidney or heart transplant center. Fantastic constructs of the gadget category also are found in *La saga/fuga*, as exemplified by the enormously complicated and bizarre smoke organ built by a secondary character. A huge, rambling series of towers, miles of pipes and tubes and orifices, this whimsical creation serves no practical purpose whatever, although its creator upon rare occasion stokes up a labyrinth of boilers and produces a "concert" of smoke, playing upon a simulacrum of a keyboard. The description of this particular creation evokes the architectural fantasies of Gaudí, especially the unfinished Church of the Sagrada Familia in Barcelona, but this association is insufficient reason to attribute to Torrente an intent to satirize. Actually, the smoke organ does not constitute an anti-fact in the sense of being contrary to known scientific principles—it would be theoretically possible to construct a machine such as is described, just as it is within the capacities of present technology to construct Torrente's "*maquina de matar pronto*." The convention which is contravened here is a moral one (Irwin devotes a chapter to fantasies of "organized innocence" which transgress not natural or scientific principles but other attitudes, values, and moral conventions).

Neither novel is totally fantastic; both display veins of satiric *costumbrismo* cementing together a mosaic of fantasy and parody, an intricate interplay of anti-fact or fantastic "facts" as perceived by illuminated psyches such as those of JB and the guru, and a thoroughly mundane, pedestrian reality perceived by society at large. Given the fugal form of the first novel and the bifurcation and splintering of the second, we are not dealing with a single, continuous narrative of the impossible, but a number of relatively extensive, semi-independent story threads presented in contrapuntal fashion. The appeal of the fantastic sequences is to the intellect rather than the emotions, which Irwin points out is characteristic of fantasy as opposed to ghost stories, Gothic romances, fairy tales, and related forms which feed the human appetite for wonder, excitement, and horror (Irwin, *Game*, pp. 89–92). Torrente's fantasies invite the intellectual game-playing and speculative participation by the reader that Irwin associates with the fantastic (Irwin, *Game*, p. 96).

NOTES

1. Fantasy elements occur in the ballads, such as that of the Conde Alarcos and his magical boat; in episodes of the Golden Age theater (as at the end of *El burlador de Sevilla o el convidado de piedra*); in the *Sueños* of Quevedo and later works such as *El diablo cojuelo*; in pastiche in much eighteenth-century theater, especially *refundiciones* of Calderón; in many Romantic novels; in the *Leyendas* of Bécquer; and closer to the present, in the use of the supernatural in Valle-Inclán and some works of Casona. There is fantasy even in so unfantastic a writer as Machado ("La tierra de Alvargonzález"), and what but fantasy is the moon's appearance in the smithy in Lorca's "Romance de la luna, luna" or the use of the *duendes* in *Don Perlimplín*? Fantasy elements have become more frequent during the past decade, and Ramón Nieto's *La señorita* is a fantastic allegory of Falangist Spain. Some contemporary novelists (e.g., Alvaro Cunqueiro, Ramón J. Sender) have cultivated fantasy intermittently throughout long careers. And fantastic elements abound in the theater of J. Ruibal and other members of the "underground" dramatists group.

2. Tzvetan Todorov, *The Fantastic: A Structural Approach to a Literary Genre*, trans. Richard Howard (Cleveland: Case-Western Reserve University Press, 1973); hereafter cited in the text. I do not follow Todorov's definition of the fantastic in this paper for many reasons, but the most important is that in reducing the fantastic to a matter of reader-text relationships—the reader's period of hesitation between a natural and supernatural explanation of events described—Todorov is left with a "genre" which has no objective existence. "The fantastic is defined as a special *perception* of uncanny events" (p. 91), and thus its "reality" is an attitude fleetingly present in the reader's mind, not something with which the literary historian or critic can work. Todorov posits for his putative reader a universality which the individual reading experience does not possess, and he does not come to grips with the logical difficulties inherent in analyzing something which no longer exists. Covertly, Todorov is aware of the problem, for he explains that the fantastic work cannot be reread (pp. 89–90).

Many other objections to Todorov might be raised: he is sloppy in his documentation, with an index of works cited but no bibliography; he customarily omits dates and places of publication; he refers to a host of secondary sources either by author's name alone or simply by title; and he quotes without pagination and does not use footnotes. While supposedly employing scientific method (proceeding from the specific to the general), he makes sweeping and impressionistic generalizations, often based on no more than two or three examples.

By fiat, in his conclusions, Todorov limits the fantastic largely to a specific historical period, beginning at the end of the eighteenth century and almost disappearing by the end of the nineteenth. He does not elucidate why only texts written in these years provoke hesitation, and he summarily abandons that category in the second half of his essay. It is evident that Todorov proceeds from certain presuppositions (of which he may himself be unaware) as to the nature of the fantastic: it occurs chiefly in the nineteenth century; it is predominantly a brief genre (he analyzes mostly short stories and one or two novellas and makes only passing reference to novels); and—on the basis of the texts selected for comment or analysis—it consists of the bizarre, the magical, the macabre, the diabolical on the one hand, and drug-induced hallucination, sexual perversion, and erotic illusion on the other.

3. W. R. Irwin, *The Game of the Impossible: A Rhetoric of Fantasy* (Urbana: University of Illinois Press, 1976); hereafter cited in the text. Irwin concentrates on long prose fiction, the "extended narrative which establishes and develops an anti-fact, that is, plays the game of the impossible"; such literature is pervaded by "what we generally think anti-natural or impossible and contravenes intellectual conventions in such a manner as to become temporarily within credence" (p. 4). He defines fantasy as a story "based on and controlled by an overt violation of what is generally accepted as possibility; it is the narrative result of transforming the condition contrary to fact into 'fact' itself" (p. 4). He later notes that most fantasies employ "presentational realism," a simulacrum of realistic method, to establish the anti-fact as fact. Fantasies are seemingly objective, realistic accounts of an impossibility. Broader and more inclusive than Todorov's definition, Irwin's has the virtue of being more objective; it appeals not to reader-hesitation but to what is generally accepted as fact or possibility, and does not require two other artificially created genres (the uncanny and the marvelous) to locate its limits. For Irwin's reader, temporary credence is part of the "game of the impossible," while Todorov's, apparently, is not playful but dead serious.

4. Gonzalo Torrente Ballester, *La saga/fuga de J. B.* (Barcelona: Destino, 1972); hereafter cited in the text.

5. Gladys Crescioni Neggers, interview, "GTB, nuevo académico," *La Estafeta Literaria* 546 (15 May 1975), 9.

6. Lewis Spence, *The History of Atlantis* (1948; reprint ed., New York: Bell, 1967), pp. 186ff.

7. Irwin has indicated that the "erotic content of genuine fantasy is slight" (*Game*, p. 90). In this he differs from Todorov, who distinguishes two broad thematic groupings, fantasies of the self and of the other, the latter being primarily sexual judging by his examples and analyses.

8. Gonzalo Torrente Ballester, *Fragmentos de apocalipsis* (Barcelona: Destino, 1977).

9. Kingsley Amis, *New Maps of Hell: A Survey of Science Fiction* (New York: Harcourt Brace, 1960), p. 18.

10. Ibid., p. 22.

11. Torrente, *Fragmentos*, p. 290.

12. See Mark Hillegas, *The Future as Nightmare: H. G. Wells and the Anti-Utopians* (New York: Oxford University Press, 1967).

II. FANTASTIC CREATURES

The world of fantasy is not populated by down-to-earth Silas Laphams and George F. Babbitts like the world of realism but by grotesque, unearthly creatures, both human and nonhuman. Critics generally have ignored literature involving supernatural or infranatural beings or have dismissed it as melodramatic grotesquerie. In the essays in this section, however, the double and Frankenstein's monster, the golem, the indefinable Other, and the vampire are considered as psychic archetypes and are related to such Jungian or Freudian themes as individuation, initiation, projection, narcissism, and Oedipal conflicts.

Narcissism and Beyond: A Psychoanalytic Reading of *Frankenstein* and Fantasies of the Double

Rosemary Jackson

I am no god. I am no demon.
I come from yourself.

Alfred de Musset, *December Night*[1]

Literary fantasy is a rich area for psychoanalytic investigation since it is a mode dealing with an expression, a manifestation, of unconscious desires and fears. Since psychoanalysis deals with the material reality of ideas in society, examining how individual human beings come to inherit and inhabit the laws which determine cultural life on an unconscious level, it can be used in the interpretation of literature—and its perpetuation of those cultural norms—in ways analogous to those used by Freud in interpreting dreams and neuroses. Many fantasies contain a desire to break with social conventions and betray an impulse toward transgression of cultural law, but there is almost invariably an eventual neutralizing of that impulse, resulting in its ultimate defeat or deflection into "safe" forms. In *Fantasy: The Literature of Subversion*, I argued that the most challenging texts are those which defer this safe resolution until the last possible moment or try to refuse it altogether.[2] Unlike the utopian fantasies of fairy tale, religious myth, or romance, the modern fantastic refuses supernatural, magical explanations of strangeness and, in place of a "transcendental" reality, presents or re-presents a weird, refracted world, transformed through the mind of the perceiver and his or her unconscious projections into the world.

By imaginatively protesting against and even fantasizing the destruction of social codes, only to renew and confirm their validity, literary fantasies can dramatically articulate social tensions within themselves. This is particularly the case in fantasies of dualism, where the narrative center, often the protagonist himself, is divided into two sides, one subverting and one upholding the dominant social order. The main focus here will be on a few selected tales of the double and shadow, but the argument can be extended to a wide range of texts. For stories of the double are graphic depictions of the alienation which is involved in becoming "human" at all: they protest against and then reenact that drama of insertion into human culture which is the time when, with the acquisition of identity, our many protean selves, our undifferentiated elements, are "unified" and stabilized as "one" character—the ego, the I, the self, indivisible and integral, upon which society depends.

Recent studies of the double in literature have acknowledged its shift in the Romantic period from a supernatural motif into an increasingly self-conscious psychological function. From its appearance in Jean-Paul's *Hesperus* (1795) onward, the double has been recognized as originating from *within* the human subject.[3] Mary Shelley's *Frankenstein* (1818) and James Hogg's *The Private Memoirs and Confessions of a Justified Sinner* (1824) are particularly interesting in that they are remarkable transitional works. They represent an explicit shift from a presentation of a demonic "other" as supernaturally evil, the devil in a conventional iconography, toward something much more disturbing because equivocal, ambiguous in its nature and origins. Hogg's *Confessions* preserves a brilliant and puzzling ambiguity about the genesis of the demonic presence—is it natural or supernatural?—and the text eludes any definitive interpretation by suggesting it is both and neither. Hogg's fantasy sees the devil move from one identity to another. It "is" the sinner himself, and his brother George, and also other characters, as well as a traditional prince of darkness. Yet conventional explanations of a "supernatural" devil figure are betrayed, within the text itself, as redundant. The reader is left stranded, unable to know who or what the shadow is, forced to recognize it as a reflection of every self, a shifting and distorting mirror image of anyone, alienated or metamorphosed into a distant, unfamiliar "other." The double then comes to be seen as an aspect of the psyche, externalized in the shape of another in the world.

Mary Shelley's *Frankenstein* operates similarly but is more explicit about the link between the self and its monstrous projections into the shape of another outside itself. Despite the apparently supernatural powers of the monster, it is literally a product of scientist Frankenstein's own ideas and actions, and it is to be located entirely within a *human* scheme of things. The monster functions as a parodic mirror image of Frankenstein: "My form," it mocks him, "is a filthy type of yours, made horrid even from the very resemblance." Frankenstein feels it to be demonic and laments his tragic destiny: "I was cursed by some devil, and carried about with me my external hell,"[4] but he confesses that the monster is really self-generated, "the being whom I had cast among mankind . . . [was] my own vampire, my own spirit let loose from the grave, and forced to destroy all that was dear to me."[5]

It is no accident that the monster is anonymous or that in the popular imagination it has come to be confused with Frankenstein himself and frequently given his name, for it is his grotesque reflection, his unnamed, unformed selves. Naming the double is impossible for both Frankenstein and Hogg's sinner since it *is* themselves in alienated form, an image of themselves before they acquired names. At the heart of both works, as indeed of all fantasies, is the problem of identity, a problem given particular prominence in tales of the double. Hogg's convoluted narrative dramatizes uncertainty as to the coherence of the "I" and expresses the sinner's sense of loss of any viable identity: "I seemed hardly to be an accountable creature . . . I was a being incomprehensible to *myself*. Either I had a second self, who transacted business in my likeness, or else my body was at times possessed by a spirit over which it had no control."[6] Mary Shelley's creature is similarly lost, crying out, "I had never yet seen a being resembling me, or who claimed any intercourse with me. *What was I*? I have no relation or friend on earth."[7] Their preoccupations, indeed obsessions, with identity point to the Oedipal drama which is at their centers, though displaced. Their recurrent question is: Who am I? Where do I come from? How can I feel whole?

Despite the possibility of simplistic readings of stories of the double as simply allegories of the "good" and "evil" sides of mankind—particularly in less complex fantasies such as Robert Louis Stevenson's *The Strange Case of Dr. Jekyll and Mr. Hyde* (1886)—fantasies of dualism have more to do with a quest for wholeness and integration than with mere moral division. They are driven by a desire to *reverse* the process of alienation which occurs in the earliest stages of human development, and their quest is focused upon an ideal beyond or before the formation of the ego.

This desire is best understood in relation to Freud's theories of human growth, especially as elaborated by the French psychoanalyst Jacques Lacan.[8] For the incredible proliferation of doubles in Romantic and post-Romantic literature points to an identical unconscious structuration lying behind them. As Marianne Wain writes, "It is astonishing, when one goes through Romantic writing generally . . . to see how this preoccupation with the lost center of personality is a veritable obsession."[9] Following from Jean-Paul's novels, William Godwin's *Caleb Williams* (1794), Charles Brockden Brown's *Wieland* (1798), Heinrich von Kleist's *Penthesilea* (1808), Adelbert von Chamisso's *Peter Schlemihl* (1814), Benjamin Constant's *Adolphe* (1816), E. T. A. Hoffman's *Doppelgänger* and *Elixirs of the Devil* (1816), C. R. Maturin's *Melmoth the Wanderer* (1820), Edgar Allan Poe's *William Wilson* (1839), Feodor Dostoevski's *The Double* (1846), Charles Dickens's *A Tale of Two Cities* (1859), Oscar Wilde's *The Picture of Dorian Gray* (1891), Henry James's *The Jolly Corner* (1908), and Joseph Conrad's *The Secret Sharer* (1912) all share a similar psychic structure which cannot be explained away as merely literary influence or coincidence. They fantasize a fragmented or dualistic existence as part of a process of returning to a pre-Oedipal stage of being as reference to Freud and Lacan will clarify.

The Oedipal complex—that knot of both hostile and loving wishes which the child has toward its parents and which, in its positive form, appears as a sexual desire for the parent of the opposite sex—occurs between the ages of three and five and is crucial in structuring the individual personality and its desires. However, preceding this period are equally important and determining stages. Freud identified three distinct but overlapping states in the child—and in culture as a whole. The first is a stage of primary narcissism or self-love. In a paradigm of "normal" development, this has to give way to an attachment to objects outside the self, a relinquishing of self-love, which eventually leads to the third stage, an acceptance of the laws of the world, its "reality principle" and necessities of self-repression for the sake of cultural continuity. In this tripartite scheme, the most crucial sequence is between the first and second stages, in the transition from primary narcissism (love for self) to attachment to love objects (love for other). For what the child has to relinquish here is a state of undifferentiation, in which it has not yet learned to make any difference between self and other. Lacan has termed this "*le stade du miroir*," the mirror stage, when the self is recognized as separate, as an object constituted by the look, the look of others. It is in the mirror phase that there is a progression from what Lacan terms an "asubjectivity of total presence" to the establishment of a coherent and unified subjectivity—the human subject, the ego, the I. This precedes the Oedipal stage and *its* establishment of gender difference.

With the mirror stage, there are now two I's: one to perceive, one to be perceived. The process of becoming an ego, becoming a human subject, involves acquiring duality: alienation is at the heart of identification. Prior to this, there is no sense of a whole, distinct, separate body, but fluidity, instability, incoherence, presence. Part of the notion of the pre-Oedipal is this idea of the non-whole, fragmented body, termed by Lacan "*le corps morcelé*," the body in pieces. It is worth extending a description of this state because of its relation to *Frankenstein*:

At this stage the infant has no organisation of data into those associated with its own body and those associated with its exteriority. It has no sense of its physical separateness or of its physical unity. This is the moment referred to retroactively after the "mirror phase," by the phantasy of the "body in fragments." The mirror phase is the moment when the infant realises the distinction between its own body and the outside; the "other." The infant sees its reflection in a mirror and identifies with it. . . . The image with which the infant identifies, which Lacan says can be described as the "Ideal-I," is positioned in the world *exterior* to the infant. . . . The ego results from the entry of the I into an identification with an object in the other (the non-infant).[10]

What seems to happen in fantasies of dualism is a reversal of the Oedipal drama *and* a reversal of the mirror stage—a repudiation of the dominance both of the Father and of the Ideal ego, the I, formed with the subject. It is an unlearning of the distinction between body and what lies outside it, a non-identification with the reflection in the mirror, and its ego outline, a desire for that state *preceding* the fall into alienation. It is an attempt to loosen, or to lose, the ego and its dominance by uncovering something less fixed, less formed, less nameable, and, inevitably, less social. Lacan has termed this longing for an original state of undifferentiation as the central unconscious longing in every human being: it is "an eternal and irreducible human desire . . . an eternal desire for the non-relationship of zero, where identity is meaningless.''[11] It is this desire which is fulfilled in the unity of mysticism and of oneness with God, but which in Western secular culture—where all our Romantic and post-Romantic fantasies are placed—takes more frustrated and agonized forms.

The motif of the double in literary fantasy can be regarded as a variation on a theme of alienated identity, also evident in related motifs such as the reflection, the shadow, the ghost, the monster, the magic portrait, the stranger. Behind these variants lies the idea of the mirror and its production of reflected selves, for the mirror establishes a different space in which the ''real'' or ''normal'' is inverted or broken. Behind the mirror is a space both familiar and unfamiliar: it sets up distance and difference. Leo Bersani writes that the mirror is ''a spatial representation of an intuition that our being can never be enclosed within any present formulation—any formulation here and now of our being.''[12] It is in precisely this metaphorical capacity that the mirror entered the language of psychoanalysis, and a reversal of the mirror stage can be seen as a metaphor for the production, or recovery, of other multiple selves.

Lacan stresses that the establishment of identity, the construction of the ego, inevitably involves a sense of loss and anxiety, in which there is an uneasy memory trace of previous union now apprehended as unattainable. A relation between the two I's, self and ideal ego, develops into one of hostility and resentment, with the ideal I, like the eye, constantly on the watch, judging, controlling, condemning, preventing any attempts of the subject to fall away from a strict coincidence with its limited, monistic, integrated social identity. Like Freud's notion of superego, this I acts as censor and judge and is the source of an internal awareness of guilt, apprehension, even paranoia. The double, a fantasy of evading this monistic I/eye, has a difficult relation to the unitary subject, haunting him/her with a reminder of all that has been excluded and amputated in the process of social formation. It is this which gives the double its subversive function, for as Bakhtin writes in his discussion of Dostoevski's version of dualism, through the double, ''the possibilities of another man and another life are revealed. . . . The dialogical attitude of man to himself . . . contributes to the destruction of his integrity and finalizedness.''[13]

The double functions as a figure onto which are externalized inadmissible and tabooed desires. They are products of projection, by which is meant ''the operation whereby qualities, feelings, wishes or even 'objects,' which the subject refuses to recognize or rejects in himself are expelled from the self and located in another person or thing. Projection so understood is a defence of very primitive origin (and is at work especially in cases of paranoia).''[14] It involves a defiance of the rule of the Father, an attempt to elude the threat of castration which hangs over the child, and to recover a state of union with the mother and of primary narcissism. Freud's collaborator, Otto Rank, in the first psychoanalytic study of the double, wrote that the double represents man's relationship with himself and that it ''personifies narcissistic self love.''[15] Freud, influenced by Rank's work to investigate narcissism more deeply, realized that the double was, in its original formation, ''an insurance against the destruction of the ego,'' ''an energetic denial of the power of death,'' the modern inheritor of the idea of the immortal soul as the double of the physical body. For the production of a reflection or of multiple selves defends against a fear of not-being, by creating a being immune to space, time, change, or mortality. The double, according to Freud, is a preservation against extinction, a product of the fear of castration and of a desire for immortality, and he finds the source of such ideas in ''the primary narcissism which dominates the mind of the child and of primitive man.''[16]

The least interesting fantasies of the double use it merely as an allegorical means of dramatizing moral assumptions. Stevenson's *Dr. Jekyll and Mr. Hyde*, for example, has Jekyll as the Ideal I, censoring and judging those aspects of himself which are socially unacceptable and projected onto Hyde. Their names signify their functions: Jekyll means I kill—pointing to the murderous side concealed within his respectable role and projected onto Hyde, all that is hidden. Stevenson's ideological position prevented him from fully exploring the complexities of such a relationship—though there are moments when his fantasy does open onto pre-Oedipal possibilities—and his text is reduced to a rather simple fable. Much more complex dramatizations of subjectivity are found in Hogg's *Confessions* and in William Godwin's much neglected and brilliant story of paranoia and persecution, *Caleb Williams*. It was this tale of guilt which was a major source of inspiration to Godwin's daughter, Mary Shelley, in her writing of *Frankenstein*, and it is her particular version of monstrous doubling which I shall examine in more detail, since it has become such a potent and popular modern myth, lying behind many literary and film texts.

As was suggested above, Oedipal questions are at the heart of *Frankenstein*: the monster's tormented quest for identity is but a vast echo of the searchings of Walton—the first narrator—and Frankenstein, the second. ''Who was I? What was I? Whence did I come? What was my destination? These questions continually recurred, but I was unable to solve them.''[17] Frankenstein creates the monster to fill a gap—the absence caused by the death of his mother—and it is the quest for a lost mother which informs the whole text. By becoming an unnatural mother, ''giving birth'' to another, who is a reflection of himself, Frankenstein is able to *be* the mother he lacks, to supply to himself his own need for a mother. Behind his link with the monster—the same sex as he—and their love/hate relationship is a need close to the one Freud described in his essay on homosexual love as ''proceeding from a narcissistic base . . . homosexuals look for a man whom they may love as their mother loved them.''[18] Significantly, the monster is made up of bits and pieces of corpses, dead bodies of others, reconstructed from the region of death where the mother now lies. Frankenstein's creation is a displaced desire to be at one with the mother again and through her to reattain that primary narcissism of undifferentiated existence. A drive for reunion with the mother dominates each section of *Frankenstein*: there are four family units and each one is characterized by the *lack* of a mother; and the same drive lies behind the central fantasy itself, the production of a

LEARN MORE

$35 million
raised for literacy

38 million
books donated

475 million
books reused or recycled

87 million
customers served

BUY BOOKS · DO GOOD · DO GOOD · BUY BOOKS

monstrous, transgressive but mirror-imaged "other," a pre-Oedipal, unnameable shade.

Soon after its genesis, the monster murders Frankenstein's intimates: the brother who displaced him in his mother's affections, the innocent girl who had taken over his mother's caring role after her death, then his bride and half-sister, Elizabeth. Elizabeth is murdered on their wedding night, at precisely that moment when the incest taboo is about to be transgressed, for Elizabeth is a replacement for the mother in Frankenstein's desires and in the family constellation. Thus the monster acts to save his maker from castration—the punishment for breaking the taboo—and is, on yet another level, a defense against the fear of castration.

Behind a desire for the mother, however, is a desire for that "non-relationship of zero, where identity is meaningless," the stage of primary narcissism, which the production of the double is an attempt to regain. Frankenstein's monster is a fantastic example of the idea of "*le corps morcelé*," the body-in-pieces, for it is actually made up of dismembered, disjointed bodies, not one but many. It *is* the fragmented body which precedes the unification and identification of wholeness in the mirror stage, a literal reanimation of our dead and buried selves, those pieces of our otherness from which we have been severed in the act of becoming ego-bound. Initially, this body is not evil—it is outside moral issues, beyond good and evil—but it has evil thrust upon it and gradually comes to assume a more conventional role as an evil monster. *Frankenstein* is one of the most radical and tense modern fantasies—and it is no accident that it was produced by a *woman* writer, on the periphery of Romanticism and unconsciously questioning its ideals of wholeness and ego-integrity—precisely because of its *refusal* to accept moral categorization of the monster. The monster is like a child, at first without form or language, and it is a fantasy version of Frankenstein's pre-Oedipal existence.

Part of the work's radical position lies in its refusal of closure. Unlike other tales of the double, where the shadow side is murdered, or reassimilated, or seen as illusory, *Frankenstein* insists on the creature's constant presence. There is no reconciliation of the two sides of the self, and their mutual haunting and obsession with each other in a complex symbiotic relationship never really ends. After Frankenstein's death, the monster wanders disconsolately into the ice and snow, toward an unknown vanishing point. The text itself, which had opened with a Chinese-box structure of letters within letters, is not resealed: the monster's shapeless form is the last image to be witnessed. What remains, through this refusal of closure of the narrative, is a radical *open-endedness* of being, of both text and reader, an opening-up made possible through the introduction of a fantasy or pre-Oedipal life. The bond between Frankenstein and monster is unresolvable precisely because of its *internal* origin, and in life there can be no overcoming of their condition of alienation as the two I's. As Irving Massey writes, "The monster is something completely internal. . . . The monster may be simply solipsism itself, or an unhappy form of narcissism . . . the monster is an aspect with which Frankenstein cannot or will not come to terms. . . . And so they must resume their endless dialectic of conflict, until, in death, they spiral into one again."[19]

If the ending of Frankenstein is compared with the ending of a more moralistic and allegorical fantasy of doubling and projection, its radical position is made even more clear. George MacDonald, for example, uses shadows and reflections in his Victorian fantasies, and even in their "high" religious fantasy a similar unconscious structuration can be detected. *The Golden Key* (1867), *At the Back of the North Wind* (1871), *The Princess and the Goblin* (1872), *The Princess and Curdie* (1883), *Phantastes* (1858), and *Lilith* (1895) can all be read as fantasies of rejection of the Oedipal moment and as attempts to return to a pre-Oedipal stage. *At the Back of the North Wind*, a popular children's story, fantasizes a movement into a changeless, timeless zone—really a landscape of non-being—through the entrance into a woman's womb. MacDonald's proliferating shadows and doubles in his more "adult" fantasies, *Phantastes* and *Lilith*, are attempts to ward off castration and to evade the law of the Father, but there is little real struggle or conflict with or through them.

Lilith, for example, has its narcissistic hero Vane—his name signifying his vanity—moving from an anxious inquiry as to his origins and real identity ("What is behind my *think*? Am *I* there at all? Who, what am I? I could no more answer the question. . . . I gave myself up as knowing anything of myself or the universe") to a submission to the Father's expulsion of him from the mother's place.[20] After rediscovering and lying next to his mother in a strangely dead landscape—indeed an almost farcical scene of fantasized incest—where he is "blessed as never was man on the eve of his wedding" (MacDonald, *Lilith*, p. 247), Vane is ejected by a male figure, Adam, the first man/father, and he apologizes: "I ought not to have lain down without your leave" (p. 248). Vane reenters the living world a wiser and better man, for he has accepted the symbolic castration which this scene represents. The "great shadow," which has been hovering throughout the story, is at last dispelled—because Vane has incorporated it into himself.[21]

The shadow/double figure at the end of *Lilith* is written out of the text, not because a pre-Oedipal unity has finally been attained, but because the desire for pre-Oedipal undifferentiation has been repressed. Instead it is displaced onto a transcendental ideal of unity, a sublimated heavenly state in which dualism is unknown. This is a displacement of desire which is common to all transcendental fantasies—a removal of contradiction from a human to a religious or supernatural scheme of things. MacDonald's words betray the unconscious wish-fulfillment behind this ideal, when his narcissistic Vane admits to his maturity in these terms: "I have never again sought the mirror" for "that life which, as a mother her child, carries this life in its bosom" (p. 274). A desire for pre-Oedipal fluidity and non-identification has been displaced here onto a more socially acceptable ideal of union with a divine mother/father.

The difference between works like *Frankenstein* and *Lilith* may have to do with the different genders of their authors, since these will have produced different formations of the social being through the Oedipal drama. However, there are further implications in their treatments of the double motif. *Frankenstein* suggests that there can be no satisfactory resolution of the conflict between the Ideal ego and the fragmented, protean selves outside its formation. It is an open-ended work, leaving in tension various parts of the psyche, creating a sense of contradiction and dissatisfaction with social constructs—of identity, language, morality, law, knowledge, reason, time, and space. It subverts the notion of a unified character or ego and implies that *there are unknown and unexpected forms of subjectivity, or pre-subjectivity, which are repressed and concealed in or through the normal and normalizing process of identification*. Produced from the edge of the Romantic movement by a female writer, it fantasizes the continued existence of pre-Oedipal states, of pre-moral and pre-male undifferentiation. It takes a negative, almost tragic form because of Mary Shelley's positioning as she wrote from within that male culture and its ideals, but it can be interpreted as an attempt to break or dissolve the ego by un-doing the process of its formation.

MacDonald, through his fantasy of submission and of eventual sublimation of a desire for the pre-Oedipal state, reconstructs the ego. He ends by rewriting, reinscribing, patriarchal values onto the human body, producing a text which, as might be expected from a male theologian at the core of Victorian conservatism, is deeply reactionary in its equation of a preordained cosmic *and* social harmony. By contrast, Mary Shelley's writing takes much more cognizance of the real consequences of inhabiting a post-Romantic, secular, patriarchal culture. *Frankenstein* provides a tense dramatization of the problematic nature of identity, its cost, its alienation of "self" from potential selves, from others, from the world which is quite unlike the facile wish-fulfillments of magical unity found in the dream works of MacDonald and those "high" fantasy writers in his wake.[22] Mary Shelley's version of dualism, which is, in effect, more of a fantasy of pre-Oedipal multiplicity, opposes itself to the idealism and the universals of Romantic and transcendental art, ultimately putting into question the very premises on which our materialistic, rational culture is based and exposing its promises of fulfillment. As Julia Kristeva writes: "The call of the unnameable . . . issuing from those borders where signification vanishes, hurls us into the void [which] appears henceforth as the solidary reverse of our universe, saturated with interpretation, faith, or truth."[23]

NOTES

1. Epigraph of *The Student of Prague* (1913), an expressionistic film on the theme of the double.

2. Rosemary Jackson, *Fantasy: The Literature of Subversion* (London: Methuen, 1981). Other works discussing the contradictions embedded in Gothic fantasy include Robert Kiely, *The Romantic Novel in England* (Cambridge: Harvard University Press, 1972) and David Punter, *The Literature of Terror: A History of Gothic Fiction from 1765 to the Present Day* (London: Longman, 1980).

3. See Ralph Tymns, *Doubles in Literary Psychology* (Cambridge, England: Bowes & Bowes, 1949); Masao Miyoshi, *The Divided Self: A Perspective on the Literature of the Victorians* (New York: New York University Press, 1969); Robert Rogers, *A Psychoanalytic Study of the Double in Literature* (Detroit: Wayne State University Press, 1970); and C. F. Keppler, *The Literature of the Second Self* (Tucson: University of Arizona Press, 1972).

4. Mary Shelley, *Frankenstein, or the Modern Prometheus*, ed. M. K. Joseph (Oxford: Oxford University Press, 1969), p. 203.

5. Ibid., p. 77.

6. James Hogg, *The Private Memoirs and Confessions of a Justified Sinner*, ed. John Carey (Oxford: Oxford University Press, 1969), p. 182.

7. Shelley, *Frankenstein*, p. 121.

8. Freud's ideas referred to in this essay can be found in "Three Essays on the Theory of Sexuality" (1905), vol. VII, of *Standard Edition of Complete Psychological Works of Sigmund Freud*, 24 vols., ed. James Strachey (London: Macmillan, 1953). The most accessible introduction to Lacan's work is Jacques Lacan, *The Language of the Self*, trans. Anthony Wilden (Baltimore: Johns Hopkins University Press, 1968).

9. Marianne Wain, "The Double in Romantic Narrative: A Preliminary Study," *Germanic Review* 36 (1961), 260. See also Louis Vinge, *The Narcissus Theme in Western European Literature up to the Early Nineteenth Century* (Lund: Gleerup, 1967).

10. Steve Burniston, "Lacan's Theory of the Constitution of the Subject in Language," in *On Ideology* (London: Hutchinson, 1978), p. 212.

11. See Lacan, *Écrits: A Selection*, trans. Alan Sheridan (London: Tavistock, 1977), particularly the chapter "The Mirror Stage as Formative of the Function of the I," which is reprinted as "The Mirror-Phase" in *New Left Review* 51 (1968), 71–77.

12. Leo Bersani, *A Future for Astyanax: Character and Device in Literature* (Boston: Little, Brown, 1976), p. 208.

13. Mikhail Bakhtin, *Problems of Dostoevsky's Poetics*, trans. R. W. Rotsel (Ann Arbor: Ardis, 1973), p. 96.

14. J. Laplanche and J. B. Pontalis, *The Language of Psychoanalysis*, trans. Donald Nicholson-Smith (London: Hogarth Press, 1973), p. 359.

15. Otto Rank, *The Double: A Psychoanalytic Study*, trans. Harry Tucker, Jr. (Chapel Hill: University of North Carolina Press, 1971), p. 95. See also Stanley M. Coleman, "The Phantom Double," *British Journal of Medical Psychology* 14 (1934), 254–73, and J. E. Downey, "Literary Self-Projection," *Psychological Review* 29 (1912), 299–311.

16. Freud, "The Uncanny," *Standard Edition*, XVII, 217.

17. Shelley, *Frankenstein*, p. 128.

18. Freud's essay "On Narcissism" (1914), *Standard Edition*, XIV, 75–76, shows the influence of Rank's study of the double in literature.

19. Irving Massey, "Singles and Doubles: Frankenstein" in *The Gaping Pig: Literature and Metamorphosis* (Berkeley: University of California Press, 1976), p. 128. Other pertinent discussions of the unconscious drives behind Mary Shelley's work include Marc A. Rubenstein, " 'My Accursed Origin': The Search for the Mother in *Frankenstein*," *Studies in Romanticism* 15 (1976), 165–94; U. C. Knoepflmacher, "Thoughts on the Aggression of Daughters," and Peter Brooks, "Godlike Science/Unhallowed Arts: Language, Nature and Monstrosity," both in *The Endurance of Frankenstein: Essays on Mary Shelley's Novel*, eds. George Devine and U. C. Knoepflmacher (Berkeley: University of California Press, 1979).

20. George MacDonald, *Lilith* (New York: Ballantine Books, 1969), p. 14; hereafter cited in the text.

21. Robert Lee Woolf, *The Golden Key: A Study of the Fiction of George MacDonald* (New Haven: Yale University Press, 1961) provides a biographical version of the formative years of MacDonald's life, relating a sense of the absent mother in his work to his early weaning and his mother's premature death.

22. Stephen Prickett in *Victorian Fantasy* (Hassocks, Sussex: Harvester Press, 1979) sees MacDonald's work as part of a tradition of "high" fantasy, characterized by a strongly Platonic idealism and evident in the writings of Charles Kingsley, John Ruskin, Lewis Carroll, Walter de la Mare, and Edith Nesbit. This tradition also includes C. S. Lewis, J. R. R. Tolkien, and other contemporary fabulists.

23. Julia Kristeva, *Desire in Language: A Semiotic Approach to Literature and Art* (Oxford: Oxford University Press, 1980), p. x.

Meyrink's *Der Golem*: The Self as the Other

Lee B. Jennings

Writers sympathetic toward Gustav Meyrink's work have stressed that he was a serious and devoted student of mystical and esoteric doctrine.[1] Less sympathetic critics, especially those favoring a sociological approach, have tended rather to treat his work under the rubric of *"Trivialliteratur."* We should bear in mind, however, that for this latter school any dominant concern with inward self-realization or affairs of the soul, let alone a receptivity toward occultistic thought, is likely to appear as evidence of counterproductive, asocial subjectivism and is bound to be entered on the debit side of the ledger when the overall merit of a work is considered.[2]

To be sure, Meyrink's *Der Golem* does show some naively awkward features. Because of the basic premise of the novel, no clear line can be drawn between visionary and paranoid perceptions, and the hero's tendency to sense menace in the most innocuous objects approaches the ludicrous at times. Ghostly messengers appear as if on cue. The inner narrator, Pernath, may seem an unlikely candidate for enlightenment, since he suffers throughout from a frenzied, expressionistic befuddlement. The erotic relationships smack of wish-fulfillment fantasy, and the overt story line, with its adventure and intrigue, appears contrived. The subsidiary characters are little more than stereotypes, and the depiction of some of the Prague ghetto dwellers as saintly figures does not quite outweigh the predictable depravity of the Jewish villains.

Nonetheless, even a casual reading should bear out the author's serious endeavor to provide a fictionalized account of the mythical struggle toward the higher self. In various works, Meyrink draws upon different areas of esoteric lore to symbolize this struggle; in this novel, the Kabbala, the tarot, gnosticism, and alchemy are favored.[3] His eclectic use of such lore makes it difficult to trace the provenance of any one motif or idea, arousing, no doubt, the suspicion of an exploitative popularization of the occult as well. This suspicion is uncalled-for, since Meyrink, like C. G. Jung, treats occult and arcane doctrines as a general repository of archetypal symbols of psychic change. The symbolic nature of visions is expressly mentioned in the novel, and within it they attain a quasi-objectivity as glimpses, shared by different observers, of a hyper-real order of things.[4]

A summary of the action may be helpful. A man troubled by puzzling dreams gradually resolves into the figure of Athanasius Pernath, a gem engraver living in the Prague ghetto. He is recovering from mental illness and cannot remember his past life because of amnesia hypnotically induced in the course of therapy. Just this amnesia, however, is said to be a prerequisite for his awakening to a higher state of being, the first step of which occurs when an uncanny stranger, later identified as the dread Golem, delivers a mysterious old book for him to repair. Pernath finds that he can now better grasp the hidden connections of events, especially as they are revealed to him in dreams and visions and in remarks of his mentor, the saintly quasi-rabbi Hillel. Hillel's daughter Mirjam, to whom Pernath is increasingly attracted, is nearly as spiritual as her father and is a naive believer in miraculous coincidences. The diabolical schemes of the obsequious, harelipped secondhand dealer, Aaron Wassertrum, are opposed by his natural son, the half-crazed, impoverished, tubercular student, Charousek, who has sworn blood revenge against Wassertrum and aids Pernath to the extent that it furthers his own cause. Less significant figures are the coquettish, aristocratic Angelina, who is carrying on an extramarital affair in a room adjoining Pernath's quarters, and Pernath's tavern cronies, wry commentators on the ghetto scene. The subplots (there is no main one except for Pernath's meandering quest) involve the protection of Angelina's secret (and Pernath's temporary infatuation with her) and Charousek's revenge-plotting.

Due to Wassertrum's conniving, Pernath is eventually imprisoned on a false charge of murder. On being released, he finds that the ghetto has been largely torn down, and he sets about seeking Hillel and Mirjam, who now seem in some way to hold the key to his fate. He apparently glimpses them as he is fleeing a burning building by climbing down a rope. They are in a mysterious, doorless (but windowed) room which the Golem was once reputed to inhabit and in which he himself once spent an eerie and sleepless night. He loses his hold, the rope breaks, and he falls.

At this point we discover that Pernath's history, though apparently true, was dreamed by yet another man, who now awakes. The dream was caused by his inadvertently wearing Pernath's hat. This unnamed frame-narrator sets out to trace Pernath and finds that approximately forty years have passed since the last events of his dream. Nevertheless, he finds Pernath and Mirjam, untouched by the ravages of time, living in a mysterious house familiar to him from his dream. The house is now a kind of shrine, decorated with symbolic depictions of the hermaphrodite and the god Osiris. He is not allowed to enter this sanctuary, but he glimpses the pair from a distance and is able to exchange hats. In a note brought by a somewhat golemesque servant, Pernath expresses the hope that his hat has not caused its bearer any headaches.

The peculiarly depressing tenor of the work seems to arise not only from its questioning of reality, but also from its nearly complete separation of spiritual awakening from the conventional moral values. The path of awakening is said to depend on a free decision, a vocation from within, but in effect this vocation seems little more than a blind and arbitrary urge, the small manifestation of a vast ultramundane plan extending over generations. Life, for Pernath, is predominantly absurd, perhaps more so after his "awakening," which, although it increases his sensitivity and intuitive understanding, does nothing to improve his poor judgment or to dampen his occasional murderous urges. No indulgent deity presides over his obscure strivings, only the stern god Osiris. A powerful virtue emanates from his mentor, Hillel, who, however, is separated even from his own family by a glass wall of sanctity. A synthesis of the infinite and finite worlds is hinted at, but the dominant concept is that of a spirituality quite incompatible with the world of the senses.

Hillel's delineation of the Ways of Life and Death evidently is intended to provide the key to the world order presented here. There are those "bitten by the serpent," "pregnant with the spirit of life," who are destined to awaken from the sleep of ordinary consciousness. Others go the Way of Death, though most humans follow no particular path in their aimless drifting (Meyrink, *Golem*, pp. 87–89). The Way of Death in its pure form, then, is rare. We gain insight into its nature from one of the novel's visionary events. Pernath, in a trancelike state, is accosted by a phantom with stumps for legs, its head a nebulous globe (a classical Jungian archetype of the whole self). The Phantom proffers seven seeds; not knowing whether his salvation lies in accepting or rejecting them, Pernath hits upon a third alternative and knocks them out of the Phantom's hand (pp. 181–85).

The exegesis of the vision is provided by Laponder, a confessed rapist-murderer and somnambulist who shares Pernath's prison cell, a saintly figure in the Dostoevskian sense. Laponder once had the same vision; in his version, he accepted the seeds and was forced to go the Way of Death. Accordingly, during his moon-induced trances, he becomes a robotlike instrument of alien spiritual forces. It is hinted that his crime represented a dim realization of the hermaphrodite image, the symbolic incarnation of the whole human being. By knocking the seeds out of the Phantom's hand, Laponder explains, Pernath has mobilized magical powers that will remain in the custody of his ancestral spirit counterparts until ready for use (pp. 307–14).

Thus, in Meyrink's usage, the concept of "life" is largely limited to the domain of the spirit. All of the things we regard as vital connote mortality and thus belong to the realm of death. When Pernath experiences vernal stirrings of the blood, he is distracted from his quest. The path of Eros is a false one. In this light, the figure of the Golem becomes more understandable. Though thematically central, this figure is rather subsidiary to the action. It is only loosely related to the legendary animated clay figure of Rabbi Loew and his predecessors. Its manifestations are explained in two fairly unrelated ways. First, the Golem incorporates the collective unconscious of the ghetto in times of spiritual crisis. The speculation here is that the legendary rabbi created a mental image which has ever since craved some form of embodiment. Usually it appears as a vaguely Asiatic, zombilike figure wearing old-fashioned clothes. Second, the Golem acts as a psychic double or alter ego for some individual, in which case it appears as a frightening but not altogether malevolent figure (pp. 54–58). To Hillel, who sees self-confrontation as the ultimate mystery, the Golem-double is "breath of the bones" (p. 141)—a puzzling term since the figure actually represents "bones" (corporeality) of the "breath" (spirit).

The doppelgänger aspect is forcibly driven home. Pernath imagines himself to be the Golem on two occasions, and when he stays in the doorless room (which he recognizes as a symbol for the recesses of his own psyche) he dons what appear to be the Golem's cast-off clothes to keep warm, causing general consternation upon his emergence (pp. 23–25, 64–66, 122–31). In this respect, the Golem is like the Jungian "shadow," which is often confronted at the beginning of a crisis of psychic growth, but it lacks the individual features that might bear out such a function. Perhaps it stands as a general reminder of the deadness of merely physical things and of the basic abstractness of the animating life-force, thus signifying the ultimate separateness of body and spirit.

Though the dread accompanying the Golem's appearances is stressed nearly to excess, Hillel explains that such demonic apparitions are not to be taken altogether seriously. They are the psychic growing pains of those who witness them, and their mental abrasiveness can be compared to the polishing of a silver mirror. When the mirror is completely reflective, that is, when the soul is clear, the unpleasantness will cease (p. 87). Hillel thus anticipates the classic psychedelic enthusiast's explanation of a "bad trip": the demons represent the ego's struggle in the face of its own temporary or permanent extinction. Likewise, although evil is clearly manifested in the rascally Wassertrum, its role in the cosmic scheme is slight. Evil is a chance imperfection, as Laponder suggests in his elaborate likening of human minds to glass tubes with different colored balls rolling through them (p. 313).

To further illustrate his arcane thesis, Meyrink calls upon the symbolism of the tarot cards. According to Hillel, these cards contain the entire wisdom of the Kabbala in the form best suited to its communication (p. 140). Pernath, while shivering in the doorless room, passes the time by contemplating the Pagad or Fool, the joker of the tarot deck, and this figure seems to materialize before his eyes. The Fool can be understood in two ways: as the materialist and sensualist, oblivious to the treasures of wisdom in his knapsack, about to walk over a precipice; or as the pure innocent whose wisdom is still undeveloped. In either case, he represents man as yet unawakened.[5]

The second tarot card mentioned, the Hanging Man, is somewhat more complex in its significance (pp. 128, 206). It depicts a man hanging upside down by one foot, his left leg folded behind the right, with a halo around his head. Pernath is unable to guess at its meaning. The symbol seems to be objectified twice in the novel. According to local legend, a workman helping to search for the Golem was lowered on a rope to look into the window of the concealed room. Just as he reached his destination, the rope broke and he plunged to his death (p. 53). Pernath reenacts the scene in his fall at the end of the dream narrative. For a moment he hangs "head down, legs crossed, between heaven and earth" (pp. 335–36). Strangely, this is the one detail that the frame-narrator is unable to substantiate; the house had never burned (pp. 346–47). The meaning of the image, in any case, is clear. The breaking of the rope means the severing of connections with the world of the senses. The Hanging Man is a Prometheus or redeemer figure, the immortal self temporarily enmeshed in the tangled yarn of mortal karma.[6] Pernath, when the frame-narrator last sees him, apparently has shuffled off, or at least loosened, the mortal coil. In his union with Mirjam in the hermaphrodite-temple he is in the world but not of it, an Immortal, demonstrating in his own being the fusion of male and female elements to form a purified and complete entity.

Meyrink's symbolization of the psychic integration process is no less valid because it draws upon occultistic lore. Pernath may seem an unworthy recipient of higher wisdom, but the archetypes of psychic transformation play no favorites and mock our moralistic expectations. Jung has noted Meyrink's use of the hat motif in connection with assumed identities.[7] Trite as it may first appear, the device conveys a legitimate message. Illumination, by its very nature, cannot readily be conveyed. The reader-pupil can vicariously follow the process, as the dreamer can understand awakening, only up to a point. Beyond that, he must discard the spurious headpiece and wear his own hat or go forth bareheaded.

NOTES

1. See Eduard Franke, *Gustav Meyrink: Werk und Wirkung* (Büdingen-Gettengach: Avalun, 1957), and Joseph Strelka, "*Das grüne Gesicht* Gustav Meyrinks," in his *Auf der Such nach dem verlorenen Selbst* (Bern: Francke, 1977), pp. 28–37. See also E. F. Bleiler's introduction to the English translation of Meyrink's *The Golem* and Paul Busson's *The Man Who Was Born Again* (New York: Dover, 1976).

2. See Theodor Schwarz, "Die Bedeutung des Phantastische-Mystischen bei Gustav Meyrink," *Weimarer Beiträge* 12 (1966), 716–19. Siegfried Schödel, "Über Gustav Meyrink und die phantastische Literatur," in *Studien zur Trivialliteratur*, ed. Heinz Otto Burger (Frankfurt: Klostermann, 1968), pp. 209–24, finds Meyrink's occultistic intent to be inadequately realized, but he is patently unsympathetic toward the occultistic intent also. Schödel takes issue with Hans Sperber, "Motiv und Wort bei Gustav Meyrink," in *Motiv und Wort: Studien zur Literatur- und Sprachpsychologie* (Leipzig: Reisland, 1918), pp. 5–52, who had selected Meyrink's work for his study precisely because it shows "*das Gepräge einer starken Eigenart, einer unverfälschten sprachlichen und*

erzählerischen Erfindungsgabe'' (''the stamp of a strong individuality, a genuine linguistic and narrative inventiveness'').

3. Cf. Bella Janse, ''Über den Okkultismus in Gustav Meyrinks Roman *Der Golem*,'' *Neophilologus* 7 (1922), 19–23.

4. Gustav Meyrink, *Der Golem* (München: Kurt Wolff, 1915), p. 310; hereafter cited in the text.

5. Cf. Ralph Metzner, *Maps of Consciousness* (New York: Collier, 1971), p. 61.

6. Ibid., pp. 66–67.

7. C. G. Jung, *Psychologie und Alchemie* (Zurich: Rascher, 1953), p. 80.

Wondrous Vision: Transformation of the Hero in Fantasy through Encounter with the Other

Karen Schaafsma

> How can we contrive to be at once astonished at the world and yet at
> home in it? How can this world give us at once the fascination of a
> strange town and the comfort and honour of being our own town?... We
> need this life of practical romance; the combination of something that is
> strange with something that is secure. We need to view the world as to
> combine an idea of wonder and an idea of welcome. We need to be
> happy in this wonderland without once being merely comfortable.
>
> (G. K. Chesterton, *Orthodoxy*)[1]

Chesterton's description of the "main problem for philosophers" also describes
a central concern of fantasy: perhaps more than any other modern genre, fantasy
literature attempts to renew our sense of the world as both mysterious and
familiar, as at once our own and a marvelous, unexpected gift. Or as Sam
Gamgee says of Lothlórien, "It's like being at home and on holiday at the same
time."[2]

In evoking the mystery at the core of experience, fantasy performs a function
formerly carried out by myth and religious ritual. The experience of wonder,
which Tolkien describes as "the primal desire at the heart of faerie," is closely
related to the experience of the sacred.[3] As Rudolf Otto has shown, both experiences are inspired by a mystery at once awful and desirable (*"mysterium:
tremendum et fascinans"*).[4] Fantasy is the only modern genre which takes as its
subject man's relationship to this supernatural or numinous reality; only fantasy
affirms that relationship as the source of positive values for man. Although
fantasy is sometimes seen as being only superficially different from science
fiction, the latter genre deals with an unknown reality which is ultimately subject
to rationalization. Thus most science fiction concerns itself with man's efforts
to bring the unknown under his control, to transform it into the familiar and

therefore manageable, while fantasy explores man's relation to a reality that eludes his conscious control and his rational comprehension.[5] Horror fiction, the only other modern genre treating the supernatural, represents it as inherently alien and threatening. In this respect, horror fiction, more than realistic fiction and science fiction, is the polar opposite of fantasy. Both rely for effect on our sense of a reality beyond immediate apprehension; both play on our feelings about the mysterious, hidden aspects of the visible world. Both describe the human hero's encounter with that reality, but horror fiction typically represents man as isolated and helpless before a malicious, alien, often chaotic force, while fantasy represents the possibility of an intimate, harmonious relationship between man and the supernatural Other.

Fantasy constructs a bridge between the natural and the supernatural, the human and the nonhuman, the objective, material world and a subjective, spiritual realm. The world view typical of fantasy is essentially religious, and it tends to be mystical in tone; the human hero confronts the Other directly without mediation of institution or ritual; the hero becomes the mediator between the Other and the larger community. Although many fantasies, like those of George MacDonald or C. S. Lewis, reflect their authors' Christian faith, the vision that informs their works is compatible with, even akin to, that expressed in non-Christian fantasy like that of Ursula K. Le Guin, Lord Dunsany, or Peter Beagle. All affirm that positive value is to be discovered in an order of reality that transcends the human and the rational.

There are a number of reasons why fantasy, especially, lends itself to the expression of this theme. Although the fantasy novel is a modern genre, its resemblance to myth and fairy tale and its archaic flavor render it an apt mode for the expression of an almost anti-modern outlook (one that implies, for instance, the inadequacy of empiricism). Since it is a non-realistic genre, which does not pretend to mirror the real world, it avoids the issue of literal belief in the supernatural, while presenting it as compellingly attractive. Because it describes the hero's confrontation with a reality he can neither rationally explain nor manipulate at will, it provides built-in parallels with religious experience. Finally, while fantasy borrows many elements from fairy tale and myth, it also shares many of the characteristics of the modern novel, characteristics which make it more accessible to the modern reader. The heroes of fantasy are drawn more realistically than those of myth and fairy tale; often, like the reader, they are initially unfamiliar with the supernatural, and they respond to their first experience of it as the reader would, with shock, fear, and bewilderment. Similarly, the landscapes of fantasy are more fully and concretely rendered than those of traditional literature; many fantasies include a detailed map. Modern fantasy, then, unlike myth and fairy tale, allows for the reader's lack of familiarity with the supernatural; at the same time, through an identification with the hero and through a vivid sense of place, the reader is invited to a more intimate encounter with that reality.

The central event in fantasy, for which both the hero and the reader must be prepared, is the encounter with the supernatural Other. It is the catalyst for the hero's transformation and for the restoration to health, physical and spiritual, of the larger community. The centrality of the hero/Other relation in fantasy is one feature distinguishing that genre from romance as defined by Northrop Frye.[6] Although fantasy obviously shares many characteristics of romance (the quest, the archetypal characters, the cyclical imagery), Frye describes the central event in romance as the conflict between the hero and his foe, a monster or demonic figure. Although the hero may be aided in his struggle to overcome the monster by supernatural helpers, these figures are always subordinate in importance to the hero and his antagonist. Fantasy has sometimes been described as a simplistic contest between good and evil. In most fantasies, the relationship which develops between the hero and a benevolent supernatural figure is of equal or greater significance. A direct contest between the hero and the antagonist is rare in fantasy; even more rare is a contest resolved by physical strength (as is typical in romance). In Tolkien's *The Lord of the Rings*, Peter Beagle's *The Last Unicorn*, and Patricia McKillip's *The Forgotten Beasts of Eld*, for instance, the antagonist is destroyed either by his own act or as an indirect consequence of some positive act by the hero. The fundamental act for the hero is not the defeat of evil, but the affirmation of the value inherent in the Other. Ultimately, fantasy suggests that those who oppose themselves to that value are doomed by their own alienation, while those who recognize the spiritual and moral authority of the Other attain a superhuman status.

The supernatural Other is represented in many forms in fantasy (it may be a unicorn, a dragon, or a wizard), but it is typically characterized by a paradoxical combination of qualities. On the one hand, it is powerful, awesome, mysterious, and impersonal; on the other hand, it is revealed as vulnerable, subject to loneliness, sorrow, and loss. The unicorn in Beagle's fantasy can kill a dragon or heal a king with a touch of her horn, but it is only through the mutual love and loyalty that develop between the unicorn and the human heroes that her quest is accomplished. The elves in Tolkien's trilogy are a mysterious, remote, and powerful race; their magic has sustained a timeless, edenic realm, untouched by any evil. Yet despite their magic and their immortality, they are vulnerable to the passage of time; the inevitable dwindling of their powers which must accompany the destruction of the ring creates an element of pathos throughout the trilogy.

The same combination of power and remoteness with vulnerability can be seen in the figure of Deth in McKillip's Riddlemaster trilogy, in the dragons of Le Guin's *The Farthest Shore*, in the lion Aslan in C. S. Lewis's Narnia books, and in the Dun Cow of Walter Wangerin's *The Book of the Dun Cow*. With few exceptions, the supernatural beings in these fantasies do not act independently of the hero, nor are they the primary agents of the central action. Often, like the unicorns in Beagle's fantasy, they are passive, themselves the object of the hero's quest. More often, they act indirectly, through the hero, transferring their strength to him. In C. S. Lewis's fantasies, for example, the lion Aslan does directly influence events in Narnia on occasion, but more often he lays the burden of action on the young heroes, while providing them with spiritual guidance. The elves in Tolkien's trilogy and the Dun Cow in Wangerin's novel function in the same way; they inspire the hero with their power of vision but take no part in the central action. Beagle's unicorn and Le Guin's dragons are less spiritualized figures, closer to the natural order, yet they also represent for the hero concrete embodiments of the values which give meaning to existence.

Although the hero's encounter with the supernatural Other is the central event in fantasy, it is the hero's transformation with which we are most concerned and which best illustrates the themes of fantasy. At the beginning of most fantasies, the hero is naive, provincial, and self-centered, ignorant of the world at large and of his relation to the order which governs it. Frodo, at the beginning of *The Lord of the Rings*, is reluctant to leave the homely, familiar comforts of his hobbit hole and is scarcely confident of his ability to carry out the dangerous quest which has been laid on him. Ged, the main character in Le Guin's Earthsea trilogy, is initially only interested in using his magical talents to increase his own power and status. Mr. Vane, the hero of MacDonald's *Lilith*, believes himself able to right all wrongs singlehandedly, and his arrogance leads him to ignore the advice of those wiser than he. Schmendrick, the magician in Beagle's *The Last Unicorn*, imagines himself an inept bumbler, a sideshow magician who must prostitute his talents in order to survive. Sybel, the sorceress in McKillip's *The Forgotten Beasts of Eld*, lives alone in a crystal dome, knowing nothing of the world of men, indifferent to their fate, incapable of love or pity.

In every case, the hero is called out of himself by some external event or presence which intrudes on his isolation and demands a response.[7] Thus Gandalf shows up at Frodo's door to tell him that all he holds dear in the world is in imminent peril and that he, Frodo, holds the key to its fate. Ged's irresponsible act, calling up a ghost to impress a rival, looses a nameless and terrifying shadow which haunts him until he confronts it. Mr. Vane suddenly is faced with his responsibility for the lives of a group of innocent children; Sybel is handed a baby to love, and so on. The challenge which the hero must face takes many forms, but always the welfare of the larger community hinges on his ability to meet that challenge. He is forced to act, often for the first time, for the sake of something other and larger than his own interests.

The hero, then, is called upon to right some injustice or to recover some lost object of value, but he is not required to accomplish his quest singlehandedly, relying only on his own resources. On the contrary, his success or failure depends upon his willingness to accept a subordinate role in relation to a larger order. It is through his encounter with the supernatural Other that the hero gains an understanding of his proper role. For the hero, the Other functions as a kind of living symbol, representing in microcosm the true order and value of all existence. Only through his experience with this concrete manifestation of ultimate value is the hero able to comprehend a reality which transcends rational understanding.

In Beagle's *The Last Unicorn*, Prince Lir is called upon to play a sacrificial role. If the quest is to succeed, Lir must give up the human girl he has come to love and allow the magician to restore her to her true self, an immortal unicorn. He is able to accept the sacrifice because he has learned that

the true secret of being a hero lies in knowing the order of things. . . . Things must happen when it is time for them to happen. Quests may not simply be abandoned; prophecies may not be left to rot like unpicked fruit; unicorns may go unrescued for a long time, but not forever. The happy ending cannot come in the middle of the story.

"You were the one who taught me," he said. "I never looked at you without seeing the sweetness of the way the world goes together, or without sorrow for its spoiling. I became a hero to serve you and all that is like you."[8]

In *The Farthest Shore*, the third volume of Le Guin's Earthsea trilogy, young Prince Arren accompanies Ged on a quest to correct an imbalance in the Equilibrium, the sacred pattern of nature. The health of the pattern depends on a balance of life and death, but a corrupt wizard has found a way to create a hole between the underworld and the land of the living. The hole exerts a powerful negative attraction, drawing all life into itself and transforming Earthsea into a wasteland. It requires an affirmation of mortality to defeat the power of the void and restore Equilibrium.

To Arren, the concept of Equilibrium is an abstraction; he cannot understand why the desire for immortality is destructive, or why death is the necessary counterpoint to life. However, in the course of their quest, Ged and Arren encounter the dragons, the most ancient living beings in Earthsea. They provide for Arren a living symbol of the value which arises out of the balance of life and death:

As Lookfar approached the islands, Arren saw the dragons soaring and circling on the morning wind, and his heart leapt up with them, with a joy, a joy of fulfillment that was like pain. All the glory of mortality was in that flight. Their beauty was made up of terrible strength, utter wildness, and the grace of reason. For these were thinking creatures, with speech and ancient wisdom; in the pattern of their flight was a fierce, willed concord.

Arren did not speak, but he thought: "I do not care what comes after; I have seen the dragons on the wings of morning."[9]

To close the hole and restore Equilibrium, Ged and Arren must descend into the underworld, but their path is only made clear by the sacrifice of the dragon Orm Embar on the sword of the enemy. For Arren, and for the reader, that sacrifice represents the heroic affirmation of a value that transcends death.

In *The Lord of the Rings*, the heroes encounter the supernatural in many forms, but it is in Lothlórien that Frodo finds a vision of light which can drive back the darkness. Lórien is a timeless land "where no shadow lay"; it provides Frodo with an image of the world as it was when first created:

It seemed to him that he had stepped through a high window that looked upon a vanished world. A light was on it for which his language had no name. All that he saw was shapely, but the shapes seemed at once clear-cut, as if they had been first conceived and drawn at the uncovering of his eyes, and ancient, as if they had endured forever. He saw no colours but those he knew, gold and white, and blue and green, but they were fresh and poignant, as if he had at that moment first perceived them and made for them names new and wonderful. (Tolkien, *Lord*, I, 365)

In Lórien, Frodo sees for the first time the magical, numinous aspect of the world around him. He sees objects in nature as separate from himself and as possessing an intrinsic, irreducible value: "He laid his hand upon the tree beside the ladder; never before had he been so suddenly and so keenly aware of the feel and texture of a tree's skin and of the life within it. He felt a delight in wood and in the touch of it, neither as a forester nor as a carpenter; it was the delight of the living tree itself" (Tolkien, *Lord*, I, 366). Although the nature which Frodo experiences in Lórien possesses a kind of concentrated purity and vitality, the value he finds there is not unique to the eleven lands; Lórien is the most enchanted realm in Middle-earth, but because it also is experienced as "home" the value discovered there is universal.

The insight that Frodo achieves in Lórien is essential for the hero of fantasy; he must recognize that the world is not his for the taking, that nature has a value apart from its use. In *A Wizard of Earthsea*, the fledgling wizards are taught that power comes from knowing the true names of things, which is to know their essence. Thus the mage Ogion instructs Ged: "When you know the fourfoil in all its seasons, root and leaf and flower, by sight and scent and seed, then you may learn its true name, knowing its being: which is more than its use."[10] It is only when the hero recognizes the value of things-in-themselves, separate from his desires, that he is able to use power wisely.

The heroine of Patricia McKillip's *The Forgotten Beasts of Eld* is a powerful young sorceress, Sybel, who lives alone in a crystal dome, her only companions a collection of magical creatures she can summon and command at will. Only one creature eludes her call, the Liralen, a beautiful, moon-white bird on whose wings she could "fly away to the end of the world . . . to the edge of the stars."[11] Sybel's desire is for a freedom that is ultimately sterile and empty; her call fails because she sees the Liralen as a means to escape the painful burden of relation rather than as a being itself bound by love. When Sybel uses her powers to enslave others to her will, she betrays that quality of inviolable otherness which the Liralen embodies; a vision warns her of the consequences: "beneath her mind's eye the image clarified and she found a moon-white bird with twisted, trailing wings, the curve of its smooth neck snapped back against itself."[12] The image forces Sybel to confront the cost of her egotism and to recognize her own earth-bound nature, the needs and desires which bind her to others. Only when Sybel frees the animals in her collection and renounces her power over others does the Liralen come to her freely.

The effect of the hero's encounter with the supernatural is to shock him into an awareness of otherness. The supernatural being is experienced as irresistibly attractive and inherently valuable, yet it may not be possessed or manipulated at will: it acts in accordance with its own nature, rather than conforming to his desires. If the hero is receptive, the encounter can produce an initiation into wisdom; in recognizing the value of the Other, he gains an understanding of the "order of things," of the "way the world goes together." In serving the Other, the hero relinquishes, to a great extent, his personal identity; he leaves behind family, friends, and his place in the community and takes on an overwhelming responsibility. However, the demands made on the hero call out in him a corresponding strength, reinforced by his relationship to the Other. Thus, Sybel's devotion to the Liralen sets free the "soaring thing" within herself. Ged learns to subordinate his desire for power to the absolute priority of the Equilibrium; he becomes its guardian and the Archmage of Earthsea, with the power to seal the boundary between life and death: " 'It will be shut,' Ged said, coming beside them; and the light blazed up now from his hands and face as if he were a star fallen on earth in that endless night" (Le Guin, *Shore*, p. 183).

Throughout *The Lord of the Rings*, images of light are associated with the elves. When Frodo leaves Lórien to continue on his quest, the elf-queen Galadriel gives him a crystal vial to be "a light to you in dark places when all other lights go out" (Tolkien, *Lord*, I, 393). Twice in the darkness of Mordor, Frodo and Sam call on the vial of Galadriel, and her name, to drive back the evil creatures that menace them. However, during Frodo's final confrontation with the powers of darkness, he himself becomes a commanding figure of white light. Here he confronts Gollum, who blocks his path to the very peak of Mount Doom, the final goal of his quest:

Then suddenly . . . Sam saw those two rivals with other vision. A crouching thing, scarcely more than the shadow of a living thing, a creature now wholly ruined and defeated, yet filled with a hideous lust and rage; and before it stood, stern, untouchable now by pity, a figure robed in white, but at its breast it held a ring of fire. Out of the fire there spoke a commanding voice:

"Begone and trouble me no more! If ever you touch me again, you yourself may be cast into the Fire of Doom." (Tolkien, *Lord*, III, 221)

The light with which the heroes become identified is a sign of their spiritual maturity, their power of vision. In fantasies which present a conflict between good and evil, it is always the hero's vision of positive value, inspired by the Other, that enables him to defeat the powers of darkness.

The figures of evil in fantasy are characterized by their insatiable greed for and alienation from the source of true value. Often the antagonist is a being reduced to mere blind appetite; his power arises, paradoxically, from the negative force of his need. In *The Last Unicorn*, King Haggard is driven to capture all of the unicorns in the world because, as he says, "I must have that. I must have all of it, all that there is, for my need is very great" (Beagle, *Unicorn*, p. 186). In *The Lord of the Rings*, in *The Farthest Shore*, and in George MacDonald's

Lilith, evil is termed "the shadow"; it is a thing without substance which can only hunger endlessly for its opposite. The wizard Cob in Le Guin's fantasy is like a "spider dried up in its web" (Le Guin, *Shore*, p. 170), attempting to draw "all light and life" into itself, to fill up its "emptiness" (p. 180). In Tolkien's trilogy, we never meet the Dark Lord himself, but Frodo sees his searching eye in Galadriel's mirror; "the black slit of its pupil opened on a pit, a window into nothing" (Tolkien, *Lord*, I, 379). Mr. Vane, the hero of *Lilith*, experiences the horror of the "shadow" as it hovers, predatory, over Lilith:

Gradually my soul grew aware of an invisible darkness, a something more terrible than aught that had yet made itself felt. A horrible Nothingness, a Negation positive enfolded her; the border of its being that was yet no being, touched me, and for one ghastly second I seemed alone with Death Absolute! It was not the absence of everything I felt, but the presence of Nothing. The princess dashed herself from the settle to the floor with an exceeding great and bitter cry. It was the recoil of Being from Annihilation.[13]

The antagonist in fantasy serves as a foil to the hero, but he also represents his double or shadow. Frodo resembles Gollum in those moments when he succumbs to the seduction of the ring; Ged's violation of the Equilibrium in the first volume of the Earthsea trilogy is identical in nature to Cob's act in volume three. Frequently, the evil figure is an alienated member of the same family or original community as the hero. Lilith is the estranged first wife of Adam; King Haggard is the adoptive father of Prince Lir; Gollum is also a hobbit; Cob, like Ged, is a member of a select society of wizards. Ultimately, however, the hero and antagonist are distinguished by their different responses to the Other. The hero recognizes its intrinsic value, independent of human desire, but the corrupt figure sees everything in relation to himself. Lilith is obsessed with a desire for total autonomy; her one cry is "I will do as my Self pleases—as my Self desires."[14] Because nature possesses a vitality, spirit, and purpose of its own, she regards it as a threat; to paralyze the natural cycles of birth, death, and regeneration to which she would otherwise be subject, she gathers all the waters of the land into a tiny bead which she holds tightly clutched in her hand; ultimately, the hand must be severed from her wrist before the waters can be freed and the wasteland renewed. The White Witch in C. S. Lewis's Narnia books is a similar figure; she keeps Narnia under a spell of eternal winter and transforms those who defy her into marble statues. Haggard's imprisonment of the unicorns is likewise an attempt to seize and control the very essence of life.

Despite their power, the antagonists in fantasy are typically starved, emaciated figures like T. S. Eliot's "Hollow Men." Their vulnerability lies in their isolation; in clinging to the Self, and in seeking to transform all that is Other into Self, they cut themselves off from the true source of life and power. In *The Farthest Shore*, Ged tells Cob, "You sold the green earth and the sun and stars to save yourself. But you have no self. All that which you sold, that is yourself. You have given everything for nothing" (Le Guin, *Shore*, p. 180). The powers of evil are all negative; they can destroy, but they cannot create; they can imprison, but they cannot liberate; they can deny, but they cannot affirm.

Although the precise value of the Other cannot be defined, it is always identified with the creative, regenerative potency in nature. In the Narnia fantasies, the lion Aslan is associated with the light, warmth, and vitality of the sun; his arrival in Narnia ends the long, deadly winter imposed by the White Witch. In *The Farthest Shore*, the dragons also are associated with the benevolent, healing powers of the sun; after Ged and Arren's defeat of Cob, they are physically and spiritually depleted. They accept the dragon Kalessin's offer to carry them home, and as they mount his back, "Both felt a warmth come into them, a welcome heat like the sun's heat, where they touched the dragon's hide: life burnt in fire beneath that iron armor" (Le Guin, *Shore*, p. 193). When the unicorns are freed in Beagle's fantasy, the wasteland of Haggard's kingdom is similarly restored: "The withered earth was brightening with a greenness as shy as smoke. Squat, snaggly trees that had never yet bloomed were putting forth flowers in the wary way an army sends out scouts; long-dry streams were beginning to rustle in their beds, and small creatures were calling to one another" (Beagle, *Unicorn*, p. 235). Similar transformations occur in *The Lord of the Rings* and in MacDonald's *Lilith*. The liberation of the Other revitalizes both the natural order and the community of men.

The happy endings of fantasy affirm that the value found in the Other is infinite, inexhaustible, yet the defeat of evil is never accomplished without sacrifice. The hero in fantasy is always called upon to relinquish the very thing the antagonist is unwilling to give up—his personal desire, his ego. In *The Last Unicorn*, Lir must renounce his desire for the Lady Althea; in *The Forgotten Beasts of Eld*, Sybel frees her animals and gives up her desire for revenge. However, the sacrifices of the hero often are more profound; Lir also gives his life to save the unicorn. At the end of *The Lord of the Rings*, Frodo must leave the land he has struggled to save, in company with the elves, whose powers have been sacrificed in the defeat of Sauron. Similarly, when Ged returns from his descent into the underworld, he is no longer Archmage; he has exhausted his wizard's powers, and, like Frodo, he withdraws from the community of men. Although the value of the Other transcends the individual and even death itself, the sacrifice made by the hero is no less real or costly. In *The Farthest Shore*, Ged attempts to explain to Arren the paradox of a timeless value embodied in the unique and temporal:

"Look at this land; look about you. This is your kingdom, the kingdom of life. This is your immortality. Look at the hills, the mortal hills. They do not endure forever. The hills with the living grass on them, and the streams of water running. . . . In all the world, in all the worlds, in all the immensity of time, there is no other like each of those streams, rising cold out of the earth where no eye sees it, running through the sunlight and the darkness to the sea. Deep are the springs of being, deeper than life, deeper than death." (Le Guin, *Shore*, p. 165; Le Guin's ellipses)

Compared to the "mortal hills," individual life is fragile indeed; it is the hero's acceptance of the need for sacrifice in the face of this fragility that enables him to defeat the powers of evil and to incorporate the value of the Other within himself.

Finally, the hero serves as a mediator between the supernatural Other and the larger community; he or his representative becomes the bridge uniting the material world with the numinous presence. Frodo leaves Middle-earth, but his companion and counterpart, Sam, returns to the Shire to restore order, bringing with him soil from the garden of Galadriel. Ged retires as Archmage, but he sees his spiritual son, Arren, crowned as king. Prince Lir inherits his father's kingdom, and he will rule it wisely, having been touched by the unicorn's horn.

For the community of readers, the work of fantasy itself serves a similar mediating function, presenting us with a vision of the world revitalized by a numinous presence. The journey on which fantasy takes us is not without risk; the encounter with mystery can disrupt our systems of meaning, but the purpose of such disruption is not, as Eric Rabkin suggests, to reveal the "chaos" of reality, but rather to restore our receptivity to an underlying order and value to be discovered in experience.[15] The journey in fantasy is a circular one, taking us "There and Back Again": we lose our way in the wilderness of fantasy so that we may find our way back home.[16]

NOTES

1. G. K. Chesterton, *Orthodoxy* (1909; reprint ed., Garden City, N.Y.: Image Books, 1959), p. 11.

2. J. R. R. Tolkien, *The Lord of the Rings* (Boston: Houghton Mifflin, 1965), I, 376; hereafter cited in the text.

3. J. R. R. Tolkien, "On Fairy-Stories," in *The Tolkien Reader* (New York: Ballantine, 1966), p. 14.

4. Rudolf Otto, *The Idea of the Holy* (1923; reprint ed., New York: Oxford University Press, 1958), pp. 12–31.

5. For further discussion of differences between the two genres, see Colin Manlove, *Modern Fantasy: Five Studies* (Cambridge: Cambridge University Press, 1975), pp. 3–8; see also Robert H. Boyer and Kenneth J. Zahorski, "Science Fiction and Fantasy Literature: Clarification through Juxtaposition," *Wisconsin English Journal* 28 (1976), 2–8.

6. Northrop Frye, *Anatomy of Criticism* (Princeton: Princeton University Press, 1957), pp. 189–97.

7. Because the call comes from outside the hero and usually fills him with dismay, W. H. Auden characterizes the quest in fantasy as "religious." See "The Quest Hero" in *Tolkien and the Critics*, eds. N. D. Isaacs and R. A. Zimbardo (South Bend: Notre Dame University Press, 1968).

8. Peter S. Beagle, *The Last Unicorn* (New York: Ballantine, 1968), p. 212; hereafter cited in the text.

9. Ursula K. Le Guin, *The Farthest Shore* (1972; reprint ed., New York: Bantam Books, 1977), p. 147; hereafter cited in the text.

10. Ursula K. Le Guin, *A Wizard of Earthsea* (1972; reprint ed., New York: Bantam Books, 1977), p. 17.

11. Patricia K. McKillip, *The Forgotten Beasts of Eld* (New York: Avon Books, 1975), p. 82.

12. Ibid., p. 188.

13. George MacDonald, *Lilith* (1895; reprint ed., New York: Ballantine, 1969), p. 221.

14. Ibid., p. 216.

15. Eric S. Rabkin, *The Fantastic in Literature* (Princeton: Princeton University Press, 1976), p. 213; but see also p. 218; "The wonderful, exhilarating, therapeutic value of fantasy is that it makes one recognize that beliefs, even beliefs about reality, are arbitrary."

16. *There and Back Again* is the subtitle of J. R. R. Tolkien's *The Hobbit*.

Rite of Passage: The Vampire Tale as Cosmogonic Myth

Ronald Foust

"Das beste des Menschen liegt im Schaudern."

Goethe

Since its inception in the late eighteenth century, Gothic fiction has been such a popular and influential literary form that "an understanding of the literature of the last two hundred years requires a knowledge of the nature of Gothic."[1] Despite its popularity, however, the "Gothic novel has not fared well among literary critics" who typically "treat the subject with chilly indifference or condescension."[2]

Of course, this general critical indifference has extended to the vampire tale. For example, Devendra Varma has called *Dracula* "probably the greatest horror tale of modern times,"[3] and yet criticism has not treated it seriously and, more surprisingly, has made no effort to connect it to the Gothic tradition.[4] This aversion to the vampire motif includes even aficionados of "weird" fiction. Thus, although Peter Penzoldt admits that "the psychological problem at the root of the Vampire archetype is a complex one," he nonetheless concludes that "the vampire motif is crude and primitive" because he can see in it merely a projection of Freudian somatic wish-fulfillment.[5] Such critical aversion ignores the fact that the vampire motif has been employed in many of our greatest literary works, beginning with Book XI of *The Odyssey*.[6]

As Varma has pointed out, the tale of terror appeals "to some deeply rooted instinct; an irresistible, inexplicable impulse drives us toward the macabre."[7] Thus, despite critical neglect, Gothicism continues to thrive among a mass audience because it satisfies a hunger for an experience that is otherwise proscribed by social conventions. This experience constitutes for the reader-protagonist a psychological "rite of passage" based upon an imaginative encounter with the chthonic doppelgänger that Jung called the Shadow.[8] Since this encounter is ultimately purgative—defamiliarizing and thus enriching the reader's diurnal experience—it is desired; however, since it initially awakens a dim species memory of man's original separation from and conquest of natural chaos, it involves him in peril (the "madness" that is a favored metaphor of the form) and is therefore feared. Finally, the uncanny effect that characterizes the vampire tale is attributable to the fact that the demonic adversary is a projection of the "buried Self," a dark double of both the reader and the fictive protagonist.

The earliest prose narrative of this kind is John Polidori's *The Vampyre* (1819), which is based on a five-page fragment by Lord Byron.[9] In it we meet Lord Ruthven (Byron), the original Undead, a nobleman pallid and burdened with ennui whose "dead grey eye . . . pierce[s] through to the inward workings of the heart," causing awe in all who meet him (p. 265). He takes an orphaned "young gentleman of the name of Aubrey" (p. 266) as his traveling companion, and together they set off on a Grand Tour.

Ruthven proceeds to debauch everyone he meets as the pair travel across Europe. Finally, in Athens, Aubrey falls in love with a Greek girl, Ianthe, who tells him "the tale of the living vampyre" (p. 271). Aubrey laughs at the superstition but is rebuked by the peasants who "shudder at his daring thus to mock a superior, infernal power" (p. 272). Later, while examining some ruins, he becomes so engrossed in his research that night falls and a storm breaks before he remembers to return to the village. Suddenly he hears a woman's cries coming from nearby. He rushes into a dark hovel and is "gripped by one whose strength seemed superhuman" (p. 273). As his attacker flees, the storm abruptly ceases and he discovers Ianthe dead: "upon her neck and breast was blood, and upon her throat were the marks of teeth having opened the vein" (p. 274). Still later Ruthven is shot during a struggle with bandits; on his deathbed he extracts an oath of silence from Aubrey concerning his habits and his fate. He dies and his body is placed on a rock so that it is "exposed to the first cold ray of the moon that rose after his death" (p. 277). Aubrey then returns to England to live with his sister, whom he takes to a ball where he sees "Lord Ruthven again before him, . . . the dead rise again!" (p. 279). Shock at seeing this revenant brings on a depression that deepens into temporary insanity as Aubrey broods over the mystery and power that Ruthven represents. Even when he learns that his sister has become engaged to marry "the monster," he cannot expose him, for each time he tries, a voice telepathically bids him "remember his oath." Although he feels powerless before Ruthven's supernatural reality, he finally rouses himself to action on the day of his sister's wedding and writes a note to her guardians exposing Ruthven. They rush to protect her but arrive to find that Lord Ruthven has disappeared and that Aubrey's sister has "glutted the thirst of a VAMPYRE!" (p. 283).

Polidori's novel both initiates the modern vampire story and adumbrates the major elements that will become the archetypal staples of the form. These include the vampire's "evil eye" or hypnotic power, its tremendous strength, its pallor and association with the moon, its immortality, its identity as a self-absorbed egotist who brings ruin on individuals and societies, its thirst for blood (an ancient attribute of the dead), and its associations with the grave (the hovel), with Satan, and with the love-crime that Mario Praz feels is at the heart of the vampire story.[10] Thus, Polidori's narrative initiates the prose tradition of the vampire as waste-maker and introduces the master-slave relation that obtains between the demonic monster and the representatives of ordinary decency and innocence. In addition, we note that Aubrey is both drawn to and repelled by Ruthven and that both he and the guardians are ineffectual in protecting the treasure (the virginal sister). I shall return to the meaning of the relation between the vampire and a treasure; here I will merely point out that the vampire con- stitutes a threat to the integrity of a beloved object in Polidori's flawed original version of the theme.

The first full treatment of the motif occurs in Sheridan Le Fanu's beautiful but neglected "Carmilla" (1872), a minor masterpiece that greatly influenced Bram Stoker.[11] It is the story of an eighteen-year-old English girl, Laura, who lives in Styria with her father, a retired English soldier, some miles from a ruined village, the former domain "of the proud family of Karnstein, now extinct" (p. 223). Early in the narrative, Laura recounts a dream she had as a child in which "I saw a solemn, but very pretty face. . . . It was that of a young lady who was kneeling, with her hands under the coverlet. . . . She caressed me with her hands, and lay down beside me on the bed, and drew me towards her, smiling. . . . I was awakened by a sensation as if two needles ran into my breast" (p. 225).

As this image implies, "Carmilla" is a story of lesbianism, which is the love- crime that is so necessary to the vampire motif. As the story begins, clouds of mist gather on Laura's estate as a servant discusses the moon's magnetic influ- ence. Suddenly a runaway carriage approaches, "thundering along the road . . . with the speed of a hurricane" (p. 230). Since it is a lunary avatar, the vampire enters at night in moonlight and in mist. Furthermore, the images of thunder and of hurricane are appropriate to the vampire motif for reasons that will become apparent. The carriage overturns and its passenger, Carmilla Karnstein (stone- flesh), is invited to remain as Laura's guest. The two are mysteriously drawn to each other, and Laura recalls that Carmilla "used to place her pretty arms about my neck, draw me to her, and . . . murmur with her lips near my ear. . . . 'In the rapture of my enormous humiliation I live in your warm life, and you shall die— die, sweetly die—into mine. . . . [You will] learn the rapture of that cruelty, which is yet love.' '' Carmilla's algolagnic passion is "like the ardour of a lover" and creates in Laura "a strange tumultuous excitement" that is com- pounded of both pleasure and "a vague sense of fear and disgust" (p. 240). In keeping with the vampire's role as lunar deity, Carmilla is pale and languid, eats nothing and appears only late in the afternoon. Her chthonic nature is implied when she is likened to a fish and to a cat. In addition, she has the gleaming eyes and the passionate gaze that are attributes of the vampire. As the two girls grow increasingly close, Carmilla makes her climactic demand of Laura: "You

must come with me, loving me, to death. . . . Love will have its sacrifices. No
sacrifice without blood'' (p. 251). Love, blood, and death: it is this insistence
upon *Liebestod* that most clearly reveals the vampire motif to be the epitome of
Gothic *Schauer-Romantik* and that relates both to the Romantic tradition.

The vampire tale is a projection of the ancient theme of demonic possession.
As Laura is being possessed, a friend, General Spielsdorf, arrives. His adopted
daughter has died under odd circumstances, and he is convinced that she was
the victim of their beautiful guest, Millarca (like Carmilla, an anagram of Mir-
calla, the vampire's true name), who sometimes takes ''the shape of a beast''
(pp. 275–76) and who Spielsdorf is convinced is a revenant or vampire. His sole
mission in life is now to find and destroy the monster in ''the usual way, by
decapitation, by the stake, and by burning'' (p. 278). Together they travel to
the ruined Karnstein village where they meet the original vampire-killer, Baron
Vordenburg, a ''fantastic old gentleman'' (p. 283), who helps them find the
monster's lair in a deserted churchyard. There they corner Carmilla, whose
features undergo ''an instantaneous and horrible transformation'' (p. 282); they
grapple with her and are overwhelmed by her prodigious strength; and she then
returns to her ''amphibious existence'' in the tomb (p. 288). They eventually
discover her coffin and, ''in accordance with the ancient practice,'' drive a stake
through her heart. Carmilla shrieks, writhes, and dies, whereupon the hunters
decapitate her (p. 285).

It is primarily in the manner of the vampire's destruction that one most clearly
recognizes the myth of the dragon-battle that underlies the modern vampire tale.
In its tremendous strength, destructiveness, and manner of dying, the vampire
is a displaced version of the ancient image of the dragon that menaces a social
unit, the members of which are individually powerless, until its threat is collectively overcome. Thus the conquest of the vampire represents at one level
the victory of conventional society over a powerful, ancient, attractive but lethal
prehistoric foe representing natural chaos.

Le Fanu elaborates all of Polidori's materials, including the vampire's association with mist, moonlight, and storms; the ambivalently attractive and re-
pulsive effect it has upon its victim; its identity as a destroyer (the ''deserted
village'' theme); its algolagnia (the love-crime), and its shape-shifting. In addition, Le Fanu adds the important elements of the picturesque castle, the vampire's chthonic anti-Christian connotations, and the mythopoeic importance of
the dragon-battle culminating in staking and beheading as the effective means
of liberating society from its ambiguously hated and loved Enemy.

Bram Stoker's *Dracula* (1897) is the masterpiece of *Schauer-Romantik* and
the culmination of Gothic as a genre.[12] It is Stoker's work which has been drawn
upon by filmmakers and imitated by epigones such as Stephen King in *Salem's
Lot*. Since *Dracula* is the most complete embodiment of the displaced myth of
the dragon-battle that generates all vampire fiction, I shall discuss it at some
length.

It opens as Jonathan Harker, an ''orphan'' who is engaged to be married, travels by carriage on May 4, "the eve of St. George's Day" (p. 6), from the village of Bistritz in Transylvania through the Borgos Pass toward the mountain that the native population calls "Isten szed!—God's seat!" (p. 10). Dracula's forbidding and ancient castle adorns the peak of the "cosmic mountain"; that is, castle and mountain together constitute a sacred center, a threshold that opens onto the three levels of heaven, earth, and the underworld. During the trip the coach rocks and sways through the darkness like a ship in a storm, and the vampire's association with the chaos of storms is again established (pp. 11–12). As the journey continues, Harker feels that he is "simply going over and over the same ground again" (p. 14). Thus the journey is the fictive equivalent of the mythic night-sea crossing in which the young initiate leaves the security of his home, is disoriented by experience, and enters a labyrinth. The mazelike quality of the temporal journey will be duplicated spatially in the form of the interior of the castle itself. This induction of the initiate into experience is a central feature of all Gothic fiction and is the narrative equivalent of the myth of engorgement, of being swallowed into a monster's belly.

When he arrives at the castle, Harker enters a courtyard which is constructed as a labyrinthine maze. He then meets Count Dracula, who introduces himself as a hunter—and indeed he is. The novel divides evenly into two parts based upon the metaphor of the hunt. During the first half, the vampire hunts his human prey; the narrative movement is from Transylvania to England as Dracula's power waxes to fullness. During the second half, his menace wanes as the human society wrests power from him and becomes the hunter, tracking him from civilization back to Transylvania, where his power disappears as they stake and behead him on the mountaintop at the foot of the castle. The story's form, then, is that of a circle divided, Yin-Yang-like, into sigmoid halves. This structure, suggestive of the waxing and waning of the moon, is apropos of the narrative's latent meaning, since the vampire tale is a modern displacement of an ancient myth in which a demonic lunar avatar is combated and finally overcome by a solar hero.

Harker's induction into supernatural reality soon deepens into horror as he realizes that he is Dracula's captive. Imprisoned at the top of the castle, he is visited by three of Dracula's sister-brides; they are succubi, "phantom shapes," who simply materialize from the moonlight. He pretends to sleep as one of them bends over him and prepares to kiss his throat. He feels "longing and at the same time deadly fear," a "voluptuousness which was both thrilling and re-pulsive"; Dracula arrives "in a storm of fury" and saves Harker for his own purposes. At his arrival the succubi suddenly "fade into the rays of the moon-light" (pp. 50–52).

In desperation he decides to explore Dracula's room, which he enters perilously by scaling a portion of the castle wall. It is empty, and all that he discovers is a large pile of gold in one corner, all of it at least three hundred years old. He passes through an open door, a threshold, which leads "through a stone passage to a circular stairway." It is yet another maze, and he descends to the bottom where, in the bowels of the earth, he enters "a dark, tunnel-like passage, through which [comes] a deathly, sickly odor." There, in the interior of an ancient, dilapidated chapel, he finds the count lying in a coffin in the moribund state that is the nocturnal vampire's lot during the half of each day that is dominated by the influence of the sun (pp. 63–65). Later, when Van Helsing and the others corner Dracula in England, Harker slashes at him with his knife, tearing Dracula's clothing, from which falls a stream of gold. Thus Harker's discovery of Dracula's treasury is a crucial scene establishing the vampire as the guardian of a treasure hoard. I shall return to the meaning of this important motif. Harker finally escapes by scaling the castle ramparts and drops out of the narrative; we later learn that he has lain in delirium in a hospital in Budapest for weeks. In the meantime, Dracula has chartered a ship, the *Demeter*, which arrives covered with mist on the English coast during a storm. The ship's crew is missing, and only a corpse is found lashed to the helm. However, the ship's log is discovered, and it recounts the events aboard the *Demeter* for the month of July, during which time Dracula systematically has destroyed the ship's entire "society." It is important to note that the height of the vampire's power occurs in midsummer at sea where, taking the shape of mist, he creates yet another ruin, just as he has depopulated the area surrounding his castle. It is in its role as destroyer of social organizations that the modern vampire most clearly reveals its kinship with the mythic dragon which is its prototype.

In England, Dracula preys on Lucy Westenra, Arthur Holmwood's fiancée. Throughout this section Dracula's chthonic attributes are insisted upon: he is associated with mist, moonlight, and bats and seems "more like a wild beast than a man" (p. 13). As Lucy declines, the orthodox physician, John Seward, calls for assistance from his former teacher, Abraham Van Helsing. A more complex version of Le Fanu's Baron Vordenburg, Van Helsing, the vampire-killer, is a shaman: he is a physician, a teacher, a jurist, and a priest whose most effective medicines are the Christian armaments of crucifix, holy water, and the sanctified Host. Two things of importance now occur: Van Helsing adopts the members of the beleaguered society—Seward, Quincy Morris, Harker, Arthur, Mina, and Lucy each becomes "my child"—and he begins to use vegetation metaphors as analogies for human action. "My friend John, when the corn is grown . . . while the milk of its mother-earth is in him . . . the husbandman will pull the ear . . . I have sown my corn [i.e., made his plan of action], and Nature has her work to do in making it sprout" (pp. 161–62); Dracula has come to England where humanity grows "like the multitude of standing corn" (p. 429).

Lucy progressively weakens as Van Helsing struggles to save her life. Finally he is forced to give her blood transfusions from each of the four men to sustain her life. Nevertheless, she dies and becomes another of Dracula's brides. After her death, Arthur is in such shock that "his stalwart manhood seemed to have shrunk" (p. 226). Thus, possession by the Undead has a clear psychosexual dimension which gives a special urgency to the hunt for Dracula conducted throughout the remaining portion of the text. Lucy is now a lamia preying upon the children of London. When Van Helsing discovers this, she is tracked to her lair, where the men look upon her with loathing, and her transformed flesh is likened to that of Medusa. Van Helsing warns Arthur that "you are now in the bitter waters, my child" and must master this terror in order to drink "of the sweet waters" (p. 286); that is, he must undergo this initiatory experience to achieve his manhood and Lucy's freedom. Thus, Arthur, looking "like a figure of Thor," hammers the stake into Lucy's heart. At this the "thing in the coffin writhed; and a hideous blood-curdling screech came from the opened lips. The body shook and quivered and twisted in wild contortions" (p. 290). The small band of humans, a microcosmic social order, by now associate Dracula with Satan and pledge to destroy the vampire, emblem of Night and chthonic chaos, in order to set "the earth free from a monster of the nether world" (p. 314).

The possession of Lucy, a love-crime occurring about midway in the story, represents the climactic point of the vampire's power. The division of the plot into halves is a structural device reifying Stoker's treatment of the motif since, among other things, the vampire is a lunar deity (hence its paleness, its languor, and its association with moonlight), whose progress is associated with the four cycles of the moon. The first half of the narrative is equivalent to the waxing of the moon and its fullness of influence; the second half recapitulates in dramatic form its waning and disappearance. This lunar association explains several important aspects of the vampire tale. As J. E. Cirlot points out, "Man, from the earliest times, has been aware of the relationship between the moon and the tides, and of the more mysterious connexion between the lunar cycle and the physiological cycle of women." Thus the vampire is a personification of the moon, "the Master of Women." In addition, the moon's phases are "the source of inspiration for the Dismemberment myth" since the moon "is the being which does not keep its identity but suffers 'painful' modifications to its shape."[13] The moon is the primordial and original shape-shifter, and this is a partial explanation of the vampire's ability to alter its form, as well as its association with that other archetypal shape-changer, the *loup-garou* or werewolf. However, there is another explanation of the vampire's ability to alter its form to which I shall return.

After his encounter with Dracula, Harker suffers so severely from the malady that had afflicted Arthur that Mina begs Van Helsing to restore her husband (p. 284). Harker's journal entry explains the malady: "I felt impotent," he writes, and Van Helsing "made a new man of me" by his vigorous resistance to the vampire (p. 252). Indeed, the making of an adolescent into a man is the novel's buried theme. The essential point is that the vampire does not produce the future—children through sexual union—but only a static, changeless present. He is an egotist who possesses others for the purpose of reproducing images of himself through an asexual "vamping" of the innocent. This is the psychological import behind the multitude of ruins the vampire creates and rules, as well as its association with the moon.

It is now October as the small band of humans turn hunter and stalk their enemy, whose power, though waning, remains great. The vampire is able still to attack and wound Mina in a hideous parody of the Christian sacrament of marriage. As she sleeps, Dracula comes to her as a red-capped column of mist during the full moon and performs a mock marriage ritual by chanting: "And you . . . are now to me, flesh of my flesh; blood of my blood; kin of my kin . . . my companion and my helper" (p. 386). The men rush to her bedroom only to see the vampire holding her in a "terrible and horrid position, with her mouth to the open wound in his breast" (p. 382). Upon their arrival Dracula becomes savage, and they banish him with the sacred wafer and crucifix. Mina honestly admits that her unnatural mating with the vampire was horrible but that, "strangely enough, I did not want to hinder him" (p. 386). The remainder of the story constitutes an act of ritual atonement, the result of which is the union of a cleansed Harker and Mina, the divine pair, in a marriage resulting in the restoration of sexual vitality and in childbearing.

We are now in a position to see a pattern emerging: the vampire threatens the cosmic *hieros gamos*, the "sacred marriage," that is the primordial model of human social organization. Lord Ruthven destroys Aubrey's Ianthe (and Aubrey's self-confidence, his "manhood") and then, on her wedding night, his sister; Carmilla seduces Laura and offers a lesbian substitute for marriage and reproduction; Dracula blasts Arthur's and Lucy's fruitfulness and then turns his ruinous passion upon Mina. Having rendered Harker impotent, he begins his seduction of Harker's bride, and he taunts his human enemies thus: "Your girls that you all love are mine already . . . my creatures, to do my bidding and to be my jackals when I want to feed" (p. 412).

However, his boast is forced; from this point on, the vampire's power is clearly on the wane as the human band organize against him, find and sterilize all but one of his coffin-homes, and force him to take flight. A white-haired but rejuvenated Harker takes command of the hunters, who track the vampire back to Transylvania. The experience of the ancient Enemy has been so estranging that the hunters begin to lose track of modern "objective" time and instead become "accustomed to watch for sunrise and sunset" (p. 503); that is, they are perilously close to falling back into the rhythms of nature.

It is now November and snow is falling around Castle Dracula as the little band overtake the gypsy wagoneers who are conveying the vampire's coffin to the castle. A struggle ensues at the peak of "God's seat," the gypsies are overcome, and in the *sparagmos* or ritualistic tearing to pieces, Harker is able to slash Dracula's throat with his Kukri knife as Quincy Morris, fatally wounded, plunges his bowie knife into the vampire's heart at the exact moment that the sun falls behind the horizon. With this ritual act of staking and dismemberment, the curse passes away, and Mina stands cleansed and bathed in rosy light (p. 507).

A "Note" is appended in which Harker relates that "Seven years ago we all went through the flames"; in the meantime, Mina has given birth to a boy who is given a "bundle of names" that link "all our little band of men together" (p. 507). Harker and Mina also return to Castle Dracula—which stands "as

before, reared high above a waste of desolation'' (p. 508)—but now the labyrinth, divested of the Minotaur at its center, is harmless and merely picturesque.

We now are prepared to understand both the myth of which the vampire tale
is a displaced version and the crypto-religious nature of the reader's encounter
with this epitome of Gothicism. It is no accident that Harker's initiation into
supernatural reality begins on the eve of St. George's Day. The vampire tale is
the most powerful modern reenactment of the ancient myth of the dragon-slaying,
of which the contest between St. George and the dragon is the premier English
version. In the myth society is threatened by a waste-making dragon, chthonic
emblem of the forces of Night and Chaos; a solar hero reestablishes social order
(i.e., rescues a treasure, often in the form of a virginal maiden, or alternatively,
the reawakening of the fertility of the land) by pursuing, destroying, and dis-
membering the *feond mancynnes*, mankind's ancient Enemy. Typically, the
sparagmos or dismemberment ushers in new life and returned social vigor.

The reader's encounter with the vampire reenacts perhaps our most ancient
ritual experience and ''one of the oldest battles in literature,'' which is ''the
fight between the sun-god and a monster deity.''[14] The best-known version in
Anglo-American mythology is the legend of St. George, although its origins are
much more ancient and extend backward in time through the Norse legend of
Thor and the Midgard Serpent, to Greek tales of Zeus and Typhon, Apollo and
the Python, and Cadmus and the founding of Thebes from the dragon's sown
teeth. However, the original version is contained in our oldest written document,
the *Enuma Elish* (*Babylonian Genesis*, circa 1500 B.C.). There the solar god,
Marduk, ''combats the evil she-dragon, Tiamat,'' his mother.[15] She is also the
spirit of salt water who symbolizes ''evil or primeval chaos,'' which explains
the dragon's frequent association with storms and the ocean.[16] The serpentine
Tiamat ''was the first dragon, and her awesome ever-changing image has haunted
mankind ever since.''[17]

This is the myth that informs such later mythico-religious documents as *Beowulf*, where, we recall, the solar hero encounters ''the serpent, the dread malicious spirit,'' the ''people's foe, the dread fiery dragon,'' and strikes it in the
head with his sword.[18] The dragon then takes Beowulf's ''whole neck between
his sharp teeth'' and inflicts a mortal wound, as Wiglaf strikes ''the vengeful
stranger a little lower,'' killing it (p. 155). The wounded Beowulf cuts the dragon
in half and bids Wiglaf enter ''the lair of the serpent, the ancient creature who
flew by twilight'' and bring out the treasure the dragon had guarded. There
Wiglaf finds ''glittering gold lying on the ground'' (p. 158). (As in Stoker's tale
the gold in *Beowulf* has lain in the ground for three hundred years.) Beowulf
dies, and his men push ''the dragon, the serpent, over the cliff,—let the waves
take the guardian of the treasure, the flood enfold him'' (p. 175). The dragon
is buried in the sea because that is the chaotic natural element it emblemizes.
Thus, the modern vampire's attributes—its power, its chthonic characteristics,
its ritualized manner of dying—are the necessary results of the requirements of

the archetypal story, that of the dragon-battle, that lies at the heart of all Gothic fiction.

"The Dragon is the greatest of all serpentes and bestes," says a Medieval document. It "dwelleth in depe caves of the ground"; it also "fleeth in to the ayre & bethet in the ayre in such wyse that it semeth to be a gret tempest in the ayre & his wynges . . . be facyoned lyke the wynges of a batte that flyeth in the twy lyght & where the dragon abideth there is the ayre dark and full of venymous corruption."[19] Mythographically considered, the vampire is a displaced form of the dragon. When discovered and staked, it writhes and agonizes because that is the ritualized behavior of the dragon symbol of chaos and is thus associated with the moon, storms, fogs and mist, and the night. It is also a chthonic divinity and thus a shape-shifter, appearing now as a bat, now as a wolf, now as an elemental mist or dust motes, and is likened to cats, fish, serpents, and lizards. It is, in effect, the personified spirit of the multitudinous power of the various elements of primordial Nature wreaking vengeance on social organizations *because* they are organized and, thus, "unnatural." Its prime targets, then, are marriage and the family since these constitute the cornerstones of civilization. Hence the vampire's typical victim is a young, marriageable innocent tremulously poised at the vulnerable turning point between childhood freedom and adult responsibility.

The popularity of all Gothic fiction, especially the vampire tale, is understandable in terms of the reader's repressed desire to experience vicariously this myth in which the villain, always some displacement of the dragon, threatens the reader's psychological integrity with "possession." The resultant effect is what Freud called "the uncanny," the ambivalent desire and dream which are the result of experiencing the alien Other as a projection of our own buried impulse toward disorder and, perhaps, death. It is projected repeatedly in these fictions as a wish-fulfillment in which the threatened innocent—Aubrey, Laura, Mina, or Harker—is momentarily overcome by the loved and hated Other, only to be rescued by the archetype that Jung called "the wise old man." The villain is the Shadow, the "negative side of the personality" of which the reader must become aware by "recognizing the dark aspects of the personality as present and real." The villain, then, is a psychopomp, "a mediator between the conscious and the unconscious and a personification of the latter."[20]

Psychologically considered, the fictive dragon-battle "has three main components: the hero, the dragon, and the treasure."[21] Dracula sleeps at the foot of a passageway linked to a treasure hoard because he is a modern manifestation of the dragon. The treasure represents the hero's Self, his maturity which must be won from a serpentine adversary who represents a fear of "relapse into the body-bound chthonic world of animality."[22] Thus, the vampire tale constitutes an initiation ritual, a "rite of passage," for the reader-protagonist. As Mircea Eliade has pointed out in another context, the initiate must pass "beyond the profane, unsanctified condition" and discover "the true dimensions of existence" before he can "assume the responsibility that goes with being a man . . . [since]

access to spirituality is expressed "in a symbolism of death and rebirth."[23] Only when Harker has slain the chthonic dragon of his own primordial animality can he "cleanse" Mina and redeem the sexual function necessary for the regeneration of society.

Dracula begins in May and ends in November, spanning the six-month vegetation cycle; the vampire charters a ship, the *Demeter*, in July and while at sea (where, being an avatar of Tiamat, he has his greatest strength) he destroys an entire microcosmic society as he had done before. He then threatens a new society, characterized by preparations for multiple weddings, with similar ruin. His destructive efforts partially succeed until he is overthrown by a "solar youth" and a "wise old man." Together they dismember him in ancient fashion, and from this act new life arises.

Overcoming the dragon constitutes an imaginative cosmogony; that is, it recapitulates the myth of an originative creative act of consciousness by which primordial man imperfectly separated himself from the preconsciousness of Nature. The vampire, therefore, is not merely a "crude motif"; rather, it is a hierophany, an "*act of manifestation* of the sacred" in which the reader shares.[24] The reader experiences what may be called crypto-religious emotions in his purely imaginative encounter with the numinosity—the power, the mystery, the awesomeness—of the vampire. As Glen St. John Barclay notes, "The inherent appeal of the story of the occult lies in its capacity not to exorcise faith in the unknown, but to reinforce it," since any fiction that "refers to the intervention of the supernatural in human affairs necessarily affirms that the supernatural exists."[25]

The vampire tale can be thought of as the climactic development of the Gothic novel, the appeal of which lies in its ability to satisfy an ancient hunger for numinous experiences repressed by the reader's conscious understanding of the limits of reality. Behind the lurid image of the vampire lurks the shadowy dragon, our repressed double, psychopomp of the Id, our barely buried "secret sharer." Thus, the vampire tale is the epitome of Gothic fiction, an understanding of which is essential to a complete literary history, since "the study of dragons is the study of the human mind."[26]

NOTES

1. Andrew Wright, ed., *The Castle of Otranto*; *The Mysteries of Udolpho*; *Northanger Abbey* (New York: Rinehart, 1963), p. viii.

2. Robert D. Hume, "Gothic versus Romantic: A Revaluation of the Gothic Novel," *PMLA* 84 (March 1969), 282.

3. Devendra Varma, *The Gothic Flame* (New York: Russell and Russell, 1957), p. 160.

4. Mark M. Hennelly, Jr., "Dracula: The Gnostic Quest and Victorian Wasteland," *English Literature in Transition* 20, no. 1 (1977), p. 13. The writings of recent critics such as Hennelly and Charles S. Binderman, "Vampurella: Darwin and Count Dracula," *The Massachusetts Review* 21 (Summer 1980), 411–28, imply a growing awareness of

the centrality of the theme of vampirism to the late Victorian social imagination. However, criticism has neither interpreted the motif from a Jungian perspective nor placed it in the broader context of modern literary history.

5. Peter Penzoldt, *The Supernatural in Fiction* (New York: Humanities Press, 1965), pp. 37–38.

6. An impressive list of writers who have used the vampire motif is contained in Mario Praz, *The Romantic Agony*, trans. Angus Davidson (London: Oxford University Press, 1933), pp. 76–78. See also M. M. Carlson, "What Stoker Saw: An Introduction to the History of the Literary Vampire," *Folklore Forum* 10, no. 2 (Fall 1977), 26–32.

7. Varma, *Flame*, p. 225.

8. I have treated the concept of the chthonic doppelgänger at length in "Monstrous Image: Theory of Fantasy Antagonists," *Genre* 13, no. 4 (Winter 1980), 441–53.

9. In *Three Gothic Novels*, ed. E. F. Bleiler (New York: Dover, 1966); hereafter cited in the text.

10. Praz, *Romantic Agony*, p. 76.

11. *In a Glass Darkly: Stories by Sheridan Le Fanu*, introd. by V. S. Pritchett (London: John Lehmann, 1947); hereafter cited in the text.

12. Bram Stoker, *Dracula* (New York: Grosset and Dunlap, 1979); hereafter cited in the text. This honor is usually accorded to Charles Maturin's *Melmoth the Wanderer*, but, as Praz has shown, Melmoth "is a kind of Wandering Jew crossed with Byronic vampire" (Praz, *Romantic Agony*, p. 76).

13. J. E. Cirlot, *A Dictionary of Symbols*, trans. Jack Sage (New York: Philosophical Library, 1962), p. 204.

14. Paul Newman, *The Hill of the Dragon* (Totowa, N.J.: Rowman and Littlefield, 1979), p. 17.

15. Ibid., p. 6.

16. Peter Hogarth and Cal Clery, *Dragons* (New York: Viking, 1979), p. 17.

17. Ibid., p. 16.

18. *Beowulf and the Finnsburg Fragment*, trans. John R. Clark Hall (London: George Allen and Unwin, 1911; rev. 1950), pp. 154–55; hereafter cited in the text.

19. Quoted in Hogarth and Clery, *Dragons*, p. 155.

20. *The Portable Jung*, trans. R. F. C. Hull (Princeton: Princeton University Press, 1970), p. 152.

21. Erich Neumann, *The Origins and History of Consciousness*, trans. R. F. C. Hull (Princeton: Princeton University Press, 1970), p. 152.

22. Ibid., p. 311.

23. Mircea Eliade, *The Sacred and the Profane: The Nature of Religion*, trans. Willard R. Trask (New York: Harper and Row, 1961), pp. 191–92.

24. Ibid., p. 11.

25. Glen St. John Barclay, *Anatomy of Horror: The Masters of Occult Fiction* (London: Weidenfeld and Nicolson, 1978), pp. 8–9.

26. Hogarth and Clery, *Dragons*, p. 206.

III. FANTASY AND THE MEDIA

The protean nature of fantasy and its suitability to a wide range of subjects and forms are illustrated in this section by analyses of fantasy in television (Budd, Craig, Steinman), in horror films (Telotte), in comic books (Whitlark), and in surrealistic film and drama (Lalande). Since such instruments of popular culture are motivated chiefly by considerations of profit, they are sensitive and responsive to public demand. People's imaginations today seem attuned to things that never were rather than to realistic representation of things as they are. The prevalence of fantasy in the mass media indicates its widespread popular appeal at the present time.

Fantasy Island: The Dialectic of Narcissism

*Michael Budd, R. Stephen Craig,
and Clay Steinman*

> As therapeutic points of view and practice gain general acceptance, more
> and more people find themselves disqualified, in effect, from the
> performance of adult responsibilities and become dependent on some form
> of medical authority. The psychological expression of this dependence is
> narcissism. In its pathological form, narcissism originates as a defense
> against feelings of helpless dependency in early life, which it tries to
> counter with "blind optimism" and grandiose illusions of personal self-
> sufficiency. Since modern society prolongs the experience of dependence
> into adult life, it encourages milder forms of narcissism in people who
> might otherwise come to terms with the inescapable limits on their
> personal freedom and power—limits inherent in the human condition—by
> developing competence as workers and parents. But at the same time that
> our society makes it more difficult to find satisfaction in love and work, it
> surrounds the individual with manufactured fantasies of total gratification.
> (Christopher Lasch, *The Culture of Narcissism*)[1]

For Lasch, the conflict of personality within advanced capitalism destroys the
possibility of independent adulthood. Instead he finds on the one hand dependence
and frustration, and on the other "manufactured fantasies" of omnipotence and
gratification. Although promising autonomy without anxiety, therapy—instruction in how to cope from interested agencies—in effect seals dependence. From
doctor's couch or television tube, bureaucrat's office or printed page, therapy
becomes the very cure that makes the sickness permanent, the analysis
interminable.

The culture of commodities increasingly represents itself as therapy for the
very dissatisfactions it produces, but the falseness of its promises generates a
dialectic of containment and excess. Not only are the fantasies manufactured by
the culture industry unable to contain, or "use up," the real excessive desires

of human beings, they also produce—to the extent that they are successful in their appeal—more dependence and hence more excesses and frustrations. Analysis of them can reveal contradictions between fantasy as desire and fantasy as product, as sham. At any moment between 10:00 and 11:00 P.M. on 17 January 1981, an estimated thirty-three million people were more or less engaged in this process as they tuned in to an episode of *Fantasy Island* as it was broadcast over ABC.[2] And it seems likely that every week most of them return. Presumably this Saturday night experience—commercials and all—in some measure arouses and gratifies their desires.

Fantasy Island, like most American television entertainment, consists of stories presented in what has been called the style of classical Hollywood narrative. This industrial form is such a dominant tradition that for most viewers it is either the only conceivable visual narrative structure or does not seem to be a structure at all. Closely imitated in virtually all commercial television, classical cinema is a *realist* mode characterized by techniques (of editing, camera work, sound, and performance) designed to make themselves invisible while making visible imaginary yet coherent story spaces with psychologically motivated characters.[3] Pioneered and refined in Hollywood, firmly established by 1920, it has nearly total world hegemony today; it provides the flattering appearance of simple, "natural" certainty and unity, the illusion of mastery over experience in its way of presenting stories to viewers everywhere.

Because of this, the fantasies of total gratification that Lasch sees as being so crucial to the formation of the narcissistic personality of our time are promoted in movies, not so much by any particular story or star as by the very way virtually all films are constructed—by classical narrative realism itself—and the corresponding ways these are consumed. Yet the alienation from watching a Hollywood film may seem mild and unrefined compared to that from watching American commercial television, which uses classical narrative forms to sell products as well as itself and commodifies them to an unprecedented degree. In part, this works precisely because commercial television seems to be free. With the rise of adult viewing to an average of over four hours a day in this country, the reality of dependence not only contradicts real and manufactured fantasies of omnipotence as Lasch argues, but also takes its place more and more *within* those fantasies, dependence and gratification locked in a tightening circle, generating their own polarization even as they become more intertwined. Television is a virtual factory of narcissism.

Programs such as *Fantasy Island* trade on human desires in order to produce audiences for commercials; networks and stations sell viewers on programs in order to fulfill a more basic economic purpose—to sell viewers to advertisers in the form of demographic categories of potential buyers for whatever the advertisers might produce to sell. Because the audience for *Fantasy Island* is primarily adult women, it is not surprising to find most of the commercials aimed at them. Commercials are placed in six "pods" (network lingo) or groups at approximately 2, 15, 28, 40, 50, and 58 minutes into the hour. The synopsis below is followed by a schematic outline focused on the relation between the program segment immediately preceding the "pod" and the first (and sometimes the second) commercial, abstracting the program material to its narrative function, the commercials to their dramatized situations. Of the transitions below, all move from "Elizabeth's Baby" to a commercial except the fourth, which moves from "The Artist and the Lady." If it is true that programs function to provide audiences for commercials, then flow into a group of commercials will be more important than flow back into the program.

SYNOPSIS: THE 17 JANUARY 1981 EPISODE

The opening credits are shown over aerial shots of a tropical island. A seaplane lands and Fantasy Island residents hurry to meet it. As the guests leave the plane, Roarke (Ricardo Montalbán) summarizes the backgrounds and hoped-for fantasies of the episode's two guests—high school art teacher Kermit Dobbs (Donny Most) and housewife Elizabeth Blake (Eve Plumb). Kermit, in "The Artist and the Lady," wants to possess the talent to paint just one masterpiece. Elizabeth, in "Elizabeth's Baby," wants to see the future of her unborn child, whose birth she knows will kill her.

Pod I: Duncan Hines Cake Mix Billboard / Life Cereal (40 seconds).

Roark calls on Elizabeth; together they look into the future and see Elizabeth's daughter, Lisa, now aged five, playing happily with her father, Steven (Don Reid). Kermit visits Roark and learns that his fantasy will be realized by borrowing the talent and identity of a visiting artist, Patrick O'Herlihy (Peter Brown). Unknown to Kermit, however, is O'Herlihy's reputation as a womanizer. Roarke magically transfers to Kermit not only O'Herlihy's talent but also other aspects of his identity. In her second look into the future, Elizabeth discovers that her husband Steven has moved, remarried, and has two additional children. Lisa, now aged twelve, feels left out and unloved.

Pod II: Caldecort Salve / Carefree Panty Shields / Local News Promo / Local Promo (*All in the Family*) / Station ID (1:55)

Kermit is painting a billboard-size rear view of a nude woman on a Fantasy Island building. Among the crowd gathered to watch are a Texan, Hud (Don Sutton), and his wife, Maybelle (Jenny Sherman). When Hud spots a familiar birthmark on the hip of the woman in the painting, he accuses his wife, punches Kermit in the jaw, and begins chasing him. Another onlooker, Mike (Mike Henry), spots a second birthmark and suspects his girl friend, Deborah (Michelle Pfeiffer). Roarke and Elizabeth again visit the future, where they find that the grown-up Lisa (Alison Arngrim) has become a prostitute. Roarke gives Elizabeth twenty-four hours to restore her to her family, on the condition that Elizabeth not reveal her true identity. Mike and Deborah argue over the birthmark on Kermit's painting. Mike punches Kermit and begins chasing him, while Deborah becomes infatuated with the painting and caresses it. Kermit hides from Hud and Mike. Elizabeth enters a bordello to find Lisa and defends her against pawing customers. Lisa's pimp (Jerome Guardino) grabs Elizabeth and locks her up.

Pod III: A–1 Sauce / Sucrets / Network Promos (*Those Amazing Animals* and *That's Incredible*) / *Fantasy Island* Bumper / Local Station ID / Local Newsbrief / Coca Cola / Jou Jou Jeans / Local Promo (2:45)

Roarke and Tattoo (Hervé Villechaize) meet Santa Claus in a 90-second segment not related to either story line. Elizabeth finds Lisa and tries to convince her to escape. Lisa's pimp tells her that she and Elizabeth will be auctioned off soon. Maybelle pursues and finds Kermit, thinking he is O'Herlihy, her former lover. She leaves and Deborah arrives to confess that she has fallen in love with Kermit because of the sensitivity of his painting. Kermit tries to explain that the painting is not his work but fails. They kiss.

Pod IV: Duncan Hines / Pert Shampoo / Network Promo (*Dynasty*) (1:45)

Elizabeth convinces Lisa to help her get to a phone. She calls Steven, without revealing her identity, and asks him to bring the police to rescue Lisa. Kermit fears losing Deborah's love along with his talent after his fantasy ends, but as Roarke restores him to normal, he finds that Deborah loves him anyway. Just as Lisa is being auctioned off, the door splinters and in rush the police, Steven, and Lisa's stepmother (Susan Cotton). Steven beats up the pimp and embraces Lisa with words of love and consolation. The stepmother joins the embrace as Lisa tells them of the love of her friend, Elizabeth, now invisible to them.

Pod V: Cream of Wheat / Bell System (1:00)

In the conclusion Kermit and Deborah discuss their plans. Roarke and Tattoo say good-bye to Elizabeth and present her with a photo of the future showing her grown daughter, Lisa, with her own husband and child.

Pod VI: Parkay Margarine / Mighty Dog Food (1:00)

Scenes from the next week's episode are shown, followed by closing credits over the island scene.

SCHEMATIC OUTLINE

1. *Program*: Mother's concern for child's happiness. *Commercial*: Life Cereal makes children happy.

2. *Program*: Mother perceives a problem (narrative disequilibrium). *Commercial*: Itching solved by Caldecort Salve.

3. *Program*: Mother tries to help family member (child). *Commercial*: Man helps family member (sister) with A–1 Sauce.

4. *Program*: Woman revealed as perfect wife-to-be, combining passion and wholesomeness. *Commercial*: Perfect wife/mother combines beauty and working skill with desserts by Duncan Hines.

5. *Program*: Mother unites family, generations (narrative closure). *Commercial*: Cream of Wheat reunites old friends, generations. AT&T reunites old friends, generations.

6. *Program*: Characters link the present with the future through traditional institutions.

Commercial: Parkay Margarine links the present with the past through traditional institutions (country store). Mighty Dog links the present with the past through traditional institutions (Old West).

When television was first developing its own forms in the 1950s, directors and writers learned to segment narratives to provide a buildup or suspenseful "hook" before the ads to hold the audience through the commercial break. Hollywood earlier had adapted classical narrative to sell the stars who appeared in it. With the advent of television, following the example of radio, newspapers, and magazines, the form was adapted to sell something outside—or next to, intercut with—itself as well. American television's use of commercial inserts—rather than clusters at a program's end—becomes particularly pertinent here.

Raymond Williams has examined these similarities as "flow"—a sequence of programs and commercials spanning several hours which are planned by networks and seen, but not thought of, as a unit by viewers.[4] Overriding both the spurious published lists of programs and the habitual, naturalized perception of television as composed of separate parts, flow describes a unity, a sequential wholeness. Many in the industry who think of programs as interruptions of commercials are closer to the truth than viewers, who usually think of commercials as interruptions of programs.

Sexual, familial, or other desires evoked by the program can be covered by an ad within minutes. Ads thus become an inseparable part of the repetitive flow of enticement and pseudo-satisfaction. As this episode of *Fantasy Island* demonstrates, classical narrative on television has now achieved a new level of commodification in which commercials respond fairly directly to the problems, desires, and fantasies articulated in the program's narrative by promising gratification through products. No conspiracy or hidden manipulation is necessary. The flow is possible because the iconography of television, its *mise-en-scène*, its *decoupage*, its patterns of narration in programs and its commercials are all converging. Their convergence may be due to refinements in analysis of audience demographics and psychographics which influence programs and commercials similarly. Both also have similar purposes—programs sell themselves, commercials sell products. Like the episodes of *Fantasy Island*, the commercials seek their fortunes in audience desires and therefore generally will not risk creating significant offense by confronting audiences in threatening ways. Industrial constraints on program-commercial relations exist at the network level, where contradictory material may be excluded prior to airing. More important, perhaps, constraints that structure program-commercial relations exist in the makers' rather uniform sense of what is appropriate for the audiences, and they exist in the hiring and selection decisions of network and production company executives. So the argument about convergence does not depend on anyone's conscious intentions. As far as we have been able to determine, there is no routine conscious effort to structure certain types of commercials at certain narrative points. Our argument is that there does not need to be one for flow to exist for viewers.

The historical change in television's flow is toward greater unity, programs and commercials becoming more and more alike—but not too much alike, for that would break the illusion of "interruption." As the narrative moves from problem to solution, from disequilibrium to equilibrium, from search to discovery, the product is there every step of the way, providing therapy for what ails the characters in the commercials and, less obviously, in the program as well. But the specific program-commercial interrelation changes from complementarity to harmony over the hour. Every commercial moves from problem to solution in one easy step. The program, however, moves through three narrative stages: defining the problem, making the solution visible, and closing out unsettled accounts. As a result, in flows 1, 2, and 3 the product does what the program's character herself cannot—help a family member. In flows 5 and 6 the advertised products and the *Fantasy Island* character act alike, unifying families or generations through "traditional" activity. In between, in flow 4, the product helps the character's commercial counterpart change into a perfect, loving wife (as defined within patriarchy) just after the program's character for the first time has been represented as suitable for marriage.

This returns us to the primary target audience for this flow, adult women. It is their desires that are at stake here, their dependence that is being sold to them. "Elizabeth's Baby" attempts to take up, to narrativize two concerns that may now be salient to the adult women in the audience: the anxieties of child-rearing and the future of the nuclear family. Both these problems—as they are conventionally posed by the culture industry (magazines, soap operas, best sellers)—appear to be present in displaced form in the story of Elizabeth and her daughter. The other story, with its aggressive objectification of women, would seem to be aimed more at male fantasy, but it provides a position for many women viewers as well. At flow 4, the only one which does not begin with Elizabeth's story, Deborah and Elizabeth become functionally similar at the one climactic point in each narrative. Elizabeth's is the story of the restoration of a nuclear family, and it is only at this moment that she can, through action, become what she "is"—a mother. Deborah's is the story of the formation of a nuclear family, and it is only at this moment that she becomes what she "is"—a wife, in contrast to the promiscuous Maybelle.

As the two narratives intersect at this critical moment over the question of the nuclear family, one can displace the other. And as we have indicated, Deborah is a better lead-in for the wife in the dessert commercial; both fuse variations on the stereotypes of mother and whore. The result is fantasies of feminine perfection under patriarchy, at the point in the flow when the narrative moves to align itself with the form of the commercials. For the characters of *Fantasy Island*, who within the hour ostensibly come better to understand themselves through the experience that is dramatized, there is the therapy of fantasy; for the audience, especially women, there is only the fantasy of therapy.

NOTES

1. Christopher Lasch, *The Culture of Narcissism* (New York: Warner Books, 1979), pp. 389–90.

2. These and other demographic figures are based on material supplied by the research department at ABC-TV. The 17 January 1981 *Fantasy Island* was chosen blind. We believe it typical of *Fantasy Island* episodes, and our findings seem applicable to other shows on American commercial television.

3. For a detailed description of classical Hollywood narrative, see David Bordwell and Kristin Thompson, *Film Art: An Introduction* (Reading, Mass.: Addison-Wesley, 1979).

4. Raymond Williams, *Television: Technology and Cultural Form* (New York: Schocken Books, 1974), pp. 90–93.

Children of Horror: The Films of Val Lewton

J. P. Telotte

Throughout the history of horror and fantasy narrative, children frequently have been exploited to evoke our fears or stir alarm. A child, after all, almost automatically projects a sense of helplessness and innocence which can be employed to manipulate our empathy or touch our protective instincts. As Henry James demonstrated in works like *The Turn of the Screw* or "The Pupil," the imagination can easily be provoked into a sense of uneasiness or horror simply by playing on the "helpless plasticity of childhood."[1] Through this tension between a threatened innocence and some external force of evil, a new perspective on our essentially naive or "innocent" view of reality is engendered. Probably because it is so elementally concerned with this problem of perspective, the horror film traditionally has made great capital from this sort of structural tension, and frequently by employing such child figures. Whether it is the monster accidentally murdering a little girl in *Frankenstein* or a maniac menacing unsuspecting teenagers in *Halloween*, the horror film frequently and effectively has managed to stir alarm at the absence of an effective adult protection for the young and unaware who inhabit that fearsome world the genre typically projects.

A more recent and seemingly opposite vogue in the horror film is the tendency to derive shock effects from a reversal of our expectations regarding that innocence. Films like *The Exorcist*, *The Omen*, *The Children*, and Michael Winner's "prequel" to *The Turn of the Screw*, *The Nightcomers*, suggest that it is the children themselves who may pose some threat, especially insofar as we tend to be seduced by the image of innocence they naturally present. Rather than affirm our traditional empathy, then, these films seem to caution against such a human "failing," as they warn us to suspect a sinister disparity between appearances and reality despite our normal feelings. Even as they foster this pervasive, almost paranoid doubt, however, such films hint at an essential alignment with the more traditional formula of the horror genre, for in their deepest structures both patterns establish a definite threat "out there," one external to our perspective and calling us to a constant vigilance.

In the body of horror and fantasy films produced by Val Lewton at RKO Studios we see what is arguably the most effective blending of these two different perspectives on innocence that occur in the genre.[2] The Lewton films, indeed, suggest a world full of external threats, as the very titles of films like *The Cat People*, *I Walked with a Zombie*, and *The Leopard Man* point up; however, these films ultimately imply that the greatest threats inhere not in such easily perceived menaces but in our naiveté, which causes us to dismiss or fail to recognize problems because of an implicit faith in the appearance of normality. Children, of course, offer an especially effective image of this attitude, and their appearance in most of the Lewton films suggests how well this evocative potential was appreciated: the fact that through a child a very typical *human* attitude could be represented. The children in the Lewton films, therefore, represent more than potential victims for some inhuman monster; they point as well to an adult world marked by a similar frailty of conception and self-knowledge. Furthermore, metaphoric use of the child serves to hint at another kind of threat less often seen in the horror film, a threat to that sense of self-satisfaction and well-being to which adults seem especially prone. This use of the child figure is, in fact, the key to the challenging tone in many of Lewton's narratives, which play not only on our usual fears for the safety of some innocent but our most deep-seated if often denied feelings of insecurity and doubts of our ability to cope with all that stubbornly remains unknown and unknowable in our world.

In *The Seventh Victim* Lewton achieved probably his most complex rendering of this pattern by placing the protagonist, Mary Gibson, in both child and adult roles. The film opens in a private girls' school, where children are reciting their various lessons; there we meet Mary, an orphan about to be turned out from that child's world because of adult neglect—her older sister's failure to pay her tuition. Thrust into that adult environment, one whose complexities her schooling has not prepared her for, Mary undergoes a frightful initiation which culminates in her becoming the film's love interest, supplanting her sister in a romantic relationship. In later films like *Bedlam* and *The Body Snatcher*, Lewton was to employ children in a more conventional but equally effective manner, using their victimization to prompt an adult awakening to the callousness and irresponsibility of their world. *Bedlam*, for instance, explores the problems of the insane by focusing on one of that famous asylum's inmates, a young boy painted gold to represent Reason in a play staged by the master of the institution. The boy's subsequent death from this treatment effectively indicts society's pretensions to an enlightened humanism. *The Body Snatcher* similarly depicts a child at the mercy of the adult world, Georgina Marsh, crippled in a carriage accident caused by her father. Although the famous surgeon Dr. MacFarlane promises to operate and cure her paralysis, he first needs to obtain a cadaver on which to practice the operation, and that need prompts the murder of another young girl. Thus the victimization continues, despite what appear to be the best of intentions. Throughout the body of Lewton's work, we find those children or innocents placed in such precarious positions as a warning of our need for a greater sense of human responsibility.

At the same time, though, Lewton added an element of complexity to his narratives and anticipated a more recent vogue in horror movies by also including some children endowed with disconcerting or frightening characteristics. The children who taunt Amy and exclude her from their games in *Curse of the Cat People* and the juvenile delinquents of *Youth Runs Wild* are obvious examples. The latter especially, though tame by today's standards, struck a contemporary reviewer as "extreme rather than average cases of war-neglected youngsters" and the troubles facing them.[3] In *The Leopard Man* a brief but unsettling portrait of a child occurs. Pedro Delgado, whose sister is later killed by a leopard, earlier taunts her with hand shadows of the cat she fears, and during her funeral he amuses himself by casting on a wall those same images of the killer cat. By juxtaposing such disconcerting, even threatening child characters with innocent victims, though, Lewton's film could more accurately take the measure of this world. What an overview of the Lewton films demonstrates is that their main focus was never the children themselves so much as the relationships between characters—or the lack of a proper relationship, as often occurs with parents and their offspring. The recurring child figures thus help to point up this failing and one of its main causes, namely the childish, unreflective nature of many adults. For like the children the adults in the Lewton films seem markedly unaware of the complexities of their world and often naively fumble about in their efforts to puzzle out the situations in which they find themselves.

In films like *I Walked with a Zombie* and *The Ghost Ship*, that parent-offspring motif is employed in an obviously metaphoric manner to limn the relationships of the adult characters. In the former, the widowed Mrs. Rand typically describes her two grown sons as "good boys" and the island natives over whom she watches with a maternal affection as her "children." She tries to help the natives by providing medical advice couched in the voodoo terminology they understand; with her own family, however, she is much less successful, for her sons fight over the wife of the eldest, and both the wife and the youngest son die as a result. In wrangles between generations we get an image of the sort of confusion and helplessness such relationships often involve. The latter film paints a similar relationship between Captain Stone of the ship *Altair* and his young third mate, Tom Merriam, an orphan who sees the captain as the father he never knew. After falling afoul of the captain's paranoia, though, Tom finds his life threatened, and only the intercession of another sailor who kills that murderous "father" saves him. In this instance the parent-child relation takes on an added dimension, an almost mythic quality, as it suggests an original fall from the basic human relationship, a fall which inexorably leads to the death of a stifling identity-denying parent figure. With such a mythic pattern Lewton could suggest an inborn human desire for the primal relation with its promise of protection and happiness, as well as the inevitable sundering of that relationship, the fall from innocence which comes with maturity.

Curse of the Cat People is a particularly fitting vehicle for examining Lewton's use of children because it interweaves all these various formulations of the motif. The film parallels the tensions between six-year-old Amy Reed and her taunting playmates; between Amy and her bumbling, misunderstanding father, Oliver; and between the old actress, Julia Farren, and her middle-aged daughter, Barbara; and each relationship evokes a brooding sense of anxiety or unease at an internal threat, at a person's inability to cope with his own needs or the demands of his world. Here, too, we see how similar the children and adults really are, as parents like Oliver and Julia, compared with their offspring, seem quite childish themselves, as petulant, irrational, and given to game-playing as any youngsters.

By noting the generally childish nature of many of the adults here, we might also better understand the subtle relations between this film and its more famous progenitor, *The Cat People*. Essentially, both films explore the fantasizing by which certain characters attempt to make sense of the mysterious or threatening aspects of their world, and both depict a skeptical, supposedly more-knowing figure—Oliver Reed in both cases—who scoffs at those imaginings. The problems of Oliver and Amy thus find their origin in the earlier story of the difficulties facing Oliver and his first wife, Irena. She fears being possessed by demons who might turn her into a killer leopard, but he laughs at her folk beliefs. "Irena, you crazy kid," he responds with an air of adult superiority, as if dealing with a frightened child. It is appropriate, then, that their relationship resembles that of father and daughter rather than husband and wife, their marriage going unconsummated amid Irena's fears of unleashing that murderous cat spirit. In *Curse* that asexual relationship obviously translates into the father-daughter situation; Oliver's attitude remains unchanged. In his daughter's fantasizing he senses "something moody, sickly," as if Amy were Irena's child, and he tells Miss Callahan, Amy's teacher, that from past experience he knows "what can happen when people begin to lie to themselves, imagine things." Amy's subsequent comments about an imaginary friend suggest to him that she, like Irena, dwells in a fantasy world, and he fears similar unfortunate consequences. This tension between the imagined and the real, the unknown and the known, then, informs both films, as they depict those seemingly childish anxieties confronted by a stubborn and equally childish assurance that there is no cause for anxiety, that this world is indeed a simple and secure place, one over which man exercises full control, provided he does not fall prey to his imaginings—to fantasy.

This certitude prompting Oliver's oversolicitousness can itself pose a kind of threat, though. Amy's parents are so fearful that they become too protective, stifling their child's individuality and denying her needs. As a result, parents and child seem to suffer from versions of the same problem: not an external threat, not something which, in Amy's case, a proper vigilance could guard against or vanquish, but a complex psychological problem, an anxiety in the face of anything unknown, including those forces lodged within the self. Amy's imaginings, just like her parents', stand ready to assume dark and frightening or brightly comforting shapes, depending on the pressures or reassurances she receives.

In delineating this relationship, Lewton probably drew heavily on his own experience, for he was the product of a broken home and never knew his father. To fill the void which resulted, he developed what Joel Siegel describes as a "wildly imaginative" streak, leading him to invent highly improbable tales with which he would "amuse and annoy" his elders.[4] Although not fatherless, Amy Reed closely follows this pattern, as she feels estranged from those around her and makes up for that alienation by fantasizing a more hospitable world. Both Alice, her mother, and Miss Callahan feel that this "active imagination" is one of the child's special attributes, a distinguishing feature of her personality. Oliver, however, fears the effects of that fantasizing, noting that "Amy has too many fantasies and too few friends, and it worries me." Consequently, he strives to mold her in his image of normality at all costs. In the Farren house a similar gulf separates parent and child, making Julia and the fatherless Barbara virtually strangers. Because of some illness which is never explained, Julia believes that her "real daughter" died at the age of six and that Barbara is "an imposter . . . a liar and a cheat," nothing more than "the woman who takes care of me." Barbara, in turn, has become resentful and withdrawn, suspicious of outsiders like Amy who threaten to alienate her mother's feelings further. The Farrens, like the Reeds, then, are a sundered family, and this "fallen" situation provides the basic problem facing these characters. Because of that situation, though, both children and adults can be brought to a more mature vision of the complex and often irrational world they inhabit.

The resulting impression that there are two parallel worlds—the simple environment inhabited by adults like Oliver where everything is just as it seems and that far more extensive and frightening world wherein children like Amy dwell—is the prime source of this film's consistently ironic tone. In fact, much of the complexity of *Curse of the Cat People* emerges from the irony that the adults themselves unwittingly encourage that play of the imagination which they eventually find so disturbing. They have passed on naturally the myths and fantasies of their own childhood, in some cases even created new ones for their offspring, but without considering the full impact those tales can have. The film opens on this note with Amy's class on a field trip; as the children walk along a tree-shaded lane in Tarrytown, Miss Callahan instructs them to "take a good look. . . . It may seem to be just a little valley with a little stream running through it, but there are songs and stories and lovely legends about this one blessed spot." The notion that there is more here than meets the eye gets repeated mention, but it creates some confusion for Amy when she tries to apply that principle. Informed that a misshapen tree in her yard is a "magic mailbox," she logically proceeds to "mail" the invitations to her birthday party in that special receptacle. When Oliver discovers the mistake, he attempts to explain:

"That wasn't real; that was just a story." What he has failed to understand is that such stories can leave an unpredictable residue when filtered through a receptive imagination. The familiar tale of "The Headless Horseman," which Amy first hears from Miss Callahan and which Julia later dramatizes for her, provides a striking example of this unpredictable effect, for what was intended as a quaint and entertaining legend becomes for the child a recurring nightmare, intruding its harsh reality into her fragile, formative world. Edward, Alice, and Oliver can wink at those fantasies which they by turns relate to Amy, for theirs is a secure and strictly defined reality. Oliver, a ship designer, and Alice, his former assistant, are accustomed to working with facts, figures, weights, and dimensions—things one can see and measure; and those things which fail to conform they naturally distrust or dismiss—as Oliver does Amy's reports of a mysterious friend—as "lies."

For children like Amy who have yet to go through the delimiting process of acculturation, those real and imagined realms easily coincide. As Freud notes in *Beyond the Pleasure Principle*, that fantasizing impulse is one of a child's typical methods of ordering the environment in which he lives, of asserting a meaningful world for himself.[5] Or as Eric Rabkin describes it, fantasizing is simply a "basic mode of human knowing" which enables a person to organize the random elements of his experience.[6] This impulse, though, is subject to certain "ground rules" which children learn as they grow up. Although Amy is in the process of learning those rules, she finds them frustratingly fluid, quickly changed to suit their adult arbiters. After Oliver warns her about fantasizing, Amy balks at wishing on the candles of her birthday cake. "Wishes don't come true," she asserts, only to be met with her father's confusing equivocation, "Certain wishes do." His repeated warnings about lying compound Amy's perplexity, especially since they seem so at odds with what she sees. While Amy watches, Oliver shouts at Alice that he is "not shouting," and she, after a heated exchange with him, attempts to comfort Amy by explaining that they were "not really fighting . . . just having a little discussion." It is indeed a puzzling and inconsistent world Amy observes; and it is that way because the adults live by certain unrecognized or unquestioned fictions. In Julia Farren's case the fiction of her daughter's death is simply more obvious, the truth which belies it— Barbara's very presence—so evident that we may think the old woman crazy. In most cases, though, those determinations are more problematic. As Lewton demonstrated in *Bedlam*, they largely depend on the whims and often irrational canons of acceptance established by those in power.

That unwitting employment of fictions points up the basic similarity between adults and children which these films establish. *Bedlam*'s childlike adults, incarcerated in the asylum by characters who are no more sane and are just as frightened by the world they inhabit as those inmates, are simply a later development of this motif. In *Curse of the Cat People* that parallel is underscored by the game-playing in which children and adults engage. For the children, games provide a means of organizing their energies and activities into a meaningful form, and the film fittingly introduces Amy and her classmates playing various games under the instruction of Miss Callahan. Among the many activities, they are shown playing ball, family, "pass the shoe," jacks, and tag. The very number of these games should catch our attention here, especially since it points up an equally prodigious amount of playing among the adults. This side of Oliver's character particularly is emphasized, as we see him playing with the tiddledy-winks game set out for Amy's party, building model ships, and playing cards with Alice and another couple. In the last case, Oliver is so preoccupied with Amy's troubles that he cannot concentrate on the game and lapses into a trancelike state—just as Amy does in an earlier scene. Edward's playing with Oliver's model ships and Julia Farren's acting and storytelling are other forms which that play activity takes here. Together these activities underscore a fundamental if often unrecognized similarity between children and adults, while also fostering a feeling of just how much like a game most human actions essentially are.

Having drawn this likeness, Lewton can more ironically point up the lack of understanding afflicting these characters and suggest how this deficiency starts many of the fears plaguing them. We expect children like Amy, faced with a complex and confusing world, to have some difficulty in distinguishing, as her parents insist she must, between the imagined and the real. That affecting combination of sincerity and confusion which she projects, though, throws into relief the similar inability of her parents to understand themselves or respond to her very human needs for friendship and reassurance. Oliver's obtuseness is especially marked, for he is certain that he knows what constitutes proper behavior for his child, yet that certitude rings hollow in light of his own lack of reflection. He claims, for instance, that he wants to rid himself of the troubling memories of his former wife, Irena, yet he stubbornly displays her favorite painting with its sinister cat motif, even though, as Alice points out, it ill fits the decor of their new home. When Alice asks him to destroy the numerous photographs he keeps of Irena, Oliver secretly holds back one which Amy later discovers and which provides the prototype for her "special friend" whom only she can see. This same lack of perspective is found in the relationship of Julia and Barbara Farren. In the mother it takes the form of a senility which denies her daughter's identity and the happiness of them both, while her inability to understand or accept her mother's condition leaves Barbara a bitter and withdrawn woman, suspicious of everyone with whom she comes in contact.

Such circumscribed views inevitably lead to a kind of isolation, a state underscored by an emphasis on the boundaries of the world these people inhabit. The film's opening stresses that sense of physical limitation, as Miss Callahan warns her students not to wander off, and Amy's parents echo this admonition in their worrying over her whereabouts and sending Edward after her when she wanders off. The fenced-in front and rear yards of the Reed home, like those of the neighboring houses, restate that protective attitude which the parents here all seem to maintain. Confined in this way, Amy naturally tries to broaden her world by fantasizing, turning her yard into an imaginary realm complete with that special friend she is unable to find elsewhere. The gloomy Farren house, surrounded by its high iron fence—used in the *Bedlam* set to suggest the virtual imprisonment of the asylum's inmates—and overgrown with weeds and bushes, is similarly emblematic of the reclusive life-style its occupants have adopted; no one, as Alice notes, has glimpsed either mother or daughter. The doors that mysteriously lock themselves, the shuttered windows, and the stuffed cat and birds that decorate the parlor only emphasize the hermetic and lifeless world Julia and Barbara have fashioned for themselves in their inability to understand and humanly deal with each other.

Typical of Lewton's films, that theme of enclosure finds further expression in numerous images of entrapment, visual compositions which speak of the confinement these people endure. Bar- or weblike shadows especially abound, suggesting the virtual imprisonment of the characters upon whom they are cast. Oliver, for instance, from the start seems bound by some unseen force, for he inititially is shown in a pattern of crisscrossing shadows as he attempts to explain Amy's behavior to Miss Callahan. That composition ironically suggests that he may be as bound by his imaginings as he fears Amy is. By later depicting Amy in a similar composition, Lewton underscores this likeness and confirms our suspicions. After hearing Julia's story of the Headless Horseman, Amy is shown in bed, the same barlike shadows playing upon her as she wakes up screaming, still possessed by that horror tale. Similar images recur when we see Barbara, as she is glimpsed within the shadow cast by a door or through the rails of a staircase—compositions which suggest how psychologically bound she is by her fears and insecurities. Complementing these moody images are other compositions which point up how unaware these characters are of their circumscribed situations. Repeatedly, frame-within-a-frame compositions hint at the Reed family's imprisonment within their dream of normality and their unawareness of that condition. Gathered around the Christmas tree, the family seems happy in the renewed hopes that season normally brings; we view this tableau, though, in extreme long shot through a small window whose frame imposes a sense of entrapment upon the family's obvious good cheer. When carolers come to the house, that composition recurs, Oliver, Alice, Amy, and Edward again forming a tableau as they stand in the Dutch door listening to the singers. Once more a long shot frames them within that tightly confined space and casts an ironic light on their manifest happiness. Moreover, it is an irony immediately reinforced by the appearance of Irena, serenading Amy from the rear of the house with a French version of one of the carolers' songs. The subsequent view of Amy in a similarly enclosed composition further comments upon that normal appearance which these characters all seem to project and reemphasizes their very limited perspectives.

Like the wartime society depicted in *Youth Runs Wild*, then, it is explicitly a circumscribed world within which these characters are placed, and perhaps for that reason an environment quite as threatening as that found in any of Lewton's more conventional horror films. The threat here, though, is not so much the world itself but a certain lack it points up within the human community—or the self; for these people are unable to understand or find understanding, and in that sense of isolation which results, they project a fear onto their world, one which colors all they encounter in their darkest imaginings. Not only is this the case for Amy, but for Oliver and Alice, Julia and Barbara as well. The problem is simply made most obvious with Amy's creation of an imaginary playmate, for what she conjures up is both friend and parent figure, a single entity which brings the worlds of innocence and experience, the adult and the child, into some harmony. Unable to find a real playmate, Amy wanders past the Farren house, where she hears a mysterious, disembodied voice—Julia's—inviting her to "come into the garden; it's nice and cool here. Come into the garden." Within that edenic locale she receives a special wishing ring, a gift thrown from above, which allows her to evoke her longed-for friend. The scene clearly carries pointedly mythic resonances, broadly suggesting a common human desire for some sort of primal return, a reentry into the garden of innocence; and it is a desire especially appropriate for a child engaged in the difficult initiation process. Moreover, this scene casts into relief the child's wish for a perfect world, a perfect parent, and a perfect friend as Amy increasingly finds herself thrust out from the realm of innocence by the inevitable process of growth and acculturation.

In reaction to that feeling of expulsion, Amy tries to abandon her parents' world in favor of Irena and her fantasy domain. The child always has met her friend in the yard; so when Irena vanishes, Amy pursues her disappearing image through the yard and beyond its fenced boundary. Outside of that circumscribed, protected world, though, Amy is disoriented and wanders in a dark and threatening realm; it is the sinister side of her fantasies, previously kept to the periphery of her experience, relegated to the night and dreams. Beyond those familiar boundaries lies a dense forest, transformed by the night and a snowstorm into a terrifying landscape where those darker fantasies reign. As she wanders among the trees and snowbanks, Amy finds every shape and sound threatening; the dogs used by the police to track her and an old rattling car which passes on a wooden bridge become frightening visitations of that Headless Horseman story which has periodically haunted her dreams. And those imagined threats foreshadow very real dangers facing Amy: becoming lost in the snow and freezing to death, or, after stumbling upon the Farren house, being killed by Barbara, who blames the child for stealing her mother's love. All of these potential dangers suggest that her parents' attempts to circumscribe Amy's world are not without some justification.

Inevitably, though, children must grow up and live in a world which is complex and often frightening. Denying the full breadth of human experience, including the world of fantasy, as Amy's parents try to do, can be as debilitating as that denial of love which has left Barbara a suspicious recluse. As Lewton's films all show, experience of the fantastic, the mysterious, even the frightening, can provide a person with the sort of perspective on his world and himself which he needs to function effectively. In fact, that perspective often becomes the measure of whatever maturity Lewton's young protagonists attain. In *Curse of the Cat People* we see that those apparent threats can be met and dealt with by a degree of understanding, as the climactic confrontation between Amy and a vengeful Barbara illustrates. With the child in flight from those imagined horrors of the woods and Barbara incensed by her mother's affection for Amy, we see two children threatened most by their own anxieties. Ironically, though, that fantasizing helps Amy to resolve this situation, to dispel those fears. When Barbara approaches her menacingly, the child calls upon Irena, whose image we see superimposed over Barbara in a bit of trick photography uncommon in the Lewton canon. Barbara then responds to that call of "My friend," in effect becoming that friend, her bitterness vanishing as Amy embraces her. In close-up we watch Barbara's hands, ready to strangle the child, slowly loosen their grasp and become a comforting embrace. With the advent of this new human relationship, that threatening atmosphere vanishes, to be replaced by a reassuring mood, as Amy's parents come to take her back home. There Oliver tells her that he, too, "sees" her mysterious friend and thus offers some acknowledgment of her fantasy world. In this accommodation by means of the fantastic, child and parent come together in their understanding of each other and attain some level of maturity.

Traditionally, fantasy tales like *Curse of the Cat People*, according to Tzvetan Todorov, have abided by one condition: the persistence of an atmosphere of uncertainty or ambiguity throughout the narrative. The audience is thus obliged "to consider the world of the characters as a world of living persons and to hesitate between a natural and a supernatural explanation" of the events in which they are involved, since only during this "certain hesitation" will the fantastic hold its powerful sway in their imaginations.[7] Of course, Henry James provided the enduring model of that ambiguous atmosphere in *The Turn of the Screw*, and in that conjunction of childhood innocence with the world of adult experience Lewton, too, found an effective formula for sustaining tension. What the children in his films see so readily and the adults usually see belatedly is the complex and disturbing nature of this world in which neither fact nor fancy rules, where no single explanation can satisfactorily account for the problems they continually encounter. Keeping with this pattern, Lewton leaves his viewers without a full explanation of these events. We wonder if children like Amy do perceive more than their parents, who are inured to a certain normative vision of the world. Or is that imaginative realm simply an amusing, sometimes even confusing structure of myths which must eventually be abandoned if the child is to function effectively in his culture? Following the fantastic tradition, Lewton imparts some validity to both views. At the film's end Amy again sees Irena but turns away from her—perhaps simply because, as Irena says, the child no longer "needs" her—while Oliver, though clearly not looking at her, claims that he, too, sees Irena. A lingering ambiguity results, leaving us to wonder what unknown and possible threatening elements may yet disrupt this world, what human fears still hide beneath that veneer of normality.

All of Lewton's films evoke a world that is seldom less than ominous, though the fears that seem to haunt it, they imply, derive largely from that isolation and lack of understanding to which both children and adults are prone. In the Lewton films, *Curse of the Cat People* especially, all of the characters suffer, though often simply because those nearest to them or they themselves are beset by fears and insecurities. In the problems of these people we find dramatized the common difficulties involved in that complex and lengthy process of maturation which we all undergo. The child's predicament, we see, is not dissimilar to that of many adults, especially those unwilling or simply unable to take their lives in hand and join in a world of human interaction and responsibility. Those disturbing events into which characters like Amy, Barbara, and Oliver are plunged do serve a positive purpose, though. They uniformly precipitate a kind of growth in the best tradition of the horror or fantasy film: one that starts characters along a path on which they might encounter their true selves. From a vision of some internal or external horror, they gain the perspective needed to see themselves and their world as they really are.

NOTES

1. Henry James to Dr. Louis Waldstein, 21 October 1898, *The Letters of Henry James*, ed. Percy Lubbock (New York: Scribner, 1920), I, 297.

2. The following Val Lewton films are referred to in the paper:

The Cat People, dir. Jacques Tourneur, RKO, 1942.
I Walked with a Zombie, dir. Jacques Tourneur, RKO, 1942.
The Leopard Man, dir. Jacques Tourneur, RKO, 1943.
The Seventh Victim, dir. Mark Robson, RKO, 1943.
The Ghost Ship, dir. Mark Robson, RKO, 1943.
Curse of the Cat People, dir. Gunther Von Fritsch, RKO, 1944.
Youth Runs Wild, dir. Mark Robson, RKO, 1944.
Bedlam, dir. Mark Robson, RKO, 1945.
The Body Snatcher, dir. Robert Wise, RKO, 1945.

3. Review of *Youth Runs Wild*, *New York Times*, 2 September 1944, p. 17.

4. For a more detailed discussion of Lewton's background, see Joel Siegel's *Val Lewton: The Reality of Terror* (New York: Viking Press, 1973), p. 8.

5. Sigmund Freud, *Beyond the Pleasure Principle*, trans. James Strachey (New York: Liveright, 1961). Freud's discussion of children's game-playing seems especially pertinent to the activity engaged in by the children in the Lewton films. That kind of play, he suggests, is essentially a repetition of real experience in which the children "abreact the strength of the impression and, as one might put it, make themselves master of the situation" (p. 11).

6. Eric Rabkin, *The Fantastic in Literature* (Princeton: Princeton University Press, 1976), p. 227.

7. Tzvetan Todorov, *The Fantastic: A Structural Approach to a Literary Genre*, trans. Richard Howard (Ithaca: Cornell University Press, 1975), pp. 33, 41. With this suspension

of judgment, Todorov argues, the fantastic permits ''an experience of limits'' (p. 93), not just of what we normally conceive reality to be, but of our human capacity to explain or make sense of that world we inhabit. It is in this sense especially that all of the Lewton films might be classified under the heading of fantasy.

Superheroes as Dream Doubles

James Whitlark

Addicted to progress, the civilized tend to see in themselves at least two individuals—a present self greatly in need of improvement and a future one tanta-
lizingly out of reach. Impatient to attain the latter, at least vicariously, comic-
book aficionados avidly read about the teen-ager Billy Batson, who, at the sound
of the word ''Shazam,'' instantly matures into the powerful adult Captain Marvel,
or about the army reject Steve Rogers, who, after a wonder-drug injection,
becomes the model warrior and crime fighter Captain America. This theme
(transformation from weakling to wonder) is not an invention of comics. It
descends from the long tradition of the popular adventure story. As Ralph Tymms
observes in his pioneer work *Doubles in Literary Psychology*, popular fiction
generally uses the double motif in a relatively ''superficial'' manner.[1] Particularly
in their early days, comics frequently followed the pulp tradition, seldom rising
even as high as Baroness Orczy's novel *The Scarlet Pimpernel* in their depiction
of a person divided into two selves: one ineffectual, the other heroic. Of late,
however, a new psychological preoccupation characterizes the better comics.
They clearly conform to a general tendency in literature diagnosed by Robert
Rogers in his study *The Double in Literature*: ''doubling in literature usually
symbolizes a dysfunctional attempt to cope with mental conflict.''[2] *Marvel Comics* have led the way in the portrayal of agonized heroes who come close to
schizophrenia (as will be analyzed later). What makes comic-book treatment of
the double unusual is its attempted reconciliation of these contrasting notions:
multiple personalities as psychic dysfunction or as potential for heroic action.
To combine pulp adventure and novelistic psychologizing, comics draw on yet
another tradition—the double in folk tale and its literary imitations.

For example, German folk stories and legends call the external soul or double
fylgja and identify it with such disparate phenomena as guardian angels, dream
selves, and werewolves.[3] German Romanticism refashioned it in terms of a new

religious esthetic, influencing a host of doppelgänger narratives that descend from one of the earliest Romantic fairy stories, Wackenroder's "Wonderful Oriental Fairy Tale of a Naked Saint" in *Outpourings of the Heart of an Art-loving Monastic*. Its protagonist mundanely "lives with the people who pass in the caravans, experiencing with them fear, hope, danger."[4] Indeed, his naked-ness, celibacy, and horror of time leave him acutely sensitive and vulnerable, aware of his inability to do or create anything. But he also has a latent second personality, that of an artistic "Genius," able to overcome time and ascend into the eternal heavens, feeling much as Stan Lee's "personal Jesus Christ surro-gate,"[5] the Silver Surfer, does when permitted to race through the vastness of the cosmos.

Romanticism typically depicted the psychological suffering and conflict of the artist, adventure comics the physical and psychological agony and battles of the hero; but in the so-called "Golden Age" of comics (late 1930s to early 1950s), this analogy was seldom more than implicit as in the Clark Kent/Superman dualism. The former identity is confined to daily life; the latter is a conqueror of temporal limitations as in his time-travel or in his blurring speed, sometimes represented by multiple images of himself on the page. With a few exceptions, Golden Age superheroes sublimated everyday desires for sexual reproduction (self-duplication) so that they could be totally dedicated to their roles, much as early Romantics often advocated such renunciation for the sake of art (e.g., in E.T.A. Hoffmann's "The Doubles").[6]

Since the Golden Age, particularly in the last few years, superheroes seem more human and psychologically complex, while their relationship to their cre-ators becomes more explicit. Indeed, in the July 1981 issue of *Man-Thing*, its actual writer, Chris Claremont, appears as one of the characters. Thrust into the fantastic world he has so long envisioned, he is at first inept, a pathetic form huddled over a drink; but near the end of the book, a demon transforms him into the monstrous Man-Thing (a comic-book character he invented). As this green, hulking swamp beast, he overcomes the villain, saves the universe, and returns to his human form to write about the adventure (although he also turns in his resignation to *Marvel Comics*). Similarly, in the June 1982 issue of *New Teen Titans*, both its writer, Marv Wolfman, and artist, George Perez, serve as characters who rescue the Teen Titans from a mad scientist. Another narrative in the same issue shows the character Wally West/Kid Flash drawing his own story. Although the disappearance of the line between creator and creation is a recent phenomenon still presented experimentally, sometimes even with apol-ogies, it epitomizes a growing tendency. Frequently the illustrators and writers of comics refer to themselves or to one another as heroes, even to the point of describing comics innovator Stan Lee as one of the "real all-fathers," ascribing to him a title of his superhero god, Odin.[7] Fans lionize comics creators at conventions as if they were the heroes they invent. At first, young readers who take comics too literally may send away for the muscle-building kits, karate correspondence courses, and books of magic words advertised therein; but eventually they are likely to realize that the only way they can instantly become their ideal selves is through their imaginations as consumers or creators of fantasy. Indeed, the NBC program "Drawing Power" preaches this to small children. Jules Feiffer says in the introduction to his compendium *The Great Comic Book Heroes* that his fascination with superbeings led him to a cartooning career, where he eventually used satire as a weapon against the degeneracy of the real world.[8] Ironically, in comic books per se, such social action has long been difficult because the Comics Code Authority fears relevance as controversial and champions art for dollars' sake instead. However, with Marvel's *Spiderman* magazine's winning a long-fought battle against that authority in order to publish an anti-drug fable in one episode,[9] there is more hope that comic-book makers themselves will become effective champions of justice.

Because of the Comics Code Authority, many superheroes have corresponded rather closely to what Rogers calls "superego" doubles.[10] For instance, the DC character Superman forces his unobtrusive ego-fragment, Clark Kent, to live a humdrum life, sacrificing his time to the compulsive altruism of his other role—hardly the best way to enchant a juvenile readership. Although not the first to do so, the *Marvel Comics* organization (which considerably outsells *DC Comics*) has pioneered in personifying the id as a superhero—a more exciting theme. The Man-Thing, for example, is a mass of muscle and emotions, void "of intellect [and] of the very capacity of conscious thought."[11] Also recognizable as an id figure is the Hulk, a huge, green embodiment of pain and rage, who in recent comics emerges when his brilliant scientist self undergoes stress, as if he suffers from periodic madness. In a 1972 article, Lawrence Kayton argues that in schizophrenia a "regressed portion of the ego" (analogous to a monster in its infantile emotionality) splits from the rest.[12] Numerous Marvel heroes are from time to time in fear of losing their sanity or are beyond fearing like the Man-Thing.

Many of the superheroes, most obviously the Hulk, directly or indirectly derive from Mary Shelley's *Frankenstein*.[13] The novel's title character is described as leading "a double existence: he may suffer misery, and be overwhelmed by disappointments; yet when he has retired into himself, he will be like a celestial spirit, that has a halo around him, within whose circle no grief or folly ventures."[14] His monster, a creation of his imagination (his "celestial spirit"), represents in extreme form another common Romantic motif, the difficulty of transferring a dream self into the real world. There the great power and oddity of the unconscious isolate its manifestation from an overly conventional society. Similarly, Superman's imperfect double, Bizarro, terrifies those he rescues, and, like Frankenstein, Superman unsuccessfully strives to destroy his hideous duplicate.[15] When either Frankenstein's creation or the Thing (a slightly more intelligent Marvel character than the Man-Thing) appears, mobs may attack before the creature has a chance to prove his benevolence.

Another common id image in comics is the werewolf, e.g., Werewolf by Night, the Beast, Timberwolf Boy, and Wolverine. Although the Germanic word *fylgja* could mean either a benevolent being (a guardian of individual, family, or nation) or a werewolf, it did not mean both simultaneously. The id superhero, however, to protect the innocent, draws power from his monstrous self.

Comics teach that a despised quality, an evil characteristic, an unconscious drive, or a seeming handicap may serve the forces of virtue. With sharpened senses because of his blindness, Matt Murdock, dressed as a horned red imp, undertakes daring deeds under the name Daredevil or Devil for short. Johnny Blaze, the Ghost Rider, who has sold his soul to the devil, becomes a demon in the cause of justice. Similarly, Dr. Strange "uses his Satanic powers on the side of good," performing such feats as sending forth his soul double while his body remains in trance.[16] Such a small difference separates villains and heroes that they occasionally switch from one role to the other. For instance, Jessica Drew (alias Ariadne Hyde), able to change to Spider-Woman (also called the Dark Angel), no longer belongs to the malevolent organization Hydra, but is now a superhero in her own magazine.[17]

In their early years, comics were Manichaean, glorifying a struggle between good and evil. Heroes took sadistic delight in murdering their foes. Nowadays (partly because of the Comics Code Authority), if a hero kills his enemy in self-defense, he may renounce his heroic career, as Star Boy, who, even for justifiable homicide, is expelled from the Legion of Superheroes.[18] The one-eyed god Odin tells the once-human, blind god Korgon, "without such [villains] as Wiglif and Loki, the balance is meaningless. Thou needest thy followers, Korgon, all of them, and they need thee. Shorn of his followers, a god ceases to exist . . . and too, thy followers have no reason to exist without their god."[19] This new emphasis on balance between ideal and actual, god and devotee, superhero and mundane alter ego pervades recent comics.

Even separate universes must maintain balance. In *DC Comics Presents*, "Mallo, keeper of the COSMIC BALANCE," notes: "Two parallel worlds, which you know as EARTH-ONE and EARTH-TWO, are the homes of numerous superheroes . . . with similarly powered counterparts on each world: The sole exception is the pair of ATOMS . . . and it is this lack of parallelism in their powers which is upsetting the COSMIC BALANCE!"[20] To prevent universal destruction, Mallo preternaturally exchanges the powers of the character named Atom on Earth-One with those of his double on Earth-Two. According to this theory, a countless number of other parallel universes exist, each with a double of all familiar superheroes. These universes contain all the choices not made, the alternatives not taken, the unrealized potential, what the structuralists call "absence" and identify with the unconscious. Thus the comic book entitled "What if Dr. Strange had been a disciple of Dormammu" shows a double of Dr. Strange choosing evil when the original Dr. Strange chooses good.[21] As a Marvel editor states, "the Multiple Universe Theory" presumes that time is not "flowing inexorably from past to future" but endlessly branching.[22]

The setting of each adventure comic is a time when the balance is broken (corresponding to a stage of psychic disharmony) and then restored, a scenario of regaining sanity after such psychic conflict as a Romantic artist explores and survives. Along the way, the labyrinthine mysteries of identity and of the un- conscious arise in all their seeming irrationality. The lame physician Dr. Donald Blake merges with his other self, the immortal god Thor, despite their strikingly different speech patterns, powers, and parents. Rob Reed becomes both Castor and Pollux, twin gods; Ronnie Raymond and Professor Martin Stein combine to form the single superhero "Firestorm."[23] And these super-identities appear in a context of doubling with heroes meeting clones, robot doubles, or former incarnations of themselves, or even other stages of their lives (through time- travel) until the normal boundaries between self and other, time and eternity, conscious and unconscious lose all solidity. As A. E. Crawley remarks in his classic article on the double: "It is natural that when once the notion of 'spiritual' duplication has been formed, it may be applied to anything that strikes the fancy."[24] Doubles in comics assume bizarre forms, yet despite or because of this, their readers continue to read and to write such letters to the editor as one to *Master of Kung Fu Comics* (no. 81, p. 19), in which Raymond Orkwis lauds it for helping him attain "a union with yin [universal feminine principle in Chinese metaphysics]—my anima, to use the word now in the Jungian sense [a man's conception of his soul or unconscious as a feminine form]." This example may seem excessive, but it does not transcend the aspirations of Romanticism, many of whose artists sought in their works a resolution of such psychological problems as Nerval's and Hoffman's autoscopy (literally, seeing their doppel- gänger walking near them).[25]

The superhero's reconciliation of his multiple personalities is at most tem- porary, a lull before the next adventure. Yet it is sufficient to bring empathetic readers a feeling of union with ideal selves, as powerful as the imagination and as profound as the depths of the unconscious.

NOTES

1. Ralph Tymms, *Doubles in Literary Psychology* (Cambridge: Bowes & Bowes, 1949), pp. 15, 17, 75 passim.

2. Robert Rogers, *The Double in Literature* (Detroit: Wayne State University Press, 1970), p. vii.

3. Jakob Grimm, *Teutonic Mythology*, trans. James Steven Stallybrass (New York: Dover, 1965), IV: 1571; E. Tonnelat, "Teutonic Mythology," *New Larousse Encyclo- pedia of Mythology*, trans. Richard Aldington and Delano Ames (Hong Kong: Hamlyn, 1959), p. 277.

4. Wilhelm Heinrich Wackenroder, *Werke und Briefe* (Heidelberg: Lambert Schnei- der, 1967), pp. 197–202; Marianne Thalmann, *The Romantic Fairy Tale: Seeds of Sur- realism* (Ann Arbor: University of Michigan Press, 1964), pp. 1–10.

5. Maurice Horn, *The World Encyclopedia of Comics* (New York: Chelsea House, 1976), p. 620.

6. *Selected Writings of E.T.A. Hoffmann*, ed. and trans. Leonard J. Kent and Elizabeth

C. Knight (Chicago: University of Chicago, 1969), p. 315; E.T.A. Hoffmann, *Letze Erzählungen* in *Poetisch Werke* (Berlin: Walter De Gruyter, 1962), p. 58.

7. See, for example, Stan Lee, *Origins of Marvel Comics* (New York: Simon & Schuster, 1974), p. 5; "Bullpen Bulletins," *Star Wars* no. 13 (1978), p. 30; *Thor* 1 (October 1980), 48.

8. Jules Feiffer, ed., *The Great Comic Book Heroes* (New York: Dial Press, 1965) pp. 1–17.

9. Hubert H. Crawford, *Crawford's Encyclopaedia of Comic Books* (Middle Village, N.Y.: Jonathan David, 1978), p. 345.

10. Rogers, *The Double*, pp. 9–10.

11. Chris Claremont, *The Man-Thing* 2 (July 1981), 22.

12. Lawrence Kayton, "The Relationship of the Vampire Legend to Schizophrenia," *Journal of Youth and Adolescence* 1 (1972), 311.

13. Donald F. Glut, "Frankenstein Meets the Comics," *The Comic-Book Book*, ed. Don Thompson and Dick Lupoff (Carlstadt, N.J.: Rainbow Books, 1977), pp. 89–117.

14. Mary Shelley, *The Annotated Frankenstein*, ed. Leonard Wolf (New York: Clarkson N. Potter, 1977), pp. 29, 324.

15. Michael L. Fleischer, *The Great Superman Book, The Encyclopedia of Comic Book Heroes*, No. 3 (New York: Warner, 1978), pp. 17–24.

16. *Origins of Marvel Comics*, back cover.

17. Chris Claremont, "The Wildfire Express," *Spider-woman* 1 (January 1981), 14.

18. Jack C. Harris et al., *Secrets of the Legion of Super-Heroes* 1 (February 1981), 15.

19. David Moench, et al., "The Blind God's Tears," *The Fantastic Four* 1 (December 1980), 28.

20. Gerry Conway et al., "Whatever Happened to the Golden Age Atom?" *Superman and Black Canary*, 4 (February 1981), 3.

21. Peter Gillis, "What If Dr. Strange Had Been a Disciple of Dorammu?" *What If* 1 (December 1979), 1.

22. Lynn Graeme, ed., "Paradox," *Marvel Preview* 1 (Winter 1980), 4.

23. *Thor* 1 (October 1980), 48; Gerry Conway, "Firestorm," *The Flash* 33 (February 1981), 1–8.

24. A. E. Crawley, "Doubles," *Encyclopaedia of Religion and Ethics* (New York: Scribner, 1951), III, 858.

25. Claire Gilbert, *Nerval's Double: A Structural Study*, Romance Monographs Series (University, Miss.: University of Mississippi Press, 1979), p. 40.

Artaud's Theatre of Cruelty and the Fantastic

Jean-Pierre Lalande

Antonin Artaud's use of the fantastic in cinema and theatre must be viewed in conjunction with Surrealism, that is to say, as an attempt to discover a new definition of reality and a new approach to it. For the Surrealists, rationalism cannot provide an accurate knowledge of the real because it limits reality to the confines of logic. As a result, the Surrealist movement will search for a new set of criteria whereby to define reality which, in the Second Manifesto, Breton expresses in these terms: "Everything leads us to believe that there exists a certain point in the mind from which life and death, the real and the imaginary, the past and the future, the communicable and the uncommunicable, . . . cease to be perceived as contradictory. And it is in vain that one would seek in Surrealism another motive but the hope to determine this point."[1] With Breton (and in Artaud's case without him), the Surrealists will undertake a similar exploratory task which will lead them beyond reason to the investigation of such little-known domains as the imaginary, the unconscious, the irrational, and the uncanny.

Given their goal, it is no wonder that the fantastic plays an important role in their works, both as a source of inspiration and as a means of expression. Indeed, the Surrealist and the fantastic approaches to the world share a common nature. Both are expressions of a mind determined to revolt against rules and institutions in an attempt to follow its own imaginative and unconscious inclinations. This explains why Breton writes: "The marvelous [which he does not here differentiate from the fantastic] is always beautiful, any kind of marvelous is beautiful, nothing but the marvelous is beautiful."[2]

After a brief initial period devoted to the writing of poetry, Artaud chose the theatre and cinema (in its very infancy then) as a means of expression. He felt that their reliance on visual rather than on verbal images (the latter being for him the vehicle of rational thought) might have greater appeal for the imagination and the unconscious. The cinema (at least as Artaud knew it) simply showed or suggested things instead of naming them; it also had the magical ability to conjure up illusions, thereby giving the imagination an opportunity to be creative. The same applies, of course, to theatrical productions as long as they do not merely strive to illustrate a text. Being an actor, Artaud never lost his interest in the theatre, but in a theatre which would break away from realism, for he sees realism on the stage as producing nothing but a superficial, dull, and distorted image of reality. Superficial because it takes no account of the subconscious imagination and deals only with banalities, dull because it discourages curiosity, and distorted because, for clarity's sake, it represents reality according to an order that does not correspond to its true nature: "Clear thinking is no longer sufficient. . . . What is clear is what is immediately accessible, but the immediately accessible is only the very surface of life."[3]

Initially Artaud considers both cinema and theatre as means of escape for the imagination. He wants to harness their power of suggestion in order to cause "a liberation . . . of all the dark forces of our thinking process" (Artaud, *Oeuvres*, III, 87) which have been stifled by reason and logic. By aiming toward the representation of some of the "secrets which lie buried in our consciousness" (Artaud, *Oeuvres*, III, 83), cinema helps us achieve a better knowledge of ourselves and of our environment. We should go to the cinema or the theatre to "escape from ourselves, or, if you prefer, to find ourselves again in . . . our innermost unicity" (Artaud, *Oeuvres*, II, 12–13).

These few remarks make it clear that Artaud assigns to the cinema the same definitions and purpose as Marcel Schneider and Eric Rabkin attribute to the fantastic. Schneider describes the fantastic as "a literature of escape in the sense that we escape in order to find ourselves again, in the most hidden retreat of our mind,"[4] and Rabkin comments: "In the literature of the fantastic, escape is the means of exploration of an unknown land, a land which is the underside of the mind of man. The fantastic is used to reveal the truth of the human heart."[5] Artaud himself is aware of such a resemblance when he writes: "The cinema will take after the fantastic, a fantastic which, as we realize it more and more, is actually nothing but the real in its totality" (Artaud, *Oeuvres*, III, 84).

Two of Artaud's film scripts illustrate how and to what purpose he intends to make use of the fantastic.

His first scenario, *The Eighteen Seconds*, was primarily an attempt to demonstrate the artificiality of rational thinking. Here Artaud imagines a succession of images in the same order as they come to the mind of a man who has no control over his thinking process during a time period of eighteen seconds. The author's first intention is obviously to oppose two ways of perceiving the world: the rational way with which everybody ordinarily complies and the spontaneous way which the character in the scenario follows. In order to communicate with others, the first one is mandatory because it is the only code universally recognized as legitimate and acceptable. Whoever fails to abide by it is rejected as an outsider or even a lunatic (like the character in the scenario who, as a result of ostracism, commits suicide).

Based upon this opposition, Artaud contends that what is commonly called reality is in fact only a very partial aspect of it. It is partial because it amounts to nothing more than the outcome of a rational perception of the world, that is to say, the logically ordered world where everything is assigned a significance and a function. Furthermore, he considers such an approach to reality as highly arbitrary and artificial because, as he attempts to demonstrate, it does not even coincide with the way the mind, once left to its own spontaneity, naturally operates. Logic is the result of an effort and therefore is contrived.

The author's second intention with the scenario is obviously the representation of what he considers the authentic aspect of reality. As irrational as they might be, the images that generate spontaneously in the mind of the character are illustrations of that other aspect of reality. For Artaud believes that behind the logical order lies a hidden life which the mind can detect and recognize, but which reason instantly represses.

Finally, the last and most important purpose of the scenario consists of convincing the audience of the existence of that hidden life. To this effect, Artaud turns to the fantastic and makes use of two elements that characterize the genre, the dream and the occult. Because it expresses the way in which the psyche spontaneously apprehends the world, Artaud uses the structure of a dream, which Penzoldt calls "the language of the subconscious."[6] It is also convenient in that it is a familiar and intriguing phenomenon which appeals to the imagination and arouses curiosity as well as interest by revealing unusual and unexpected facets of ordinary things. The occult, on the other hand, is equally convenient because, by suggesting the existence of phenomena that cannot be explained logically, it offers an unusual conception of the world which, therefore, appeals to the imagination.

For Artaud, the occult, like the dream, possesses a reality of its own which the cinema must express: "The cinema is essentially the revelation of an occult world with which it puts us directly into contact" (Artaud, *Oeuvres*, III, 83). A later scenario, *The 32*, is even more fantastic than *The Eighteen Seconds*.

Here the author imagines a banal setting where strange events will make a sudden eruption into everyday life. His main character, who must initially appear as a very social chemistry teacher, turns into a mad killer whenever he has hallucinations; and, in the end, it becomes known that he has killed thirty-two women and that he may indeed be a vampire. Until this moment the spectators are kept in a state of suspense and fright.

After an initial scene presenting the professor in his classroom, Artaud immediately wants to arouse the curiosity and the apprehension of his audience. He does so in the following segment, where the professor makes an appointment with a young girl for midnight on the next day. From that moment until the arrival of the young girl at the professor's house, the camera must focus on the surrounding environment. First, the dark and quiet town, then the professor's house, its dark and empty rooms, his lab where nothing can be seen besides bottles and strange instruments, the professor himself whose nervous state is evident, and finally the door of his house.

The nature of the scenario coincides exactly with Schneider's description of the fantastic: "The fantastic is not confined to the thrill of terror or to the diabolical. It must also be seen as a step toward things which are beyond appearances and discursive logic."[7] After making use of the dream and the occult, Artaud now employs fear in the same way as in a fantastic story, that is, as a means to manipulate the spectator, to make him vulnerable and receptive to what he sees, while keeping his attention. Fear stimulates the imagination as well as the unconscious and permits the audience to suspend its disbelief without realizing it. Artaud hopes that once fear sets in, the spectator will stop rationalizing what he sees and will perceive the objects presented to him by the camera, not according to their practical or logical functions, but rather according to what their appearance on the screen triggers in his imagination or subconscious: "I can visualize very well all the things of real life reorganized and crystallized according to a revolutionary order which would derive its meaning from nothing but the solicitations of the unconscious" (Artaud, *Oeuvres*, I, 38–39).

In other words, Artaud is convinced that if the camera can present the objects with enough force of persuasion, it will be able to create a certain atmosphere conducive to manipulating the spectator's mind or unconscious. The very same ordinary objects will then be looked upon differently, and, as a result, they will take on new and different meanings which, even if they are not logical, will nevertheless make sense for the observer in a process similar to the dream-work. One thing may become something else, familiar objects may become disturbing, threatening, mysterious and yet remain quite real. The professor, for example, may be seen as a solitary alchemist of sorts and his lab a setting for some black magic performance. These various potential aspects that things may take constitute what Artaud calls the "hidden life behind the logical order" or "the occult life of things."

It is now clear that Artaud uses these fantastic devices because he is in the same situation as the writer of a fantastic story. He wants to present an illogical aspect of something that he considers to be reality, and he wants his spectator to accept it as real. Therefore, he must choose a theme which will appeal to the imagination and the unconscious of his audience and which can create an atmosphere of mystery or fear so that the spectator will be sensitive to it, and finally he must present it in the most concrete way possible.

Unfortunately, nothing came out of either of the two film scripts, and, disappointed, Artaud turned again to the theatre with the same purpose in mind: to illustrate the occult nature of reality. The themes remain the same—they all pertain to the fantastic—but Artaud's use of them becomes more sophisticated and more indicative of his conception of reality.

In 1928 Artaud chose to stage Strindberg's *A Dream Play*. In this drama

Strindberg creates a world in which people are driven to misery and despair because their hopes and expectations—though reasonable—are repeatedly destroyed. These misfortunes stem from the fact that man does not see his world as it is and therefore cannot fully relate to it. Strindberg shows that too often people organize their environment logically and act accordingly, a phenomenon that invariably leads to disaster because the laws of nature are not always rational. Because things never follow their expectations, the characters are so bewildered that they can no longer differentiate between true and false, real and unreal.

Artaud is attracted to the play because it presents a situation which is both concrete and mysterious, and he attempts to emphasize these two contrasting aspects. He wants the staging to be as concrete as possible so that the reality of the action can never be challenged (in other words, he does not want the play to be looked upon as the representation of a dream or of a fantasy world). He also wants the staging to magnify the mysterious nature of things and, for that reason, he focuses on the objects themselves. But his interpretation is different from Strindberg's.

Strindberg suggests that things are deceptive because their existence is just an empty appearance without meaning or substance. Artaud, on the contrary, wants to convey that they are deceptive because we are unable to capture their full meaning and that consequently they do not answer our expectations. Here again, his staging borrows heavily from the repertoire of the fantastic but for different purposes. He now decides to intrigue the spectator by giving mysterious appearances to the props themselves. He elaborates on Strindberg's idea of using the same objects in different scenes for different purposes, to show that there is no limit to their potential. This effect, along with the atmosphere of mystery that prevails, must give the impression that things possess an occult life. But Artaud goes even further: he hopes to show the alienating effect of this occult life on the characters. He feels that because the environment is constituted of objects, man is compelled to react to them, to give them a meaning in order to organize and thereby dominate his world. However, these objects escape from his grasp as they inevitably take on other meanings. Artaud's intentional manipulation of the play consists in showing that, as a result, man can never dominate his environment and, for this reason, is eventually overwhelmed by it.

Because of financial problems, Artaud was given only one opportunity to stage the play, but very soon afterward he had several projects for new productions. At that time he was working on a translation and an adaptation of Matthew Lewis's novel *The Monk*. This growing interest in the fantastic and the occult is perhaps best reflected in a proposal he wrote in 1930 for the staging of yet another play by Strindberg, *The Ghost Sonata*. It is also in this proposal that Artaud gives full significance to elements pertaining to the fantastic.

Strindberg's play, *The Ghost Sonata*, is already rich in fantastic elements. After a seemingly realistic opening scene, the atmosphere becomes eerie. Most characters are skeletal figures, moving about in what seems to be a peaceful environment. Their behavior also seems normal until a feeling of fear and death begins to prevail without any obvious reason. For Artaud it is another perfect play to appeal to the imagination because it invites any number of interpretations. It resembles a dream in that it juxtaposes the familiar and the mysterious while not appearing to follow a rational development; and it also conveys "the feeling of something which, without being supernatural, non-human, belongs to some sort of inner reality" (Artaud, *Oeuvres*, II, 127). Through his interpretation of the play, we can understand that this "inner reality" is in fact the expression of what Artaud views as the true nature of reality, stemming from the relationship between the fantastic and the real, which theatre must manage to communicate.

Whereas Strindberg intrigues his spectator by opposing appearance and reality, Artaud wants to disorient him from the very beginning by focusing on the material objects themselves. He immediately eliminates Strindberg's seemingly realistic opening by suggesting a transparent house where some of the objects inside appear much larger than their normal size. He also wants to make it obvious that the mystery comes from the very presence of these objects and their respective situations vis-à-vis one another. In other words, before the play even begins, the objects must attract the spectator's curiosity and become the agent of the mystery. As the play unfolds, Artaud intends to continue focusing on them to maintain their power over the spectator's interest.

His staging directions revolve around the idea of an overwhelming magical attraction which would emanate from things. In order to make the audience sensitive to this magnetic power, the actors are directed, throughout the play, to appear spellbound. This is where Artaud's interpretation of the play becomes truly fantastic. The actors must give the impression that they are drawn to the house by some superior force: "This feeling of invincible attraction, of bewitchment, or magic, is oppressing, overwhelming" (Artaud, *Oeuvres*, II, 129). To create such an effect, Artaud suggests that they appear as depersonalized and lifeless near-corpses doomed to revolve mechanically and endlessly around their tiny world. He goes so far as to portray them at times in the form of mannequins.

Clearly, Artaud presents this attraction as all-powerful and universal: there is no escape; and, as in *A Dream Play*, he sees it as a destructive force which deprives each individual of his will power, turns him into a mechanical puppet, and eventually consumes him. No one will escape from destruction and death, and Artaud goes on to illustrate that this destruction is caused by the concrete world which brings about alienation. In his staging, the character of the cook (who provokes the slow death of almost everybody in the house) is represented at all times by a mannequin. Here matter literally takes life in order to destroy, and this is not an isolated instance: the old lady who brings about the death of the man who appeared to be the main character is represented by the form of a mummy coming out of a closet. At crucial moments, Artaud envisions the action as being dictated by the presence of particular objects.

As mentioned earlier, Artaud's work involves discovering a new approach to reality and a new definition of it. His interpretation of *The Ghost Sonata* reveals the main evolution of this effort. To a rational world where everything is labeled and classified, Artaud opposes a world where things are in perpetual motion and therefore impossible to apprehend, let alone explain. When he says that the theatre (and also the cinema) must help us detect the occult life of things, he means precisely that it must teach us how to perceive and acknowledge this constant transformation of things in spite of its irrationality and unpredictability.

Artaud explains the ever-changing nature of things by the existence of cosmic forces running the universe. These forces, which are active and destructive at all times, constitute for Artaud the "point" mentioned by Breton from which "life and death, the real and the imaginary, the past and the future . . . cease to be perceived as contradictory."[8] The most fundamental element of reality becomes, then, the recognition of the existence of such a cosmic fatality which accounts for all phenomena. Artaud is of the opinion that man can achieve an awareness of this destructive fatality through careful observation of his relationship with the physical world, and it is the purpose of his theatre to provoke such an awareness. This is why Artaud calls it a Theatre of Cruelty.

It is cruel because it shows man that his method of apprehending the world—namely reason—has brought about nothing but false assumptions and frustrations, as evidenced by Strindberg's two plays. It is also cruel because it compels man to realize his inability to explain and control his environment due to its constantly changing nature. He must accept the fact that the least he can do is to be aware of these changes. Finally, it is most cruel because it places man, forever alone and defenseless, before this uncontrollable and mysterious fatality which will inevitably destroy him as it has destroyed the characters in *The Ghost Sonata*. Artaud expresses this theatrical ambition in one sentence: The ultimate goal of the theatre is "to reintroduce into each theatrical gesture the idea of a cosmic cruelty without which there would be neither life nor reality" (Artaud, *Oeuvres*, V, 154).

In conclusion, we can say that Artaud's theatre is metaphysical in purpose and fantastic in nature. Moreover, aside from the author's use of such motifs as dreams, ghosts, vampires, and magic, it would be helpful to point out briefly some general characteristics which relate this theatre to the fantastic genre as defined by such critics as Todorov, Caillois, Rabkin, and Schneider.

All four agree that the fantastic is based on the existence of mysterious and sometimes frightening phenomena which disturb the familiar order of the world and which cannot be explained logically. Schneider and Rabkin emphasize the fact that the fantastic is a means of escape that allows the individual to explore the other side of himself, his imagination and unconscious. Schneider also points out that the fantastic author's originality consists in the fact that he does not change the nature of the outside world and of the objects he uses, but instead multiplies their significance and power. Artaud's theatre shares all these characteristics.

However, it does not seem to follow Rabkin's theory of a reversal of perspective. Artaud's theatre is not "reality turned 180° around." According to

Rabkin, the fantastic presupposes the presence of two contradictory orders: the natural order with its well-known laws and the supernatural order with its unknown laws. Artaud (who dislikes the term ''supernatural'' because of its misleading religious connotations) does not see the fantastic as the opposition of the natural and the supernatural, but as the coexistence of these two complementary aspects of the same reality. The fantastic for Artaud is not the reversal of reality but one aspect of it, its hidden and therefore unknown facet, because, as Todorov says, ''If a fantastic event is part of reality, it means that reality operates according to laws unknown to us.''[9]

As a matter of fact, Artaud's theatre appears most fantastic when compared with Todorov's definition of the genre. Todorov sees the fantastic as a hesitation on the part of the individual whose familiar world has been disturbed by illogical phenomena. Artaud's theatre can be seen then as provoking the ultimate hesitation. It not only reveals the presence of these phenomena which baffle all rational explanation, but it also shows the individual that his life is dramatically altered by them in a way that will always escape his understanding and consequently will leave him forever in a state of powerless hesitation in front of his own destiny.

NOTES

1. André Breton, *Manifestes du Surréalisme* (Paris: Gallimard, Collections Idees, 1967), pp. 76–77; my translation.

2. Ibid., p. 24.

3. Antonin Artaud, *Oeuvres Complètes* (Paris: Gallimard, 1970), III, 84; my translation; hereafter cited in the text.

4. Marcel Schneider, *La Littérature Fantastique en France* (Paris: Fayard, 1964), p. 407; my translation.

5. Eric Rabkin, *The Fantastic in Literature* (Princeton: Princeton University Press, 1976), p. 45.

6. Peter Penzoldt, *The Supernatural in Fiction* (London: Peter Nevill, 1952), p. 31.

7. Schneider, *La Littérature Fantastique*, p. 275.

8. Breton, *Manifestes*, pp. 76–77.

9. Tzvetan Todorov, *Introduction à la littérature fantastique* (Paris: Le Seuil, Collection Points, 1970), p. 29; my translation.

IV. FANTASY AND LITERARY TRADITION

Fantasy is timeless. It has always made up part of the fabric of literature, though it has seldom predominated in the imaginations of writers to the extent that it does today. Essays in this section relate the fantastic to themes, forms, and character types that have a long history in literature. Roger C. Schlobin finds the fool alive and well in modern heroic fantasy, and Michael Collings discusses traditional epic conventions in some modern science fiction. J.R.R. Tolkien, probably more responsible than any other individual for the renascence of fantasy since World War Two, is the subject of two essays that relate his work to Celtic and Germanic mythology (James L. Hodge) and to the classical concept of pastoral (Douglas A. Burger). Richard H. Abrams interprets *The Winter's Tale* as a study in demonic possession; Steven M. Taylor analyzes the influence of Lewis Carroll on the dramas of Fernando Arrabal; William Coyle discusses Mark Twain's use of fantasy; and Constance D. Markey analyzes Italo Calvino's use of ancient tarot cards to express contemporary attitudes.

The Survival of the Fool in Modern Heroic Fantasy

Roger C. Schlobin

The modern mentality has all but destroyed the fool in literature. Staggered by the stress on reason and science, he fell victim to the collective empiricism of Neoclassicism, Realism, Naturalism, Existentialism, and Skepticism. As a figure who denies order, mocking the society that ironically he needs to survive, the fool's power to melt the "solidity of the world"[1] became, finally, too much of an embarrassment. He has been transformed into a superficial scapegoat whose comic efforts are reduced simply to chaos rather than enlightenment, as Harlan Ellison's " 'Repent Harlequin!' Said the Ticktockman" illustrates by its pathetic marriage and Robert E. Vardeman and Victor Milan's *The Sundered Realm* demonstrates by its maimed, castrated prince who retains only the fool's license to speak freely in the presence of his demagogue sister. As Carl Jung points out in *Psychological Types*, the modern intellect recognizes everything but itself as fantasy, and being a closed system, the intellect represents fantasy activity as much as possible.[2] Therefore, the fool must die.

Ironically, as the artistic and philosophic legacies of Copernicus, Newton, Darwin, Sartre, and others gave birth to a singular stress on actuality and immediacy that emasculated the fool, the fall of the nobility and its own special order destroyed the social environment that the fool needed as the frame for his wisdom and mockery. The fool dies with the king. Enid Welsford in her classic study *The Fool: His Social and Literary History* accurately summarizes the fatal descent of the fool:

The King, the Priest and the Fool all belong to the same regime, all belong essentially to a society shaped by belief in Divine order, human inadequacy, efficacious ritual; and there is no real place for any of them in a world increasingly dominated by the notions of the puritan, the scientist, and the captain of industry; for strange as it may seem the fool in cap and bells can only flourish among people who have sacraments, who value symbols as well as tools, and cannot forever survive the decay of faith in divinely imposed authority, the rejection of all taboo and mysterious inspiration. (Welsford, *The Fool*, p. 193)

However, to believe that the fool is a victim of the modern era, one that Erich Neumann condemned so fully for its appalling inability to deal with the human soul, is to fail to recognize the fool's characteristic plasticity.[3] Smacked over and over again, he will spring back up like a Joe Palooka doll—eternal in his capacity for regeneration. To discover him, the search must be conducted among the rigidly structured social orders in which his vision and folly originally flourished. Joseph Heller, in his mock epic *Catch–22*, uses the military and the absurdity of seemingly unending bombing missions as just such an environment. When Orr finally reaches Sweden on his rubber raft, the reader shares the celebration of the fool as outsider who still manages to triumph despite repressive and ordered systems. In an instant Orr is transformed from "a permanent scapegoat whose official duty is to jeer continually at his superiors in order to bear their ill-luck" (Welsford, *The Fool*, p. 74) to the fool who is licensed to summon the "magical force of continuing life" and violate order with impunity.[4] The success of Heller's Orr as a figure who exhilarates centers of life and, thus, causes joyous laughter is also present in the immensely popular *M.A.S.H.*—Richard Hooker's novel (1968), Robert Altman's film version (1970), and the television continuation.[5]

While the bathetic characterizations of Woody Allen are indications of just how exceptional *Catch–22* and *M.A.S.H.* are, the fool has been alive and well in examples of heroic or sword-and-sorcery fantasy for some time now. He is still uncommon, for heroic fantasy's roots in saga, epic, and romance give it a predominantly solemn tone—inhospitable to the fool. Were it not for the Hobbits, for example, a study of humor in J.R.R. Tolkien's *The Lord of the Rings* would be the shortest article ever written, a characteristic that made the series so delightfully vulnerable to Henry N. Beard and Douglas C. Kenney's parody, *Bored of the Rings*. In the same vein John Jakes mocked Robert E. Howard's Conan and Solomon Kane along with other equally grim examples of sword and sorcery in *Mention My Name in Atlantis*. Nonetheless, heroic fantasy does have the necessary orderly world view and royalty to be fertile ground for the fool despite its exaggeratedly sanctimonious virtue.

In fact, fantasy, in general, is usually more rigorous in its ethical constructs than the actual world, and while it is most often socially and morally non-didactic, heroic fantasy is predominantly preoccupied with psychomachia. This stress on the polarities of good and evil also explains why the fool doesn't occur more frequently despite the suitability of the environment. The fool is most frequently an enemy of the didactic,[6] an amoral, Janus-like[7] figure who lives in ambiguity, not the clear win-or-lose conflict of psychomachia. Thus, Samwise, Tolkien's fool in *The Lord of the Rings*, becomes a functional agent only in the final struggle at the Crack of Doom between Gollum and the evil-possessed

Frodo. Here Samwise serves in the fool's role of a counterweight to whatever principle is in control.[8] Many heroic fantasies seek to make or reestablish boundaries, and the fool is a boundary-breaker,[9] as Enid Welsford also points out: "Under the dissolvent influence of his personality the iron network of physical, social and moral law, which enmeshes us from cradle to grave, seems—for a moment—negligible as a web of gossamer" (Welsford, *The Fool*, p. 317).

The fool and his folly, an agent for the freeing of the imagination, is a true alien in a heroic fantasy that has ethical and pompous extremes that are self-protective and intolerant. Examples of this are the two main characters in Italo Calvino's *The Nonexistent Knight*, a fantasy set during the wars of Charlemagne. Agilulf, a paladin, is only an empty, immaculate suit of white armor. He exists only by his will power and constant belief in himself and Charlemagne's holy cause. He never sleeps, and while fools are supposed to expose pretenders,[10] Agilulf's twenty-four-hour puritanism and meticulous attention to proper procedures are constant plagues upon his less glorified and mundane comrades. He loses his self-sustained life when his perverse comrades pressure him to discover whether or not the damsel he rescued in his youth, a feat on which Agilulf bases his entire reputation and honor, was a virgin. When it appears that she was not (via a convoluted deus ex machina reminiscent of eighteenth-century domestic drama), Agilulf literally falls apart. He is a victim of his own inability to understand the follies of the world, his comrades, and himself. He cannot avail himself of the fool's ability to protect himself from the environment,[11] nor can he be a touchstone to test the true quality of men and manners (Welsford, *The Fool*, p. 249). Interestingly, a multinamed idiot—a natural fool and Agilulf's page—does survive. He is the opposite of the paladin and is totally unaware of his own existence, thus his many names; one is as good as any other. Among his many spontaneous performances that delight everyone are his near-drownings when he forgets if he is to eat his soup or if it is to eat him and when he forgets if he's to be in the ocean or the ocean in him. He can, however, be a bit pesty when he thinks he's a fish and gets tangled in the villagers' nets. He is a "prisoner of the world's stuff," the narrator tells us. Because he is, he is allowed to survive. Agilulf has none of the "world's stuff"; therefore, he perishes. Both are too extreme to be true fools. Somewhere between them is the true conscious fool who can break down the distinction between folly and wisdom and be a slave to neither.

Another figure in modern heroic fantasy who cannot distinguish among the ambiguities of the world, although with less painful results than in Agilulf's case, is Zdim in L. Sprague de Camp's *The Fallible Fiend*. In this burlesque tale, Zdim is a demon drafted in his native realm to serve a mortal wizard in exchange for much-needed iron. Zdim's difficulty is that he takes literally everything he is told. Like Jim Eckert in Gordon R. Dickson's *The Dragon and the George*, whose mind is placed in the body of a very large dragon in an alternate world, Zdim is hilariously confused. When asked to shake, he gyrates his hips; told to devour the first person who enters the wizard's workshop, he consumes the apprentice. After he and the master decide to go on a vegetarian diet, he is incapable of devouring a true thief. Obviously, Zdim is caught in the world's paradoxes and ambiguities. The professional fool, being aware of his role, uses these for his own gain, ignoring the created laws of logic, to satisfy his own needs and exercise his special insights. However, Zdim, a demon of no small intelligence, does learn the ropes and manages to manipulate various leaders and chieftains to save his adopted city. In fact, he gets so good at it that, after he returns to his own plane, he requests another "sabbatical" on Earth.

As mentioned earlier, the fool is invariably an alien or outlaw within the social order, but as with any figure who lives by his wits, he is dependent on that same order for his existence (Welsford, *The Fool*, p. 55). He is, in part, a parasite. Yet he is a powerful leech who lives through exploitation. His power is in his ability to live with ambiguity, which is a natural characteristic of the cosmos, while the more normal characters around him keep expecting order, honesty, and justice. Thus, he is ennobled during holiday, as the incarnate Lord of Misrule, when everyone yields to natural instincts and moves to the rhythm of life.[12] In a rare example of the combination of social satire and fantasy, Charles G. Finney creates just such a figure in *The Magician Out of Manchuria*. Set in China during the "Great Leap Forward," it focuses on the magical and scandalous activities of a thief, magician, and general rapscallion. Finney's character is a picaresque figure who prefers wine to gold and who must shed his skin at the most inopportune moments due to a python in his family tree. He, his apprentice, and his ass join with a very ugly queen; she has been the victim of an attempted assassination, and with a magic balm the magician has transformed her into the Queen of Lust. The magician's strenuous amorous interludes with the Queen, after he has shed the obese skin he wears at the beginning of the novel and has become strikingly handsome, illustrate another traditional characteristic of the fool—his exaggerated sexuality.[13] More importantly, *The Magician Out of Manchuria* demonstrates the fool's role as compensator as he balances the predominant ruling order. He plays what John Danby identifies as the game of "handy dandy."[14] In this case, his whimsy, exploitation, and cunning are the comic alternative to the rote conformity of the "Great Leap Forward." As always, he mocks the artificial class distinctions that societies create from only superficial characteristics and then fervently believe in as facts. While Enid Welsford identifies the priests and their no-nonsense religions as the fool's greatest enemies (Welsford, *The Fool*, p. 180), Finney's rogue attracts more modern and more expansive threats. The social satire of the novel demonstrates how secularism, socialism, and nominalism have reduced the continual rebirth of imagination and the liberating mind-play of festivity to socially integrated and inferior portions of the supposedly "superior" utilitarian world.[15] Art is subordinated to "real" waking experience,[16] and the rhythm of spontaneous life, which the true fool so thoroughly embodies, is lost.

This role as compensator is probably the fool's most valuable characteristic in modern heroic fantasy; examples are Finney's magician, Heller's Orr, and

Walter Wangerin's Mundo Cani in the early parts of *The Book of the Dun Cow*, though late in the novel he becomes a sacrificial hero. This is Samwise's role in *The Lord of the Rings* as he attempts to place his diminutive self across the fulcrum from the deep solemnity of the trilogy's virtuous and fell forces. De Camp's Zdim, like Bink in Piers Anthony's Xanth series (1977–1982), also serves this purpose as he turns potentially horrific events into laughter. As Puck does in Shakespeare's *Midsummer Night's Dream*, the successful fool often has to stand against the potentially destructive and maiming forces of the world of experience. Sustaining vision and imagination, the fool continually tries to re-create the world by averting potential horror with kinetic folly.[17] In this he is in opposition to the hero, who is trying to conquer the world; and typically it is the hero, rather than the fool, who is featured in sword-and-sorcery fantasy, much in the manner of Northrop Frye's romance. This is why Calvino's Agilulf fails: he hasn't the balancing power of the fool or the social acceptance of the hero.

Another figure who stands against the frequently dreary and dangerous atmosphere of heroic fantasy and is a transformer of the mundane is Black, the sidekick in Roger Zelazny's series of short stories and one novel (*The Changing Land*), featuring Dilvish the Damned or the Deliverer (depending on who is speaking at the moment). Dilvish has been cursed by the Dark One, and for 200 years his body stood as a statue while his soul suffered in Hell, his punishment for saving a sacrificial virgin.[18] Clearly, Dilvish is not given by disposition to frivolity. However, Black, his burnished iron and magical warhorse, is given to speaking sardonically and even sarcastically at times. Unburdened by the morbid irony of Cugel the Clever in Jack Vance's *The Eyes of the Overworld* and no prancing jester in cap and bells, Black is a prime illustration of Robert Hillis Goldsmith's observation in *Wise Fools in Shakespeare* that the wise fool is often more ironic and less direct in his folly than the buffoon.[19] Black is characterized by his understated wisdom. He demonstrates this frequently by his droll insights and his knowledge of impending danger. For example, in "Tower of Ice," he mutters about how someone of his dignity has to pull a sled out of a ditch and explains that one day civilization will have an entire system of physics to explain what he is doing.[20] Like Elric's eternal sidekick in Michael Moorcock's sword-and-sorcery series, Black's character is determined by his Bogartesque tone, which is well illustrated by the following interchange as he carries Dilvish through a dementedly sorcerous gauntlet:

Lowering his head, Black plunged down the hillside into the fog, his eyes glowing like coals. The ground was shaking steadily now, and in the portions of which he had view, Dilvish could see cracks appearing, widening. Wisps of smoke rose from several of these, moving to mingle with the fog. The winds rose again about them, though not as strongly as before.

Leaping among large, cube-shaped green rocks in a very unhorselike fashion, Black bore steadily to the right as the ground leveled and the fog abated in patches. The sound of a terrific explosion reached them and splatters of hot mud rained nearby, though only a few fell upon them.

"In the future," Dilvish remarked, "I would prefer not cutting things quite that closely."

"Sorry," Black replied, "I was caught up in the beauty of the moment."[21]

Zelazny's Black brings up an important point about the fool in sword-and-sorcery fantasy, which is that he is often disguised and not as obvious as when he wears the conspicuous motley. This should be no immediate surprise since the wise fool frequently adopts disguises in literature.[22] In fantasy, however, there is a more critical issue because the literature's totality is already a statement of the reversal of normal expectations, a suspension of the rules of everyday in which the fictive experience itself assumes the traditional role of the fool in the reader's mundane world. Thus, in their roles of balancers, fantasy's fools are sometimes reminders of the pragmatic world the reader has left to enter the misrule of the fantasy realm.

Nowhere in modern fantasy is the use of the fool as a referent to the reader's cosmology better demonstrated than by Schmendrick the magician in Peter S. Beagle's *The Last Unicorn*. Schmendrick is one of the Last Unicorn's companions as she journeys to free her ensorceled kin from the spells of King Haggard, a twisted creature who hungers for beauty but has the crippling knowledge that nothing is worth loving since it will only die in his hands.[23] One of Schmendrick's important roles in the novel is maintaining a fatalistic optimism after he has inadvertently turned the unicorn into a maid to save her from Haggard's awesomely fell Red Bull and, as a result, introduced her to the horrors and pains of mortality. This is just another of his misfired spells, a condition he has come to expect since he has no faith in his ability to do any real magic. He has said to the unicorn, "Take me with you for laughs, for luck, for the unknown" (Beagle, *Many Worlds*, p. 58). His attitude reflects the realistic view of the reader's world that magic is really useless and only a sham, for he "can't turn cream into butter" (p. 53). Schmendrick considers himself only a storyteller, a traveling prestidigitator, and a fool; not even the unicorn's magic can turn him into a true magician (p. 59). Thus, he serves as his own foil when magical power does triumphantly take possession of him, and his humorous misadventures stand between the reader and the potential tragedy of the wondrous unicorn dying as a human and never saving her kin.

Interestingly, the one immediately recognizable fool in heroic fantasy appears in *The Last Unicorn* only briefly and is a slightly mad butterfly (pp. 32–34). This delightfully blithe creature identifies itself as a roving gambler and brings laughter to the unicorn for the first time in her arduous quest. He misdirects, rhymes, riddles, puns, and sings—all motion, whim, and impulse—before his madness suddenly vanishes for a moment and he warns the unicorn of the dread foes that await. However, in true fool fashion, he quickly recants his wisdom and lapses into balancing folly. As he flitters briefly through Beagle's wondrous novel, one is immediately provided with a vision of the perfect fool as he must have capered across the Elizabethan stage some 400 years ago.

Thus, the fool is alive and well in some modern heroic fantasy. In these works, his perennial power to melt the solidity of the world (Welsford, *The Fool*, p. 221) is augmented by his ability to maintain the dual realistic and fantastic perspective of the fantasy reader. He prevents the often violent and dangerous heroic world from tumbling into horror and fear, and his balancing act maintains wonder and intuitive wisdom. The fool prevents the yielding of the world to mankind's continual attempts to impose an artificial order that is at best boring and at worst creatively stultifying. As Don Antonio points out to Samson Carrasco, in Cervantes' *Don Quixote*, human beings need the fool:

"O sir!... may God forgive you for the wrong you have done in robbing the world of the most diverting madman who was ever seen. Is it not plain, sir, that his cure can never benefit mankind half as much as the pleasure he affords by his eccentricities? But I feel sure, sir bachelor, that all your art will not cure such deep-rooted madness, and were it not uncharitable, I would express the hope that he may never recover, for by his cure we should lose not only the good knight's good company, but also the drollery of his squire Sancho Panza, which is enough to transform melancholy itself into mirth."[24]

NOTES

1. Enid Welsford, *The Fool: His Social and Literary History* (London: Faber and Faber, 1935), pp. 55, 221; hereafter cited in the text.

2. C. G. Jung, *Psychological Types*, trans. H. G. Baynes, rev. R.F.C. Hull (Princeton: Princeton University Press, 1971), pp. 53, 59.

3. Erich Neumann, *Depth Psychology and a New Ethic*, trans. Eugene Rolfe (1949; reprint ed., New York: Harper & Row, 1973), p. 25.

4. William Willeford, *The Fool and His Scepter: A Study in Clowns and Jesters and Their Audience* (Evanston: Northwestern University Press, 1969), p. 87.

5. For further discussion of the cause of laughter, see Susanne K. Langer, *Feeling and Form: A Theory of Art* (New York: Scribner, 1953), p. 340.

6. Robert Hillis Goldsmith, *Wise Fools in Shakespeare* (East Lansing: Michigan State University Press, 1963), p. 48.

7. John Danby, "The Fool and Handy Dandy," in *Shakespeare: Modern Essays in Criticism*, ed. Leonard F. Dean (New York: Oxford University Press, 1961), p. 333. For further comment on the fool's amoral nature, see Langer, *Feeling and Form*, p. 342.

8. Ibid., p. 334.

9. Willeford, *Fool and His Scepter*, p. 27.

10. Danby, "Fool and Handy Dandy," p. 334.

11. Ibid., p. 339.

12. Langer, *Feeling and Form*, p. 349.

13. Willeford, *Fool and His Scepter*, p. 22.

14. See note 7.

15. See my *The Literature of Fantasy: A Comprehensive, Annotated Bibliography of Modern Fantasy Fiction* (New York: Garland, 1979), pp. xxii–xxiii, for elaboration of this point.

16. Herbert Fingarette, *The Self in Transformation: Psychoanalysis, Philosophy, and the Life of the Spirit* (New York: Harper & Row, 1965), p. 189.

17. Willeford, *Fool and His Scepter*, p. 99.

18. Roger Zelazny, "Thelinda's Song," *Fantastic*, June 1965, pp. 5–11.

19. Goldsmith, *Wise Fools*, pp. 11, 89.

20. Roger Zelazny, "Tower of Ice," in *Flashing Swords, No. 5: Demons and Daggers*, ed. Lin Carter, Science Fiction Book Club (New York: Doubleday, 1981), p. 53.

21. Roger Zelazny, *The Changing Land* (New York: Ballantine Books, 1981), pp. 46–47.

22. Goldsmith, *Wise Fools*, p. 20.

23. Peter S. Beagle, introduction, *The Many Worlds of Peter S. Beagle* (New York: Viking, 1978), p. xii; hereafter cited in the text.

24. Miguel de Cervantes Saavedra, *Don Quixote of La Mancha*, trans. Walter Stark (1605, 1615; reprint ed., New York: New American Library, 1957), p. 415.

The Epic of *Dune*: Epic Traditions in Modern Science Fiction

Michael R. Collings

Traditionally, the epic has been considered among the highest forms of literary expression. From pre-classical times until well into the nineteenth century, the epic held its position as second to none (or on occasion second only to tragedy) in rankings of literary forms.[1] In fact, its preeminence was so widely recognized that during the Renaissance, critics defined the epic as the ultimate creative achievement from whose rules all other genres depended.[2]

With the publication of *Paradise Lost*, however, the development of the English verse epic reached a climax. Milton so expanded the boundaries of language and form that to go beyond Miltonic epic would be to burst the limits of the language itself and turn English into a language foreign to its own speakers. Consequently, during the eighteenth and nineteenth centuries, the epic languished while simultaneously (and paradoxically) retaining its status as the monarch of poetic forms. What successful approaches there were to the epic generally were subsumed under the rubric of mock epic. Pope's two masterpieces, *The Rape of the Lock* and *The Dunciad*, depend for much of their effect on the reader's knowledge of epic conventions and on an awareness of the degree to which Pope reversed those conventions. Nearly a century later, Byron used the mock epic for *Don Juan*, consciously parodying and inverting epic expectations.[3]

By the twentieth century, many critics were arguing that the classical verse epic—in spite of attempts by writers like Whitman, Hart Crane, and William Carlos Williams—had not survived the apocalyptic consequences of *Paradise Lost*. Some suggested that the epic had died, an outworn genre inappropriate to an age of common men; others argued more reasonably that the epic impulse had merely been diverted to a new form. Poetry had always been the accepted language of the highest literary achievements, it was argued, and therefore the epic had been a verse form. But by the mid-to-late-nineteenth century, the novel had preempted the status earlier held by poetry. Perhaps, then, the epic continued within the novel, expressed in new ways more appropriate to its new form.[4] Examples of hybrids between the epic and the novel seemed easily identifiable; *Moby Dick*, for example, has been seriously considered not only as a prose epic but more specifically as the heir to the Miltonic epic impulse.[5]

Countering this point of view is the suggestion that the modern novel more often than not consciously attempts to portray ''real life,'' and nothing is more devastating to the epic spirit than an overdose of that stultifying ingredient. Worship of the common man—of the anti-hero rather than the hero—works against every tradition of the epic. Consequently, the word *epic*, while still common, has ceased to define a literary form and instead has become merely an adjective or noun appended to any work of unusual bulk. An otherwise undistinguished film is, because of its length, billed as ''an epic of the Old West''; a mini-series broadcast on six consecutive nights is thereby assumed to be an ''epic''; and novels of more than 500 pages (particularly if historical and multigenerational) are advertised as ''epic.''

These redefinitions of the word are, of course, not entirely illegitimate; it is difficult to proscribe certain usages while admitting others, particularly when new senses of words become widespread. However, modern readers have lost sight of what an epic actually is and, consequently, apply the word less discriminately than they should. For most, *epic* in its traditional sense suggests a long, archaic, and uninteresting poem.

There is, however, at least one narrow area in which the epic in its formal sense still survives, somewhat altered in external appearance but essentially the same, and that is in the science fiction novel. Not all or even most science fiction novels are included in this category, of course. Epics, after all, have been quite rare throughout history, and great ones have been even rarer. We think of perhaps twenty memorable epics that have survived in Western tradition; of those, only a handful are acknowledged masterworks; the *Iliad* and *Odyssey*, the *Aeneid*, *Paradise Lost*, and *Paradise Regained* come most readily to mind. There is little to wonder at, then, if only a few science fiction novels contain more than a few rudimentary remembrances of epic traditions. And yet there are those few, and in them the epic survives.

It would be possible to define the science fiction novel as epic by listing two dozen or so literary conventions found in traditional epics; to do so, however, would remain unconvincing since these conventions exist on the surface. Indeed, one of the characteristics of a bad epic is its slavish dependence on superficial conventions at the expense of originality, genius, and achievement. Instead, it is more fruitful to concentrate on several essential elements of the epic and to suggest ways in which they provide structure and form to a particular science fiction novel, Frank Herbert's *Dune*.[6]

The primary feature of the traditional epic was that it centered about the exploits of a hero—of a single man superior in talent and ability to common men. We think immediately of the central characters of major epics: Achilles, Odysseus, Aeneas, Adam, and Christ. In each instance, the hero is elevated beyond common mortals by particular traits, conventionally either peculiarities surrounding his birth and lineage or unusual mental and physical strength. Just as the form itself was the highest manifestation of the poetic impulse, so the character it defined was superior to other men.

In *Dune* the hero, Paul Atreides, is introduced immediately, and in the first pages of the novel we discover that he is unusual. He is aristocratic, the son of a duke and a distant cousin of the Padishah emperor. Beyond that, he is the *son* of a Bene Gesserit; indeed, he is one of only two such in the entire novel, the second being his ostensible opponent in the final duel, the Count Fenring (p. 480). This heritage is essential to the working out of the plot, since the Bene Gesserit are instructed to bear only daughters as a method of preserving the purity of the Sisterhood and of segregating essential bloodlines.

Paul's birth interferes with the breeding plans of the Sisterhood, but, more importantly, it defines him as a potential Kwisatz Haderach, the "one who can be many places at once" (p. 12). Through his father he inherits the honors and perquisites of royalty; through his mother, the genetic and psychic makeup that will allow him to pass the Reverend Mother Mohiam's Gom Jabbar—the ultimate test of humanity. Even the Reverend Mother herself, irritated though she is at Jessica's effrontery, acknowledges Paul's inherent superiority, admits that he withstands more pain than a woman could bear, and suspects that she wanted him to fail the test (p. 9).

Paul's essential difference is underscored continually in his relationships with key characters: the Imperial Planetologist Kynes is shaken by Paul's seemingly impossible ability to fit into the Arrakeen way of life without previous instruction; the Fremen (especially their tribal leader, Stilgar) immediately see in him characteristics implicit in their messianic legends, amplified through his training in the "weirding ways" of the Lady Jessica; Fenring, the emperor's executioner, refuses to meet Paul in personal combat, defying the express order of the Padishah emperor and ignoring his own knowledge that he could in fact kill the younger man. In each instance Paul impresses those about him with his superiority, both in degree and in kind (to borrow a distinction from Northrop Frye). He is set apart in the opening pages of the novel and remains isolated until the end. Even in his final victory as he assumes the Imperial throne, he remains beyond the full understanding of even the most astute observers.

His actions, like those of the traditional epic hero, are of worldwide (in this instance, galaxy-wide) impact. In classical epic the hero performs actions which alter irrevocably the history of his world: Achilles compounds the insanity of the siege of Troy, leading to the death of many warriors; Aeneas founds the Roman Empire; Adam chooses to fall and initiates mortality. Through his actions on Arrakis, Paul alters the face of his universe. As a member of the ducal family, illegally deprived of his fief, Paul wages war against the evil Harkonnens and the unscrupulous emperor. He honors his oath of fealty to the emperor as long as the Imperium recognizes his rightful ducal claims. However, when Shaddam IV chooses to abet the Harkonnens (allowing Imperial troops to support Harkonnen treachery, thus aligning himself with Paul's enemies), Paul has no choice but to resist the Empire. Through the power of his Fremen forces, he topples the static, rather degenerate Shaddam IV and breathes new life into the Imperium.

As the Kwisatz Haderach, however, Paul initiates actions which vastly overshadow his political aspirations. He becomes a reluctant messiah, in whose name religious "jihad" will sweep the galaxy, forever diverting the direction of human history.[7] As the "one who is in many places," he can foresee many cataclysmic events resulting from his actions, and he struggles to avert them.

A final characteristic of the epic hero is that he frequently is not positioned at the top of the power hierarchy. Achilles is a warrior, not a king. He owes allegiance to Agamemnon, whose decisions in part cause the conflict in the *Iliad*. During the Middle Ages and the Renaissance, this division between *rex* (king) and *dux* (leader) became more pronounced.[8] The interrelationships between the active, heroic warrior and the more passive, authoritarian ruler often blended with the heroic fable itself to lend the traditional (usually military) epics greater complexity in character development.

In *Dune* the same division between *rex* and *dux* exists—literally as well as figuratively. Paul Atreides is in fact the Duke of Arrakis; as such, he acknowledges his responsibilities to his direct overlord, the emperor. His initial skirmishes against the Harkonnens are merely to affirm his hereditary and legal (through Imperial decree) right to sovereignty on Dune. In a sense, he fights to reaffirm the legality and authority of the Empire. Only when it becomes obvious that the Empire itself is corrupt does Paul move against it—and then only as a Fremen battle-leader. In his final encounter with the emperor, Paul clearly differentiates between his roles as a duke and as a member of the imperial entourage (p. 473). As a duke, Paul responds to the conventions and limitations of the Imperial court; as Muad'Dib, the Lisan al-Gaib of the Fremen, however, he acts according to different standards.

The second major element of traditional epics involved the world of the action itself. The epic was a narrative on a grand scale—worldwide in the case of the wanderings of Odysseus, cosmic in *Paradise Lost*. The epic presupposes a conviction on the part of the author that his words are of paramount importance, that the actions he describes are essential to the human race. Frequently the epic traces the destruction of old standards and the creation of new. In the *Iliad*, the *Odyssey*, and the *Aeneid*, there are physical upheaval and literal destruction; in *Paradise Lost* the conflict is primarily spiritual. In each work, however, the definition of meaning in the universe is altered. The epics attempt to create order out of the chaos that results whenever human society undergoes drastic changes.

In a science fiction novel, the author may investigate the complexity and upheaval which characterize modern society. In a society frequently convinced of the meaninglessness of life, the science fiction novel may posit an alternate universe in which there are coherence, meaning, order, and tradition. In *Dune* the setting is obviously far-flung; the immediate action encompasses three distant planets—Caladin, Arrakis, and Geidi Prime—and through the prescient visions of Muad'Dib, the rest of the galaxy as well. Frank Herbert has successfully limned new worlds beyond the familiar earth, peopled by strange beings (not all even remotely human) and quasi-mythical beasts. The sandworms of Arrakis, for example, take on the attributes of a Demiurge and become, in fact, the basis of a new mythology. Paul's battles engage the known galaxy, with ships from every planet orbiting Dune during the final confrontation, waiting to despoil the planet when the emperor succeeds in eliminating the Fremen rabble.

In addition, *Dune* reflects the turmoil and political chaos which have characterized the twentieth century. Man's weaponry has outstripped his moral development, and instruments of destruction are turned against his fellow beings.[9] Into this seething society comes Paul Atreides, who through the force of his personality and his powers-beyond-human imposes order on disorder. He displaces the old levels of authority—the dissipated, treacherous emperor, the hired assassins, the depraved Harkonnens—and establishes a new hierarchy based on loyalty, trust, and competence. The former emperor is to be stripped of all power; in his place, Paul establishes a new, just order, bestowing titles and honors on his loyal supporters (p. 482). What seems superficially to be blatant sharing of the spoils of victory is in fact an appropriate delegation of power to those who have throughout the novel fought for order, legality, justice, and honor. Paul's followers are placed in positions of authority, not merely because they are his followers but because they are the most capable administrators within the new order.

In an epic the hero frequently undergoes heroic journeys, not the least of which is a journey of enlightenment. In one of the earliest surviving epics, Gilgamesh journeys to the dwelling of Utnapishtim to discover the secret of immortality; Aeneas journeys to the underworld and there receives a vision of the future history of the nascent Roman Empire; and Adam journeys to the mount of revelation for a vision of the history of all mankind. Through such visions, the epic transcends the immediate concerns of readers and involves itself instead with the fate of nations and of worlds. In *Dune* this tradition is an essential part of the story. Paul undertakes a desperate journey for survival, descending into the underworld figuratively (he is considered dead by both his enemies and his friends throughout much of the novel) and literally (as Muad'Dib he dwells in the subterranean caves—*sietches*—of the Fremen). More importantly, and more relevantly in terms of the relationship between *Dune* and traditional epics, he undertakes an internal journey of revelation. Descending to the lowest point of the sietch, the dungeon of a captive sandworm, Paul imbibes a drop of the unchanged poison secreted by the dying sandworm and enters a death-like trance. On recovering days later (and narrowly escaping premature interment), through the mediation of the maker's poison Paul is able to see not only the past and the future but the Now (p. 441). Like other epic characters before him, Paul emerges from his journey armed with vision and truth and with the power to create order, stability, and justice in a world of disorder, instability, and injustice.

In addition to the definition of the hero and of his milieu, a number of less important conventions have become associated with the epic, and most of them are integral parts of the plotting and structuring of *Dune*.

The traditional epic opens with either a *propositio* or an *invocatio*.[10] Lacking a muse to invoke, Herbert provides a *propositio*, a brief opening statement of the purpose of the narrative in a headnote from the "Manual of Muad'Dib" by the Princess Irulan; it identifies the hero, the time of the narrative, and the location of Dune, the planet Arrakis (p. 3).

From this point the novel moves directly into the action of the plot and in doing so fulfills a second epic demand—that the "fable" begin "in the middle of things." The first sentence of the novel indicates that events have already begun to move long before the reader is introduced to Paul Atreides. Even the structuring of the opening raises questions which can be answered only when the full background is known: "In the weeks before their departure to Arrakis, when all the final scurrying about had reached a nearly unbearable frenzy, an old crone came to visit the mother of the boy, Paul" (p. 3). Who are *they*? Why are they leaving? Where are they now, and where are they going? Where and what is Arrakis? Who is the old crone? the mother? the boy? Only as the reader becomes immersed in the complex history of vendetta and kanly, of treachery and intrigue between Harkonnen and Atreides, does he fully understand the answers to these questions. The novel does indeed begin "in the middle of things."

This convention leads to another. In classical epics background information is revealed most frequently by means of councils, which often are held in conjunction with a dinner. In *Dune* there are a number of epic councils, each with the specific purpose of revealing essential information and thus allowing the reader to understand convolutions in the plot. One of Duke Leto's first actions after arriving at Arrakis is to convene a war council with his lieutenants: Gurney Halleck, Duncan Idaho, the Mentat Hawat, and Paul. In addition to providing the reader with insights into the characters, the council provides necessary information on the history of Dune, on the Harkonnens and their tactics, and on the state of the galactic empire. Paul senses confusion in the minds of the men at the council, and for the first time he considers the possibility of defeat (p. 95). Herbert suggests that the microcosm of the council parallels the macrocosm which is the empire. The epic council simultaneously defines the characters, the situation, and the status of the plot. Shortly thereafter, Herbert includes a prolonged banquet scene, which is both an additional revelation of background (particularly in terms of Dune and its inhabitants) and a definition of Paul's emerging powers. At the banquet the boy temporarily replaces his father; within hours Leto is dead, and Paul becomes in fact the ruling Duke of Arrakis.

A final tradition which deserves attention in the context of *Dune* is the use of funeral rites. In the world of *Dune*, death is ritualized; battle is conducted along rigidly traditional lines as a way of providing controlled outlets for individual aggression. Feyd-Rautha (the Harkonnen heir) counts on this awareness of undeviating ritual in his encounter with a slave-gladiator. After arranging for an undrugged gladiator to meet him in the arena, Feyd-Rautha treacherously inverts the rules of combat by using poison on the blade that is traditionally pure. After individual combat—interspersed with the exchanging of taunts and insults typical of epic combat—Feyd-Rautha kills his opponent, relying not only on the treacherously poisoned blade but also on hypnotically implanted key words which momentarily paralyze the slave's muscles. Despite his deceptive and dishonorable tactics, Feyd-Rautha finally responds to a sense of honor. The slave fought well, coming closer than planned to killing the Harkonnen heir, and so the slave is honored in death. His body is not mutilated; he is buried intact with his knife in his hand (p. 331).

The Harkonnen's perverted attention to the ceremonial of death and of battle provides an effective counterpoint to Paul Atreides's reaction on killing his first opponent. The rites of battle in the Fremen sietch are carefully defined, down to the comments of the spectators and the ritual challenges. Paul is unaware of the rules of combat and unused to fighting without a shield, nor does he know that he must kill his opponent. He seeks to wound, to injure, to win by default. As a result, he rouses the anger of the spectators by seeming to toy with his adversary. Yet when the battle is finally over and Jamis is dead, Paul responds according to the ritual. He is named Usul, his sietch-name, secret among the tribe, and Muad'Dib, his Fremen name. He participates in the funeral rites for Jamis, listening to the formalized words intended to set the spirit of the newly dead to rest. He delays his own participation in the ceremony until urged by Stilgar, the leader, to speak. When he stands, he fully immerses himself in the ritual of death; he calls himself a friend of Jamis and sheds tears, "a gift to the shadow-world" (p. 309). Feyd-Rautha's superficial gesture of respect toward the dead earned him momentary approval by the mobs of Geidi Prime; Paul's intense and unself-conscious tribute to his opponent cemented the relationship between himself and the Fremen, allowing him to mold them into the most devastating troops in the Empire.

Throughout *Dune* the reader is exposed to devices which, originating as they do in epic traditions, elevate the worlds and characters of *Dune*, investing them with a grandeur and a significance surpassing a mere plot-summary. The reader leaves *Dune* at once enlightened and uplifted, having participated for a time in a world where heroism is still viable, where the actions of a single individual may in fact decide between order and disorder, tradition and chaos. The conventions of epic lend a dignity to the novel and to other science fiction novels that incorporate these conventions to a greater or lesser degree. In *Dune*, as in other science fiction novels, the author creates characters who provide modern man with paradigms of heroism and courage applicable to a technological society. In a post-heroic, anti-romantic, cynical world burdened with burgeoning technology and lagging moral development, the science fiction novel may, in fact, represent one of the last surviving strongholds of the true epic impulse. Here the writer can create a world in which human potential is investigated, stretched to its limits, and infinitely expanded. *Dune*, as an epic in the traditional sense of the term, falls legitimately into the category of an heir to the concerns, techniques, and impact of the traditional epic.

NOTES

1. See Aristotle, *On Poetry and Style*, trans. G.M.A. Grube (New York: Liberal Arts Press, 1958), pp. 11, 49–53; also Frederick H. Candelaria and William C. Strange, eds., *Perspectives on Epic* (Boston: Allyn and Bacon, 1965), p. 146.

2. E.M.W. Tillyard, *The English Epic and Its Background* (New York: Oxford University Press, 1966), pp. 228–33.

3. This is not to say, however, that writers did not attempt serious epics. Biblical epics, slavishly modeled on *Paradise Lost*, appeared and disappeared, largely unread. In the New World Joel Barlow attempted the definitive American epic, *The Columbiad*, a difficult amalgam of continental literary conventions superimposed on an American theme, the visions of Columbus. Wordsworth's introspective autobiographical poem, *The Prelude*, provided a new definition of the genre, in a sense bridging the gap apparent to readers and critics alike between their adulation for Milton's achievements and the necessities of contemporary poetic theory. Perhaps the most nearly epic of the major poems of the nineteenth century, Tennyson's *Idylls of the King*, was deliberately not granted the dignity and elevation of "epic" by the poet, who feared that to claim for the *Idylls* an epic dimension would bring charges of pretentiousness and self-aggrandizement down on himself and on his work: in short, he feared that if he called the *Idylls* an epic, it would go unread.

4. Paul Merchant in *The Epic* (London: Methuen, 1971), pp. 66–77, argues for the novel as the successor of the verse epic. See also Donald M. Foerster, *The Fortunes of Epic Poetry: A Study in English and American Criticism, 1759–1950* (Washington, D.C.: Catholic University Press, 1962), pp. 38, 92–112.

5. Henry F. Pommer, *Milton and Melville* (Pittsburgh: University of Pittsburgh Press, 1950); R.W.B. Lewis, "Melville on Homer," *American Literature* 22 (1950–1951), 166–76.

6. Frank Herbert, *Dune* (1965; reprint ed., New York: Chilton Book Company, n.d.); hereafter cited in the text. The following discussion could profitably be applied to a number of other science fiction novels, including Ursula K. Le Guin's *Left Hand of Darkness*, Larry Niven's *Ringworld*, and Piers Anthony's *Battle Circle*.

7. Reluctance is often a part of the epic hero's personality; he may not think of himself as a hero, and he is aware of his limitations.

8. In *The Song of Roland*, the poet specifies Roland's subordinate position to Charlemagne; the Cid is the chief warrior of King Alphonso; and Beowulf initially fights in defense of the king, Hrothgar. Even in *Paradise Lost* and *Paradise Regained*, there is a carefully defined hierarchy of authority with the hero of each poem (Adam and Christ, respectively) in the subordinate position.

9. Note the references in *Dune* to kanly, vendetta, revenge, and the concern over the possible misuse of family atomics—all of which lead to the creation of conventions to preserve even a tenuous sense of order. Roy Harvey Pearce in "Toward an American Epic," *Hudson Review* 12 (Autumn 1959), 362–67, includes within his definition of the "new epic" that it will be "one of ordering, not of order; of creation, not confirmation;

of energizing, not memorializing.'' To a large extent this defines both the purpose of Paul within the context of *Dune* and the impact of the novel on the reader.

10. The *invocatio* suggests an external source for the epic; that is, the poet conceives of himself as a transcriber, while the actual creation is left to the inspiring muse or deity. The *propositio*, on the other hand, represents an internalizing of the epic impulse. The poet speaks for himself without the mediation of muse or deity.

Tolkien's Mythological Calendar in *The Hobbit*

James L. Hodge

"You asked me to find the fourteenth man for your expedition. . . . Just let any one say I chose the wrong man or the wrong house, and you can stop at thirteen and have all the bad luck you like, or go back to digging coal."[1]

This is what Gandalf says when the dwarves experience doubts about Bilbo's qualities as a burglar. The bad luck associated with the number thirteen is familiar to everyone nowadays, and it seems reasonable—at least on a whimsical level— that the dwarves should feel a need to avoid ill fortune by avoiding the unlucky number. It is also clear that Gandalf himself will not be a part of the enterprise and cannot be counted in the group.

On the other hand, poor, fat Bombur never likes the idea from the start and would gladly break off at any point. Why not reduce the number to twelve and avoid bad luck the easy way?

Those who are acquainted with Tolkien's scholarly career will not be surprised to learn that the number "13" is mythologically necessary to Thorin's group, and that their triskaidekaphobia may be taken lightly as a superstition or more seriously as an echo of certain traditional beliefs. Although the grim, fortune-loving, mattock-wielding dwarves of *The Hobbit* are of clearly Germanic origin, the number of their party finds echoes throughout Indo-European tradition. Specifically, twelve is the number of retainers suited to a leader or ruler: "12 + 1 = king (queen) and retinue." I offer here a few examples of the mystic "12 + 1 = 13," as they are noted by Alwyn and Brinley Rees in their excellent reappraisal of Celtic mythology: Odin and his twelve counselors in Northern Germanic tradition, Conchubar and the twelve heroes in Bricriu's Hall from Gaelic mythology, Arthur and his twelve knights of the Round Table, Charlemagne and the Twelve Peers of France, Odysseus and his twelve companions, twelve (thirteen) mythologically significant geographical divisions in Ireland and Iceland, Jesus and the Twelve Disciples, as well as other Biblical twelves.[2]

Clearly, it would be an ominous breach of ritual to reduce this magically significant number. The only solution is to acquire a "semi-detached" addition who will function as burglar, cat's-paw, scapegoat, gadfly, and, eventually, hero of sorts.

The hidden significance of "12/13" is but an introduction to the hidden magic agenda of Bilbo's adventure. The journey he will take with this party of a magic number will pass not only through territory but through time, touching upon some of the most significant dates of the Celtic and Germanic calendars. The very outward appearance of Gandalf—who arrives as a harbinger of summer—implies his magical (or mythological) connections. Because of his wand as well as other characteristics, he has been compared to the sorcerer Merlin (although a comparison is just as easily made to the Welsh Math and several Gaelic gods who wield an effective "druid rod"). For his tricking of the trolls, he has been compared to Thor, the Norse thunder god, who similarly tricked the dwarf Alvis and who was an implacable enemy of the giants, also called *thursar* or "trolls." Because of his beard and clothes, he has been compared to Odin, chief of the Norse gods. This association is reinforced by a startlingly obvious but—so far as I know—thus far unnoticed detail. When Bilbo invites Gandalf to tea, he writes on his Engagement Tablet: "Gandalf Tea Wednesday" (p. 20). We must at least wonder whether the association of Gandalf with Woden's (Odin's) Day is not puckishly purposeful on Tolkien's part.

That there is no punctuation at all in this entry of Bilbo's may either be quite natural for his notation of appointments, or it may be suggestive. Rather than "Gandalf: Tea, Wednesday" or something of the sort, we have a line which could—with a stretch of the imagination—be read: "Gandalf T. Wednesday," or even "Gandalf Ti (Tiu, Tir, etc.) Wednesday," thus reminding us that Gandalf, the wizard and, ultimately, war-leader, is related through Odin, the shaman and war-leader of the Aesir, to Tiu, the old war-god of the Aesir, whose position of prominence Odin has usurped.

Be that as it may, our first notation of time is the day of the week in connection with Gandalf. The next time notations also come from Gandalf: "And Thrain your father went away on the twenty-first of April, a hundred years ago last Thursday, and has never been seen by you since" (p. 37). That is, Thrain disappeared on Thursday, April 21; "today" in the story is Wednesday, April 27; Gandalf appeared on the day before, Tuesday, April 26; and the expedition starts off the next day, Thursday, April 28. Perhaps it is significant that the days involved here are not the anonymous Moon's Day (Monday) and Sun's Day (Sunday) nor the Greek's Saturn's Day (Saturday), but the three English days of the week which are connected with the three chief male sky gods of the Germanic pantheon: Tiu's Day, Woden's Day, and Thor's Day.

The only date Gandalf explicitly mentions is that of Thrain's disappearance: April 21. This date falls within the limits of the Easter season; Easter Sunday itself may fall anywhere from about March 25 to April 26. This is also the time surrounding the vernal equinox, the time of the coming of spring and the time in ancient cultures, to say nothing of medieval Europe, which was looked upon as the New Year.[3] This season might see the Death of Winter, the Carrying out of Death, the Death of Carnival, and even, among the ancient Swedes, the ritual burning of the king as a sacrifice for fertility.[4] In other words, the Easter commemoration of sacrifice, death, and resurrection is consonant with ancient pagan customs at this time of year.

Into this order of celebrations falls the appointment of an April Fool, King of the Bean, etc.—a ritual figure who is often the subject of a mock sacrifice, thus reflecting the ancient appointment of a Fool King for a day, followed by his ritual death to insure the long life of the true ruler or to substitute for the true ruler as a fertility sacrifice.[5]

What little we hear of Thrain might easily fulfill the conditions of this ritual performance. Setting off with the map on what proves to be a fool's errand, he has "lots of adventures of a most unpleasant sort," never gets near the Mountain, and when Gandalf is forced to abandon him, he is "witless and wandering" (p. 37). There is no overt suggestion that his apparently useless death prepares for the successful return of the dwarves to their mountain, but it is through him that Gandalf comes into possession of the map and involves himself with the dwarves because it is Thrain's one wish that his son "read the map and use the key" (p. 38).

It has long since been noted that "Thrain" (spelled "Throin") appears in a list of the names of primeval dwarves in the *Prose Edda*—a repository of Icelandic verse forms and of Norse mythological material. What has not been noted is that this same "Throin" is also a by-name of Odin.[6] Thus, a possible Fool-King figure is associated through his name with an acknowledged source of the Gandalf character. Furthermore, Odin's cult included sacrifice, and he himself exemplified this by "sacrificing" himself—hanged, wounded by a spear, from the ash tree, Yggdrasil—in order to discover and interpret the Germanic runes.[7] He is the father of runic lore. All the more interesting, therefore, that the runes on Thorin's map are authentic Germanic runes, although perhaps of mixed geographical origin, and can be translated—with only a few spelling eccentricities—exactly as Gandalf and Elrond interpret them.

Gandalf arrives at Bilbo's house in April, although nearly a week after April 21. In fact, he arrives on the last likely date for Easter in any year: April 26. It is intriguing that the dreaded Wild Hunt swept through Germanic and neighboring territories not only between Christmas and Epiphany but also during the entire Easter season. The Wild Hunt is a personification of terrible storms and is usually led by a figure named "Wut," "Wod," etc., who is interpreted to be a folk survival of Odin, the god of death. The hunt is accompanied by wind and lightning and gathers souls to it along its way.[8]

It is intriguing that Gandalf should arrive at such a date, gathering souls, as it were, and that a peculiar phenomenon occurs during the gathering at Bilbo's, at the end of Thorin's enchanting song: "Suddenly in the wood beyond the Water a flame leapt up" (p. 28). Although the narrator tells us that it was probably someone lighting a wood fire, the effect is to disenchant Bilbo completely and make him shudder. Just over a page later, Bilbo is thoroughly frightened by Thorin's reference to the dangers of the journey, gives a shriek, and falls to his knees as the lamp is knocked over. When Gandalf strikes a blue light at the end of his wand, Bilbo falls flat on the floor and cries repeatedly: "Struck by lightning!"

There is never any explanation of the mysterious flame or of Bilbo's peculiar outcry. We are left to surmise that these incidences of flame (in the wood and in Gandalf's wand), the season in which the wizard arrives, and Bilbo's esoteric outcry are all reflections of Gandalf's Odinic qualities.

One further seasonal notation is made on the day the expedition starts. "One fine morning just before May," the narrator says. To some, this may suggest a cheerful, sunny day with, perhaps, a dance around the Maypole. To others, it may suggest the ancient fertility practices recorded by Frazer as occurring between the middle of April and the first of May, the ritual battle to the death between May King and Winter King, or even the great Celtic sacrificial fire-rites of Beltaine on or about May Day.[9] We may even be reminded of St. Walpurgis—English missionary to Germany and protectress against magic—whose "appropriation" of May Day was meant to supersede older heathen practices. Ironically, she is commemorated chiefly in the term *Walpurgisnacht*, which is the great gathering of witches and other Underworld figures, often taking place on, in, or near a mountain. This is the unearthly diversion offered Faust by Mephistopheles and also memorialized in *Night on Bald Mountain*.

Bilbo's great adventure begins at a portentous time of the year, marked by the Wild Hunt and Walpurgis Nights of Germanic origin and the great sun-god fires and sacrifices of Celtic origin. It is fitting that a wizard often compared to the Germanic (sky-god) Odin and the Celtic (sky-god)[10] Merlin et al. should arrive at this crucial changeover in seasons, heralding the start of an expedition against the powers of the Underworld.

From the time of leaving Bag-End, through the adventure with the trolls, to arrival in Rivendell, the party travels for about forty days. We may deduce this from the fact that departure is on April 28 and that the party stays at Rivendell for fourteen days (a magic number again?) until Midsummer, that is, about June 21–24. On Midsummer Eve, Elrond identifies the magic swords Glamdring and Orcrist and deciphers the moon-runes, mentioning for the first time Durin's Day. The party leaves Rivendell on Midsummer Day.

May Day—while notable for Germanic traditions—is one of the four most significant Celtic seasonal festivals: Beltaine. Midsummer—while marked in Celtic and other Indo-European territories by the lighting of great bonfires—is one of the four great Germanic seasonal festivals: Sommerblót or "Summer Sacrifice."[11] Its great significance is reflected late into our time by apparently Christian celebrations in honor of John the Baptist, who was particularly revered by early Western worshipers of fire, the Freemasons, and the Rosicrucians. The "Johannisfeuer" may still be seen in parts of Germany on June 24.

This is the time of the summer solstice, a significant "quarter day" and break in seasons, and may be considered the date of the death of bright Balder, most glorious of all the Norse sky-gods. It is also the festival for which Attila invites the grim and doomed Burgundians to his court and must unwillingly witness the near annihilation of his great armies, the slaughter of every Burgundian, and the bloody deaths of his son and his queen. This confluence of fateful confrontation with Midsummer is one of the great documents of Germanic literature—the *Song of the Nibelungs*—exemplifies the immense significance of this time for the early Germanic peoples.

As we shall see, Elrond's deciphering of the runes concerning Durin's Day provides the mythological framework of *The Hobbit*. Beginning with May Day and Midsummer—high seasonal festivals of the Celts and the Germans, respectively—the adventure points toward and culminates on Durin's Day, i.e., Samhain, highest and most portentous of the four Celtic seasonal festivals.[12] As the Easter season was a New Year for certain cultures, so Samhain—or Hallowe'en—was New Year to the Celts. Thus, the crucial action of *The Hobbit*—moving from early spring to the last day of autumn—also begins at a "new year" and reaches a climax at a "new year."

As if he wished to evoke echoes of Walpurgis Nights, Tolkien now leads his party into an adventure inside a mountain. Their captivity by the goblins is certainly captivity by Underworld figures whose grotesque faces and bodies are vividly reminiscent of chthonic opponents of the gods in Celtic and Germanic tradition: the ice and cliff giants, or thursar, of the *Eddas*; the Fomor of the Gaelic cycle of the gods. In cutting down the Great Goblin, Gandalf joins other sky-god figures who slay chthonic opponents: the Norse Thor who slays the giants Hymir and Thrym, among others; the Gaelic Lugh who kills the Fomor chief Balor.

Escape from this underworld *caer* is hardly accomplished when the party is "treed" by goblins and wargs and nearly burned alive. Following his evocation of May Day, Tolkien now conjures up the sacrificial rites of Sommerblót: "he could feel the heat of the flames; and through the reek he could see the goblins dancing round and round in a circle like people round a midsummer bonfire" (p. 109).

The timely appearance of the eagles is susceptible of more than one interpretation, but only one may be useful in this context. The worship of Odin brought with it a change from inhumation to cremation of the dead—presumably a freeing of the spirit to move upward to the gods of the sky rather than joining the gods of the earth. The eagle appears in two ways in Norse mythology—as a shape-shifter of the gods and their opponents and as an eater of the dead after battle. We may suspect, however tenuously, that the goblin "bon-fire" and the flight of the eagles is a vivid metaphor of death and transportation to the gods.

Like the eagle, the figure of Beorn, whose territory the party now reaches, is best treated outside the limits of this essentially calendric consideration. Suffice to say that his shape-shifter—the bear—his guardianship of the animals, and the lushness of vegetation in his vicinity are among those characteristics which unite him to such fertility figures as the Celtic Cernunnos and the Norse Freyr.

The party's experiences in Mirkwood offer two further echoes of the pagan calendar. Bombur's fall into the stream is caused by "the shape of a flying deer." This event is followed closely by "the noise of a great hunt going by to the north" and the appearance of "a hind and fawns as snowy white as the hart had been dark" (pp. 144–45). The color white, especially, is evocative of the Celtic Underworld, Annwn, which was often represented by white or red and white animals. We need not be surprised that the hart is dark, as one might expect in traditional Christian demonology, for this scene is a thoroughly mixed metaphor: the Lethe-like stream recalls the classical entry to the Underworld; the animals—or shapes of animals—suggest the interference of a (possibly Celtic) god; and, finally, the "great hunt" suggests the passing of a dangerous and ghostly retinue similar to the Odinic Wild Hunt.

Following this encounter, the party comes three times upon "a great feast. . . . A woodland king was there with a crown of leaves, and there was a merry singing, and I could not count or describe the things there were to eat and drink" (p. 149). The number three has obvious magical connotations. The feast, we know from a remark on page 146, occurs in late summer: "Outside autumn was coming on." The woodland king is, of course, King of the Wood-elves, who appears later in his own palace: "On his head was a crown of berries and red leaves, for the autumn was come again. In the Spring he wore a crown of woodland flowers" (p. 168).

It is clear that the feast encountered three times by the dwarves and Bilbo is a late-summer feast, similar to the Christian "Lammas" or "loaf-mass"—a celebration of the first fruits of harvest, circa August 1. There is, of course, an underlying pagan holiday connected with the early harvest season—the Celtic Lugnasad, which commemorates the sun-god Lugh and, according to some authorities, his marriage to a goddess of the earth.[13]

The later festival of the wood-elves and the simultaneous festival at Lake-town are clearly festivals of the fall harvest, and we are reminded on page 195 of the "waning of the year," on page 196 that "autumn was now crawling towards winter," and on page 200 of the imminence of the last week of autumn.

At last, arrived on the mountain, Bilbo discovers the "back door" when the sun and moon appear together at the turning of the year, that is, on Durin's Day, Samhain, Hallowe'en, All Saints'. It is at this time in the Celtic calendar that passage to and from the Underworld becomes easy. Accordingly, Bilbo opens the "back door" and ventures into the mountain. We may safely predict that death will result from this adventure—not merely because the villain of the piece is so powerful, but because Samhain was a time of high sacrifice for the Celts, when all firstborn were offered to Crom Cruaich.[14] Tolkien seems to acknowledge the sacred and bloody significance of this time by naming this month in his calendar "Blotmath." *Blot*, as we have seen, comes from the Germanic word for "sacrifice" and is both a source of and orthographically and audibly evocative of "blood."

As in many a good story, the climax is not also the end. The denouement of *The Hobbit* offers further reference to the pagan calendar. The journey home is broken at midwinter by a long stay with Beorn. It is by now no surprise to the reader that Tolkien does not mark Christian holidays in the year. Nor should it be surprising that he refers to the winter solstice as "midwinter," echoing the preceding (Germanic) significance of midsummer, and as "Yuletide," thus evoking the Germanic "Jol," which is similar to the Celtic Samhain in its connection with human sacrifice and its significance as the doorstep to the intercalary days haunted by the Wild Hunt, ending at what is now called Epiphany.

Beorn himself bears a Germanic name whose Northern version is Bjorn; he is a shape-shifter like Sigmund and Sinfjotli of the *Volsungasaga* among others, and he displays a *berserk* rage similar to that made famous by the Vikings. (This rage, by the way, is typical of warriors devoted to Odin.)

The cycle is completed by Bilbo's arrival at Rivendell on May Day, and at Bag-End at the summer solstice. Years later, Gandalf arrives with Balin for a visit, "one autumn evening." We may wonder whether this autumn evening is on or near Michaelmas, September 29, for then it would also be Disablót, the Germanic festival most closely associated with Odin.

If we assume this to be the case, then we may add Disablót to the following chart of Celtic and Germanic "quarter days" as they appear in *The Hobbit*:

Hobbit	Germanic	Celtic
Thrain disappears	(Wild Hunt)	
Gandalf arrives		
Departure	(Walpurgis)	*Beltaine*
Rivendell (solstice)	*Sommerblót*	(bonfires)
Woodland King and feast (Lammas)		*Lugnasad*
Durin's Day (All Saints', Hallowe'en)		*Samhain*
Beorn's	*Jol*	
Rivendell (May Day)	(Johannisfeuer)	*Beltaine*
Home again (solstice)	*Sommerblót*	(bonfires)
Gandalf's visit (Michaelmas)	*Disablót*	

The most significant portion of this chart—April 21 (Wild Hunt) to November 1 (Samhain)—displays a background of pagan rituals invoking fertility in the spring, sacrifices in the summer to insure a great harvest and protect against plague and calamity, and, finally, great appeasement sacrifices at the end of the year's fertility and beginning of the cold season, or "death" of the world. The repeated, emphasized occurrence of May Day, Midsummer and All Saints'—to name only the most important—demonstrates Tolkien's conscious and purposeful use of Western European tradition.

NOTES

1. J.R.R. Tolkien, *The Hobbit* (New York: Ballantine Books, 1965), p. 31; hereafter cited in the text.

2. Alwyn Rees and Brinley Rees, *Celtic Heritage* (London: Thames and Hudson, 1961), pp. 150–52.

3. Barbara W. Tuchman, *A Distant Mirror* (New York: Knopf, 1978), p. xv.

4. James George Frazer, *The New Golden Bough*, ed. Theodor H. Gaster (Garden City, N.Y.: Doubleday, 1961), pp. 144, 149, 150–53. Snorri Sturluson, *Heimskringla*, trans. Samuel Laing (New York: Dutton, 1961), II, 38–39; Frazer, *Golden Bough*, pp. 34, 138–39.

5. Ibid.

6. Snorri Sturluson, *The Prose Edda*, trans. Jean I. Young (Berkeley: University of California, 1954), p. 49.

7. *Poems of the Vikings, The Elder Edda*, trans. Patricia Terry (Indianapolis: Bobbs-Merrill, 1969), 34 ff.

8. Ake V. Strom and Haralds Biezais, *Germanische und Baltische Religion* (Stuttgart: Kohlhammer, 1975) in *Die Religionen der Menschheit*, ed. Christel Schroder, XIX, 1, 102; *Brockhaus' Konversations-Lexikon* (Berlin: Brockhaus, 1903), XVI, 720.

9. Rees and Rees, *Heritage*, p. 158 passim.

10. For evidence of Merlin's sky-god origins, see Charles Squire, *Celtic Myth and Legend, Poetry and Romance* (Hollywood, Calif.: Newcastle, 1975), pp. 322–25 passim.

11. Frazer, *Golden Bough*, pp. 354–56; Rees, *Heritage*, pp. 91, 158.

12. Rees and Rees, *Heritage*, pp. 89, 196, 251 passim.

13. Jan De Vries, *Keltische Religion* (Stuttgart: Kohlhammer, 1961) in *Die Religionen*, ed. Christel Schroder, XVIII, 227–29.

14. Rees and Rees, *Heritage*, Chapter 3 passim.

The Shire: A Tolkien Version of Pastoral

Douglas A. Burger

Tolkien maintains in his essay "On Fairy-Stories" that fantasies succeed when they awake "desire, satisfying it while often whetting it unbearably."[1] In his portrayal of Middle-earth, Tolkien follows his own advice by creating landscapes which appeal deeply to universal human longings and fulfill archetypal desires. Quite naturally, then, Tolkien's idealized lands share characteristics with many other literary countries of the heart's desire—the pastures of Arcadia, the forest of Arden, the fells of England's lake district, and Walden Pond—all idealized pictures of man's relationship to the land, all worlds which we may call, in a general way, worlds of the pastoral.

One of the oldest and most persistent of all traditions, the pastoral appears in many times and in many forms. But at its core, the pastoral is marked by a yearning for a simpler, more natural, more meaningful way of life. The comparison is usually with life at court or in the city. From the effete decadence of hellenistic Alexandria, Theocritus looks back with longing to the Sicilian countryside of his youth. For Sir Philip Sidney and other Renaissance courtiers, the pastoral recoil from the complexities of civilization usually manifests itself as a withdrawal from a corrupt and dangerous court to the innocent country pleasures of rural England.

In "Lines Composed a Few Miles above Tintern Abbey . . . ," Wordsworth compares his life "in lonely rooms, and 'mid the din / of Towns and cities" with his boyhood when "the sounding cataract / Haunted me like a passion: the tall rock, / The mountain . . . were then to me / An appetite; a feeling and a love." Today the pastoral impulse gains redoubled intensity because of the pervasive problems of industrial city life: ugliness, sameness, noise, and the foulness of air and water. *The Lord of the Rings* follows the same pattern and calls to those who feel tangled in the complications of urban life, out of touch with nature and with themselves.

It is in his bemused and loving depiction of the Shire at the very beginning of *The Lord of the Rings* that Tolkien most powerfully evokes the pastoral appeal.[2] The classical form of the pastoral depicts shepherds and their flocks, but Tolkien here creates the typical image of more recent pastorals: a simple agrarian life set amid green hills, fertile plains, and nice manageable woods. Reminiscent of Thoreau's beanfield, the countryside of the Southern Agrarian writers, and the fields of hay in E. M. Forster's *Howards End*, the Shire is a peaceful, cultivated land. Here the simple hobbits "play their well-ordered business of living," and most of that business is associated with the "rich and kindly" soil (Tolkien, *Fellowship*, p. 24). To the extent that Shire occupations are ever mentioned, almost all are agricultural: hobbits are farmers like Sam Cotton and Farmer Maggot or gardeners like the Gaffer and Sam Gamgee. Even the officials, the Shirriffs, are more "haywards than policemen" (p. 31). As Tolkien says, "Growing food and eating it occupied most of their time" (p. 30). The towns themselves are interlaced with gardens. At Bag-End, Bilbo's garden comes right up to the window, where he and Gandalf watch the "snap-dragons and sun-flowers" glowing "red and golden" in the westering sun; and the nasturtiums virtually take over the dwelling, trailing all over the turf walls and peeping in through the round windows of the house (p. 49). Also, it is in the very midst of Hobbiton where the Gaffer grows his crop of "taters." In fact, the distinction between village and country is scarcely relevant here, for hobbit homes blend harmoniously and unobtrusively into the bucolic setting. Made of natural materials—thatched with dry grass and surrounded by walls of turf—they are only a slight development of the ancestral hobbit holes, comfortable tunnels reaching down into the earth itself. Like the hobbit holes, several other images reflect the hobbits' closeness to the earth, both literally and figuratively. Hobbits are, says Gandalf, "tough as old tree roots" (p. 78), and surely it is no accident that Tolkien has the old Gaffer specialize in root vegetables. The hobbits' feet, being unshod, touch the ground; they prefer to wear green and yellow, the colors of growth; and hobbit women are often named for flowers: Rose, Primula, Pansy, Lobelia, Camelia. In sum, nothing could be more quintessentially hobbit-like than Sam's vision when he puts the great Ring of power in the heart of Mordor: "At his command the vale of Gorgoroth became a garden of flowers and trees and brought forth fruit" (Tolkien, *Return*, p. 216).

As well as showing the "close friendship with the earth" (Tolkien, *Fellowship*, p. 20), the Shire shares with the traditional pastoral an emphasis on the simplicity of life and freedom from the ambiguities and complications of advanced civilization. Indeed, the hobbits have no need for complex social forms or the pervasive institutions that can stultify and control. For example, since the hobbits are contented and prize peace and plenty, they lack the ambition to start wars. As Tolkien says, "For a thousand years they were little troubled by wars" (Tolkien, *Fellowship*, p. 24), and as Frodo says later, "No hobbit has ever killed another on purpose in the Shire" (Tolkien, *Return*, p. 352). Thus they need no army. They also have no real police—only the Shirriffs, who are more concerned with the strayings of beasts than the misdoings of the hobbits—not that the hobbits are by any means uniformly wise and good, but their infractions are all minor, like the spoon-snitching of Lobelia Sackville-Baggins and the trespassing of young Sancho Proudfoot in Bilbo's pantry. In fact, there are only two governmental services in the Shire: the Messenger Service and the Watch. With so little government, there is no need for governors, and the closest approximations to hobbit rulers are the elected Mayor of Michel Delving, whose duties are only ceremonial, and the Thain, now only a "nominal dignity" (Tolkien, *Fellowship*, p. 30).

In addition to manifesting a more natural way of living and a simpler, more humane society, the Shire has in common with many earlier pastorals another aspect, one which requires some explanation. In other literature, the pastoral impulse often involves not just a sense of going *away* from an unnatural, overly elaborate way of life, but of going *back*—back to an earlier age or time. In *As You Like It*, Duke Senior and his fellow refugees in the forest of Arden are said to "fleet the time carelessly as they did in the golden world" (I.i.110–11), that ancient idyllic time referred to in Ovid and in Greek myth. Virgil likewise goes back to the earlier world of the Arcadian shepherd, back from the "progress" of his own imperial Rome. More significant for what Tolkien is doing with his creation of the Shire, other poets and writers often depict not just an earlier age, but an earlier time in their own lives. Theocritus looks back to a happy boyhood in Sicily, and Wordsworth often longs to return to that instinctive primal harmony with nature that he felt as a youth. Thus the pastoral impulse often includes the desire to relive an earlier, happier time of life. On the psychological level, the pastoral return to a simpler life, to a more natural life, is a return to an idealized childhood.

The Shire amply satisfies such a desire to relive vicariously a childhood time, when all was safe and comfortable and all wants were easily supplied. Even though there are petty vexations and minor annoyances, life in this pleasant green land is as sheltered and secure as childhood, and the hobbits delight in innocent pleasures. Little could be more central to our memories than birthday parties, and the hobbits take special pleasure in them. As a matter of fact, they are always receiving presents because of their custom of giving gifts on their own birthdays. All the first chapter is suffused with the excitement stirred up by Bilbo's party: invitations are sent out by the bagful, replies are received, and the whole region is alive with anticipation. As well as birthdays and parties, the hobbits love simple wonders, like fireworks sparkling across a night sky, like the treasures they collect much in the spirit of the seven-year-old boy who stuffs his pockets with his own special "mathoms" (Tolkien, *Fellowship*, p. 25). They also love innocent plots: Bilbo takes a boyish delight in his sudden disappearance, and though there is serious loyalty in Pippin and Merry's conspiracy to follow Frodo, there is also the happy excitement and sheer fun of the secret. In addition to having childlike tastes and attitudes, the hobbits are about the size of children (two to four feet tall), and they have, literally, an extended childhood since their coming-of-age occurs at thirty-three.

Rather like childhood itself, this pastoral of childhood exists only because it is protected. The Rangers of the North keep a constant secret guard on the Shire's borders, and as Aragorn says later, "If simple folk are free from care and fear, simple they will be" (Tolkien, *Fellowship*, p. 326). The protectors of actual children, of course, are usually family members; and reinforcing the warm security the hobbits feel is their sense of being surrounded by family and friends. Clannish and provincial, they never weary of hearing and rehearsing stories of their kin, and they even find interest in the recitation of interminably long and many-branched family trees. In short, the Shire is an archetype of home, with all the related associations—the warmth, the sense of belonging, the security, even the stifling limitations. At the end of the last book, Sam returns to Rosie, sits by the fire, and takes little Elanor in his lap. After all the adventures, the dangers, the joys, he says, "Well, I'm back" (Tolkien, *Return*, p. 385). It is profoundly satisfying and fitting. We have come full circle, round again to where the trilogy began, to the wonderful ordinariness, the simple naturalness of the Shire. We are home.

The Shire, however, is not the only example in *The Lord of the Rings* of an idealized picture of a land whose inhabitants are in pastoral harmony with nature. Tom Bombadil, autumn leaves in his hair and dew on his face, is like a nature god in his beloved forest, fully in tune with the natural music of growth and the seasons. Rivendell is the last Homely House, and from its porch, Frodo looks at the scene before him: "The light of the clear autumn morning was now glowing in the valley. The noise of bubbling waters came up from the foaming river bed. Birds were singing, and a wholesome peace lay on the land" (Tolkien, *Fellowship*, p. 314). Lothlórien brings the pastoral Golden Age into the present, and the elves live in the beautiful mallorn trees in a land where there is "no stain" (Tolkien, *Fellowship*, p. 455). In Fangorn there are the literal shepherds of the pastoral, but in this case they are the remarkable Ents who watch over their flocks, not of sheep but of trees.

That the Shire is not Tolkien's only version of pastoral suggests a central aspect of his outlook. Throughout the trilogy, we are shown that there are many different, yet right and meaningful ways to live, and that each race has its own distinctive virtues and skills: the dwarves are staunchly unyielding and have great skill in metalwork; the elves are teachers and singers of tales; the hobbits astound even the wise with their unpretentious common sense. In a like manner, it is true that there are many different, yet legitimate and bountiful ways to relate to nature. In *The Lord of the Rings* the good and natural ways of life are as richly and abundantly varied as the manifold world of nature itself.

This is not to say that good and evil are relative matters: as Aragorn says, "Good and ill have not changed since yesteryear; nor are they one thing among Elves and Dwarves and another among Men" (Tolkien, *Towers*, p. 50). However, goodness may have many manifestations, and the free peoples of Middle-earth prize and try to protect the uniqueness of each land. Evil, in contrast, is marked by an appalling sameness. The enemies' terrains are all virtually undistinguishable from one another. Ash, smoke, machines, noise, befouled water, felled trees—all are features that mark Isengard as well as Mordor, or even, heartbreakingly, the Shire under the degenerate Saruman. The sameness rises from a central cause: the destruction of the multiplicity of the natural and of the special character of the landscape. Nature's abundant variousness has been reduced to a common denominator of ugliness which comes with a people's domination of the earth and carelessness about preserving its special life. Hence the very range of variation in the pastoral appeal makes an important moral point for Tolkien.

Finally, in addition to the thematic implications of the presence of several versions of pastoral, there is a significant narrative effect created by the relationship of the Shire to the other ideal lands of the trilogy. Bombadil's home, Rivendell, Lórien, Fangorn are all as imaginatively fulfilling in their own particular evocation of pastoral qualities as is the Shire. The special magic of those lands, however, is enhanced and intensified by the fact that they have been preceded by the abnormal normality of the Shire. The ordinary, down-to-earth Shire acts as a foil to set off all the more brightly the marvels that come later. Because we have become accustomed to the Shire's orchards and little woods, the great golden trees of Lórien, mighty enough to hold palatial platforms, seem all the more astonishing. Because *The Lord of the Rings* begins with the vine-covered hobbit holes, cheerful parties, and folksy music, we feel all the more keenly the wonder of the great halls of Rivendell with its high Elven celebrations and music like an "endless river of swelling gold and silver" (Tolkien, *Fellowship*, p. 307). The Shire is a touchstone, a consistent basis for contrast—and not simply because we have encountered it first and the memory lingers with us. For the Shire stays with us in the persons of the hobbits who travel to the splendid places of Middle-earth. Significantly, in each of the most wondrous, most piercingly beautiful of the lands, Tolkien takes care to focus the point of view in the hobbits, so that we experience the landscape primarily through them. We see with their simple hobbit eyes—and partly because they are dazzled, we are dazzled. In Lórien Frodo "looked up and caught his breath"; he saw familiar colors "fresh and poignant, as if he had at that moment first perceived them and made for them names new and wonderful" (Tolkien, *Fellowship*, p. 454). In Rivendell the beauty of the melody holds Frodo in a spell, and he stands "enchanted, while the sweet syllables of the elvish song fell like clear jewels of blended word and melody" (Tolkien, *Fellowship*, p. 313).

The creation of the Shire is an example of Tolkien's unparalleled imaginative and narrative skill in the making of fantasy worlds. Not only does it provide a fully satisfying and distinctive version of pastoral in all its traditional potency—its appeal to the deep-rooted human desires for a more natural way of life, a simpler society, and a recovery of a sense of home—but it also does double duty by preparing for the contrasts that create meaning and intensify the appeal of the other lands. In one of the most successful ploys of the maker of Middle-earth, it is an evocation of the pastoral at its richest and most skillful—a version that enhances other versions.

NOTES

1. J.R.R. Tolkien, *Tree and Leaf* (London: Unwin Books, 1964), p. 39.

2. J.R.R. Tolkien, *The Lord of the Rings*, 3 vols. (*The Fellowship of the Ring*, *The Two Towers*, and *The Return of the King*) (New York: Ballantine Books, 1965); hereafter cited in the text.

Leontes's Enemy: Madness in *The Winter's Tale*

Richard H. Abrams

Just before their duel, Hamlet apologizes to Laertes for his wild behavior at Ophelia's grave by placing the blame on an "enemy" that took over when Hamlet "from himself [was] ta'en away"(V.ii.234).[1] This "enemy" in Hamlet's expansion of the figure becomes virtually a possessing demon, like the "unclean spirits" (*cacodaemones*) said to afflict the mentally ill in a tradition holding from Biblical times to the Middle Ages. In the Renaissance, this view of mental illness was in retreat as evidenced by Shakespeare's broadly satiric portrait of the quack exorcist in *Comedy of Errors*, and we need not suppose that Hamlet seriously tries to escape responsibility for his actions by disowning the thing of darkness in himself. For though he speaks of reason and its adversary, madness, vying for control of his being, the very facetiousness with which he pursues this figure suggests the presence of a *tertium quid*—his assumed "antic disposition"— mediating these extremes. His apology to Laertes, which Harry Levin terms "disingenuous," may have some corrective function in a play whose chief spokesman for absolute identity ("to thine own self be true" I.iii.78) and a "psychodynamic" approach to madness ("this effect defective comes by cause" II.ii.103) is Polonius, but it is scarcely the key, though preferred by Hamlet himself, which can unlock his heart of mystery.[2]

Hamlet is not the only Shakespearean tragedy in which a superstitious definition of madness is embedded with a generally realistic character portrayal, providing false perspective on Shakespeare's method. In *Othello* Emilia's evocation of jealousy as "a monster / Begot upon itself, born on itself" (III.iv.161–62) may have ultimate bearing on the fact that Othello is essentially self-persuaded, as critics have argued, but in the immediate sense it is naive; Shakespeare provides at least the illusion of cause in the tempter Iago, who whispers Othello's jealousy to life. In *The Winter's Tale*, however, the pretense of telling "an old tale still" frees Shakespeare to explore a primitive mode of psychological explanation which, in the tragedies, he is obliged to maintain at the level of poetic figure. With his causeless, self-begetting jealousy, Leontes often has been described as his own Iago, and he exhibits a splitting of reason from madness as radical as that proposed by Hamlet in his apology to Laertes. Where Hamlet's playful invocation of his madness as "enemy" leaves off, Leontes's paranoia begins. With terrible literalness, Leontes persecutes his faithful wife, Hermione, as though she were the otherness in himself, his concretized "enemy."

Twenty-five years ago M. M. Mahood speculated, "The Elizabethans might have put Leontes' outburst down to demonic possession," but this formula resists serious elaboration. In its favor is the incredible rapidity of Leontes's change. In the space of a single line, "Too hot, too hot!" (I, ii, 108), five minutes into his opening scene, he is visited by a full-blown revelation of his wife's seeming infidelity, and this seizure radically alters his manner of speaking. With their lightning free-associations, Leontes's mad speeches suggest glossolalia, "language that I understand not" (III.ii.80), as Hermione confesses, speaking for most of the audience. Then, as suddenly as it appeared, his madness vanishes with his son's death, leaving Leontes to answer for deeds performed by his "enemy" when, in Hamlet's phrase he was "from himself . . . ta'en away": when, in his own phrase, he was "transported by my jealousies" (III.ii.158).

Strictly speaking, the possession motif gives out at this point. Shakespeare "psychologizes" evil influence, barring literal "sprites and goblins" from his winter's tale at least until Antigonus's haunting in Act III. But though we cannot speak of Leontes's possession by a particular demon (an Asmodeus, a Belial, or whatever), there survives in the Renaissance, and indeed well into the eighteenth century, an alternate tradition of "possession" by an indwelling enemy or ruling passion, for which the motif of demonic possession becomes a familiar allegory. When in a late morality play Christ casts forth from Mary Magdalene the Vice "Infidelitie" together with the ".vii. diuels which have hir possessed," the devils, identified with the seven deadly sins, are not quite invading demons but the soul's own leanings to vice, its hypostatized temptations exorcised each by its contrary virtue. When in Book III of the *Faerie Queene* jealousy causes Spenser's Malbecco to gape in lewd fascination as his wife disports with a troop of satyrs till "he has quight / Forgot he was a man, and *Gealosie* is hight" (III.x.60), the event, loosely speaking, is one of possession (hence the rebaptism), though not by an anthropomorphic agent; rather by Malbecco's *invidia*—a sick predisposition to voyeuristic pleasures, to dwell in the shadow of a virile competitor—which, seizing on the mere occasion of his wife's nymphomania, tyrannizes from within.[3] Shakespeare himself deals in this allegory of demonic possession as early as *Love's Labor's Lost* when Berowne complains that he is possessed by a "love . . . as mad as Ajax" (IV.ii.6) and Don Armado rages, "Love is a familiar; Love is a devil. There is no evil angel but Love" (I.ii.172–74). Here, as in Hamlet's apology, the metaphor of possession belongs to a rhetoric of shame that would disown its own emotions by representing them as besieging the soul rather than arising internally. Like the four humors (and "the humor of affection'' is what Armado elsewhere calls his desire) linking man's emotional makeup to the material universe, desire can be conceived as having extension both within and beyond the subject, so that as the latter notion is stressed it becomes common to speak of the soul beset, hounded, possessed, by what it feels.[4]

Now, desires healthy and otherwise are normally viewed as attendant on or generated by particular love-objects; a man sees a beautiful woman and falls in love; his wife commits adultery and he becomes jealous or angry. Sometimes, however, as in the case of Malbecco with his prior disposition to voyeurism, desire exists relatively independent of particular objects; it lives a life of its own within the subject, is ''self-begot.''[5] In *The Winter's Tale* jealousy's ''life of its own'' within Leontes is attested by his notorious apostrophe to Affection as a hypostatized enemy besieging his soul. He has just been interrogating his son, Mamillius, about Hermione's supposed infidelity (''Can thy dam? — may't be?'') and, meeting with incomprehension, he turns inward to interrogate his emotions directly:

> Affection, thy intention stabs the center!
> Thou dost make possible things not so held,
> Communicat'st with dreams — how can this be?
> With what's unreal thou coactive art,
> And fellow'st nothing. Then 'tis very credent
> Thou may'st co-join with something; and thou dost,
> And that beyond commission, and I find it,
> And that to the infection of my brains
> And hard'ning of my brows.
>
> (I.ii.138–46)

A jealous imagination, Leontes recognizes, may deal in mere conjecture. Thus, damping down his suspicions, he tells himself that his imagination ''fellow[s] nothing.''[6] But then, a moment later, a fresh suspicion is engendered. In what J.H.P. Pafford considers an argument *a fortiori*, Leontes notes that if imagination can work on ''nothing,'' it can likewise join with ''something,'' and that with regard to Hermione's supposed infidelity, it *does*. Whereas moments before he had rejected his suspicions, now he settles into the conviction that he has indeed been made a cuckold.

How, we ask ourselves, does Leontes get from ''nothing'' to ''something'' in a single step? How is his new suspicion engendered *ex nihilo*? The question is not merely of philological interest, for it restates in little the problem of where Leontes's unfounded jealousy came from in the first place. Instead of trying to answer it, however, we may reflect that the question arises only if, denying Affection's status as a thinking subject, we hold Leontes himself (i.e., Leontes's reason) wholly responsible for the flow of ideas in the soliloquy. If, on the other hand, we accept Leontes's attribution of a ''Thou,'' an originative intelligence, to this faculty, then the entire second half of his speech has the status of an interpolation. First, in other words, Leontes's reason tries to distance itself from imagination by defining it as a mind-clouding enemy ("Affection, thy intention stabs the center!"). However, in the midst of this activity, reason loses initiative. Affection takes over and, as though it "really had the power of thought," imposes an idea of its own.[7] At exactly the midpoint of the soliloquy (the caesura in the fifth of nine lines), Leontes's suspicion is reborn, which is to say that Affection almost literally "stabs the center." Conjoining with the word "nothing," or the actual nothing of the caesura, the demon Affection begets a fresh suspicion of adultery in Leontes's mind.

Under the spell of jealousy, Leontes is changed. His good angel, reason, abandons him, and the tempter, imagination, does his thinking for him. Eliminate the pneumatological machinery hinted by Leontes's "serious personification" and this much is truism. What is remarkable, though, as underscored by the mathematic symmetry of the Affection soliloquy,[8] is the degree to which Affection possesses originative power, figuring as a *malin genie* with which (or whom) Leontes shares his being. Because this other-in-himself possesses such solidity, Leontes tries to project it, lending it substance by associating it with Hermione, the most intimate "other" in his external environment. As "internal dramatist," he translates the war in his own psyche into confrontation with a pseudo-objective enemy.[9]

The Freudian model of projection is, of course, anachronistic in this regard, though the Renaissance had ready substitutes, one of which is highly pertinent to Leontes's madness. No convention of love poetry (or modern love-chat, for that matter) is more familiar than the metonymy in which the lover refers to his *inamorata*, his loved one, as "my love," calling by the name of his own passion the woman who excites it in him and without whom the passion would not exist. By similar logic of elision Leontes identifies his jealous agony with Hermione, whom he projects as its "cause" (II.iii.3). Women and their lusts are pronounced "a bawdy planet, that will strike / Where 'tis predominant" (I.ii.201–02). Leontes's metaphor of celestial influence touches incidentally on the etymology of the word "affection," which comes from *affectare*, to yield or lean toward, in turn deriving from *afficere*, to strike or influence. Instead of Affection piercing Leontes's center, this office of intimate penetration is assigned to his wife— "one / Of us too much beloved" (III.ii.4)—whose being Leontes imagines impinging on his own. "Your actions are my dreams" (III.ii.82), he accuses Hermione; she is somehow inside him, her sexual dance providing orchestration for his nightmare, so that only when she is "gone, / Given to the fire" (II.iii.7–8), only when her evil influence is exorcised, can Leontes imagine himself whole again, restored to "The purity and whiteness of my sheets— / Which to preserve is sleep" (I.ii.327–28).

Leontes's projection of enmity onto Hermione is merely paradigmatic. The mad king is well described by Camillo as one "Who in rebellion with himself will have / All that are his so too" (I.ii.355–56). Thus, not only his wife and best friend but his faithful retainers and newborn daughter, whom Leontes imagines joining the mockers when she comes of age and innocently calls him "father" (II.iii.155–56), "All that are his" are thrust into adversary roles, as though in dramatization of Leontes's quarrel with the other in himself. Of these instances, the last mentioned, that of the scapegoat Perdita, is the most important, for it leads to the fantasy-sequel of the tragedy in which we trace the afterlife of Leontes's "other" in certain ambiguous out-of-body activities of Hermione's ghost. Though Leontes's charges against his wife are groundless in the form in which he makes them, Shakespeare in a sense justifies his paranoia retrospectively by developing a darker side of Hermione's nature after Leontes himself is content to believe he "but dreamed it" (III.ii.84).

This movement toward the actualization of fantasy begins with Perdita, produced to testify as silent witness to Hermione's innocence. Leontes's refusal in Act II to "own" his own child, his insistence, three times reiterated, that Antigonus carry it off as a bastard, brings Hermione's ghost into the drama as her infant daughter's protectress. "Jove send [the child] / A better guiding spirit" (II.iii.126–27), says Perdita's godmother, Paulina; and Antigonus, carrying it into exile, echoes her: "Come on, poor babe / Some powerful spirit instruct the kites and ravens / To be thy nurses" (II.iii.185–87). The angelic advocate or tutelary genius whom these words conjure is Hermione, who, appearing to Antigonus in a dream, names her daughter in Leontes's default and safely guides it to Bohemian shores, whereupon, amid the shepherds' talk of fairies hovering, she vanishes, never to be heard from again, as the audience supposes.

Throughout the pastoral scene of Act IV, we see the wind in the reeds. Though Hermione is never mentioned, she seems to oversee Perdita's growth and fortune, teaching the lost one to find herself, to "queen it" in her mother's fashion and to find her way back to Sicilia. The theme of *dii minores*, of tutelary gods hidden in things, is maintained from the first words of the sheepshearing scene in anticipation of Hermione's revival; and in Act V, Hermione's spirit slouches toward the scene of her resurrection, sensed only by Leontes, who, in apprehension of "the ghost that walk[s]" (V.i.63), seems once more to teeter on the brink of madness. Earlier it was Affection—imagination infected by morbid eroticism—that conjured, in its own image, the figure of Hermione the temptress. Now imagination subserving a guilty consience conjures an antithetical image, yet one which curiously produces an analogous effect. Haunted by memories of his dead wife, Leontes is drained of desire for other women, as though Hermione, "sainted spirit" that she may have been when alive, now works upon her husband succubus-fashion. If ever he were to remarry, Leontes fantasizes, Hermione's spirit would newly "possess her corpse" (V.i.58) and return to the world shrieking for explanations; the ghost, possessing him, would "incense" him "To murder her I married" (V.i.61–62). This new phase of madness then—Leontes's jealousy on the dead Hermione's behalf—inverts his earlier jealousy *of* Hermione. However, there is the important difference that, whereas the adultress-Hermione was merely a projection, in the present case Leontes's imagination joins with "something" after all. He is haunted by a possibility that corresponds to "what's real"; and as the statue comes to life, the audience asks itself what Leontes's imagination *mates with*: "How can this be?"

"[I]t appears she lives" (V.iii.117), says Paulina, and if some critics stress the verisimilitude of that appearance—the wrinkles, which contradict Leontes's idealized expectations—others stress the precariousness.[10] This is and is not Hermione, as Troilus said of Cressida. Or as Oberon in *A Midsummer Night's Dream*, restraining Puck from mischief, reminds him, "we are spirits of another sort" (III.ii.388), so Hermione's resurrection is wholesome, but just barely.[11] Can we tolerate or even believe in this piece of virtue's having collaborated with Paulina in a cruel deception? And if not, how to escape the morbid conclusion that Hermione has "stol'n from the dead" (V.iii.115), that as she embraces Leontes, hanging about his neck like a succubus, he is in mortal danger? "It is required / You do awake your faith" (V.iii.94–95), says Paulina, mentioning "wicked powers"; and it is a kind of faith, surely, which not only revives the statue but also insulates generations of listeners and readers from noting the dark other meaning of Paulina's later admonition: "Do not shun her [Hermione] / Until you see her die again, for then / You kill her double" (V.iii.105–06), which results from taking the word "double" as a noun meaning doppelgänger rather than as an adverb meaning "twice."[12] Is it possible? Is this Hermione's double, not Hermione herself, whom Leontes will now install in his heart of hearts, sharing with her his being? We refuse to entertain the notion and cleave in the end to an explanation that explains nothing, in proportion to our need to believe in the saving power of love, whose two-in-one reverses the mystery of the divided self. But Leontes has entertained it—"If this be magic, let it be an art / Lawful as eating" (V.iii.110–11)—and, having recognized himself as his own worst enemy, would rather risk the terror of demonic possession than the drawn-out torment of solitary life. "I cannot be / Mine own, nor anything to any, if / I be not thine" (IV.iv.43–45), said Florizel to Perdita. So, too, Leontes must give himself away in the most radical sense—must obliterate the boundary between self and other—in order to become truly his own.

NOTES

1. All Shakespearean quotations are from the Pelican edition of *The Complete Works*, gen. ed. Alfred Harbage (Baltimore: Penguin Books, 1956) and are cited in the text.

2. Harry Levin, *The Question of Hamlet* (New York: Oxford University Press, 1959), p. 113. An extraordinary document in the blindness of psychoanalytic insight is Theodore Lidz, *Hamlet's Enemy: Madness and Myth in Hamlet* (New York: Basic Books, 1975), p. 45. Lidz commends a "psychodynamic" orientation to Hamlet's problem, undeterred by the fact that, in citing the passage in parentheses, he is following in the footsteps of Polonius.

3. The idea of lust intensifying as it passes through a filter of envy to become jealousy is a Renaissance commonplace. Thus, in the formal pageant of vices in Spenser's *Faerie Queene*, we find "lustfull Lechery" riding a goat whose green eyes are "the signe of gelosy" (I.iv.24–26), a detail that recurs in Othello (III.iii.180). Similarly, as in the case

of Malbecco, jealousy's fulfillment lies in gazing, whence the connection with *invidia*, intense looking. Spenser stresses that Malbecco, with his one good eye, can never see enough; and Shakespeare has Othello seek satisfaction in ocular proof. For an interesting modern treatment of the relation of jealousy to envy, see René Girard, *Deceit, Desire, and the Novel*, trans. Yvonne Freccero (Baltimore: Johns Hopkins University Press, 1965), 12 ff.

4. The editor of the Arden edition of *The Winter's Tale* (Cambridge: Harvard University Press, 1963), J.H.P. Pafford, cites Montaigne's essay "Our affections are transported beyond our selves," in which Montaigne writes "We are never in our selves, but beyond" (Appendix II, p. 166). Compare J. Leeds Barroll's discussion of affections as "implanted yearnings" in *Artificial Persons: The Formation of Character in the Tragedies of Shakespeare* (Columbia: University of South Carolina Press, 1974), p. 37.

5. C. L. Barber argues the "priority of desire to attraction" in connection with Touchstone's "as pigeons bill, so wedlock would be nibbling" (*As You Like It*, III.iii.66–67) in *Shakespeare's Festive Comedies* (Princeton: Princeton University Press, 1959), pp. 231–32. The chicken-or-egg question of whether desire came first or was generated in the adolescent Leontes and Polixenes by the sight of their attractive wives as temptation is under debate by Hermione and Polixenes when Leontes interrupts, moments before his jealous seizure (*The Winter's Tale*, I.ii).

6. In reading "Affection" as Leontes's own imagination rather than Hermione's supposed lust, I do not mean to limit the word's ambiguities. Complexities arise throughout the speech since metaphors used to define the act of imagination are reflected from Leontes's obscene vision of Hermione's sexual penetration (hence Leontes's later "projection" of violations onto Hermione as external enemy). Carol Thomas Neely convincingly argues a shift in the meaning of "Affection" (which moves from Leontes's imagination to Hermione's lust) in "*The Winter's Tale*: The Triumph of Speech," *Studies in English Literature 1500–1900* 15 (1975), 321–38, especially 324–27.

7. Thus Joseph Priestly discusses the trope of "serious personification" as a figure which "obtrudes itself upon [the speaker]" so strongly affecting his passions that "while the illusion continues . . . [it is] as if the object of them really had the power of thought" (*A Course of Lectures on Oratory and Criticism*, 1777).

8. The poetic strategy of the Affection soliloquy, with Affection supervening midway in the speech to change the course of Leontes's meditation, is repeated at the midpoint of the action when Time, the Chorus, pressing into the "wide gap" separating Acts III and IV, changes the dramatic mode from tragedy to comedy. For imagery establishing the Chorus's speech as geometric center of the play, see William Blissett, " 'This Wide Gap of Time': *The Winter's Tale*," *English Literary Renaissance* 1 (1971), 52–70. In addition, it may be noted that the Chorus, like the Affection soliloquy, is shaped around a geometric center. The speech is thirty-two lines long—the first part dominated by the word "I" and dealing in violent, tragic emotions, the third part dominated by Time's third-person references to himself and dealing in gentler, comic experience. The second part is transitional and introduces the second-person pronoun. It occupies lines 15–17, or precisely the central portion of the speech, with the pivotal phrase, "I turn my glass," occurring in the first half of line 16.

9. See Thomas F. VanLaan, *Role-Playing in Shakespeare* (Toronto: University of Toronto Press, 1978), especially ch. 9, "The Internal Dramatist."

10. For a discussion of the two Hermiones created by the play's improbable ending,

see James Edward Siemon, '' 'But It Appears She Lives': Iteration in *The Winter's Tale*,'' *PMLA* 89 (1974), 10–16.

11. See David Bevington, '' 'But We Are Spirits of Another Sort': The Dark Side of Love and Magic in *A Midsummer Night's Dream*,'' *Medieval and Renaissance Studies* 7 (1975), 80–92.

12. The word ''again'' in Paulina's speech is similarly unsettling.

Wanderers in Wonderland: Fantasy in the Works of Carroll and Arrabal

Steven M. Taylor

Any discussion of the work and thought of Fernando Arrabal must include a treatment of his artistic and philosophical mentor, Charles Lutwidge Dodgson, otherwise known as Lewis Carroll. As the Spanish author stated in a 1969 interview with Alain Schifres, "Everything comes from Lewis Carroll."[1] This avowal, together with other personal remarks of equal clarity, combined with the obvious borrowings of names and characters in such works as *The Song of Barabbas, The Burial of the Sardine, A Tortoise Named Dostoevski*, and *Today's Young Barbarians*, have, much like the rabbit hole which tempted Alice to enter Wonderland, provided the basis for drawing brief comparisons between the two authors by such critics as Irmgard Anderson, Alain Schifres, Peter Podol, and Thomas Donahue.[2] Yet such discussions have stopped short of giving the English nonsense writer his full due. My own exploration of Carroll's writings and Arrabal's early plays is an attempt to provide instances of deeper significance, in particular the profound similarities in the authors' conception of reality itself. Arrabal's allegiance to and fascination with the panic philosophy he shares with Jodorowsky, Topor, and Sternberg was, in my opinion, preconditioned by the upside-down universe of Lewis Carroll, his favorite author.[3] Both men formulate a world in which dreams represent truth, and games, trials, and death constitute its laws. This essay will discuss the unpredictable reality of Wonderland as portrayed by these two masters of fantasy and confusion.

Reality is confusion. For Arrabal, perception does not imply categories. There is no a priori organization of reality, even though Western man tries to impose a grid on what exists. This is done by language and logic when used in conventional ways. But the great god Pan, god of merriment, terror, and surprise, dies of strangulation in this double noose, and with him dies life itself. Thus, Arrabal reasons that all entities must be subjected to the catalyst of confusion, which is the only truth.[4] He concludes that what is human is, by his definition,

confused. Chance governs the future and thus life. Consequently, by imposing
a set of laws on reality and eliminating what is unpredictable, authors mechanize
the human condition and divorce it from reality. Because Arrabal revolts against
all constraints, life, as it appears in his theater, is chaotic and often nightmarish,
that is to say, realistic. His panic theater is, as he has observed, like Alice's
nightmare.[5] He believes that dreams are what best encompass confusion, since
they present an infinite field of possibility without the critical distance introduced
by reason. Because dream reality is continuous, Arrabal agrees with Breton that
the waking state should be considered a phenomenon of interference.[6] Like his
character Apal in *The Tricycle*, Arrabal finds reality only in dreams.[7]

In the same way, Carroll methodically destroys the normal givens of existence:
mathematics, logic, social conventions, time, and space. His most popular character, Alice, falls into the rabbit's hole, where she undergoes successive shrink-
age and expansion. She tries repeatedly to regain her bearings using normal
logic. But in Wonderland, growth depends on ingesting the proper amount of
cake or mushrooms. Once Alice learns this, she counts on this phenomenon as
an infallible cause and effect, a ''logical'' conclusion, since these results have
occurred several times. It is at this point, however, that the unpredictable fools
her by temporarily reassuming normality. After eating a piece of cake she now
expects to grow or shrink, only to find herself remaining the same size. ''To be
sure, this is what generally happens when one eats cake; but Alice had got so
much into the way of expecting nothing but out of the ordinary things to happen,
that it seemed quite dull and stupid for life to go on in the common way.''[8] A
similar effect of disorientation occurs at the Mad Hatter's tea party, where it is
Time which does not conform to Alice's expectations. In Wonderland, Time is
not a dimension but a person whom the Mad Hatter knows. The latter, having
irked Time, can no longer ask him for favors and must accept it to be always
six o'clock at his house. Further confusion results when the hosts insult the poor
girl by offering her more tea when she very correctly points out that she cannot
take any more as she has not yet received any. ''You mean you can't take any
less,'' said the Hatter. ''It's very easy to take more than nothing'' (Carroll,
Alice, p. 103). In this way Alice is tricked each time she tries to apply the normal
rules of language and logic to the confusion around her, since in Wonderland
nothing is predictable. Her world view, which organizes what she perceives, no
longer has any validity. Like Giafar in *The Song of Barabbas*, Alice thinks she
knows how to tell dreams from reality. However, the foundation of these literary
universes is dreams and therefore confusion. Consequently, mechanical categories no longer function. Carroll's works provide a comic yet terrifying vision
of the world which exists underneath the conventions of Western society.

If, as Carroll and Arrabal maintain, integral reality can be found only in
dreams, the key to their works must lie in an analysis which would provide the
ground rules of these universes where the mind can no longer organize existence
in traditional ways. Therefore, it would seem important to establish at the same
time the difference between waking and dreaming; but Arrabal's characters, like

schizophrenics, exist on the border of the kingdom of dreams and hesitate in drawing a distinction. As Cavanosa says in *The Grand Ceremonial*, "My whole life consisted of dreaming" (Arrabal, *Theatre III*, p. 192).[9] In *The Song of Barabbas*, Arlys advances the hypothesis that things must be as they seem, "Unless everything which you have told me is only a dream." To which Giafar replies, "But if what I am saying is a dream, why wouldn't what is happening now be one also?"(Arrabal, *Theatre III*, p. 79). Does existence, then, depend on dreaming? A dialectic derives from this hypothesis, of which Cavanosa proposes the following proof: "I dream that people are laughing and know that I am going to kill myself. But *I* don't know why. I don't find out until the end of the dream. And consequently those who were laughing were not a creation of my mind since they knew something that I only found out later!" (Arrabal, *Theatre III*, p. 288). In Arrabal's universe, therefore, dreams constitute the only continuous reality, in which case there is no distinction to be drawn.

Carroll, too, was obsessed by the question of reality insofar as it is conveyed by dreams. Tweedledum and Tweedledee pose this problem quite clearly in their interpretation of the Red King's dream, when they muse, "He's dreaming now, and what do you think he's dreaming about? . . . Why, about you! And if he left off dreaming about you, where do you suppose you'd be? You'd be nowhere. Why, you're only a sort of thing in his dream. If that there king was to wake, you'd go out—bang—just like a candle" (Carroll, *Alice*, p. 239). Alice cannot determine whether she exists independently or not. Like Giafar, she can no longer distinguish between dreams and reality. This same problem troubles the narrator in another of Carroll's stories, *Sylvie and Bruno*: "So, either I've been dreaming about Sylvie, I said to myself, and this is the reality; or else I've really been with Sylvie, and this is a dream. Is Life a dream, I wonder?"[10] It is unquestionable that such passages had a seminal effect on Arrabal, who, in an interview with Alain Schifres, again paraphrases these ideas, perhaps unaware of their Carrollian overtones: "Often I dream that I have gigantic ears which fall to my feet. I imagine that I can wrap myself up in them, protect myself thanks to them and, there inside, I dream that I am dreaming."[11] Based on the frequent occurrence of this theme in both authors' works, it would appear that they have not resolved this enigma. From their characters' point of view, it is clear that they would prefer their dream-reality, where the impossible happens. In it, Arrabal's Giafar can resuscitate Sylda with a kiss. Likewise, a door in an attic can open out onto the stratosphere. All bizarre events can be explained by the infinite possibilities of dreams.

However, in such a universe, it is not surprising to discover that characters profoundly shaken by the reversal of everything which they thought absolute start doubting their own identity. Alice cries, "I wonder if I've been changed in the night? Let me think: was I the same when I got up this morning? I almost think I can remember feeling a little different. But if I'm not the same, the next question is 'Who in the World am I?' Ah, that's the great puzzle!" (Carroll, *Alice*, p. 205). Giafar finds himself in the same predicament. He stammers, "I'm

so . . . disoriented . . . I would like to have confidence in something and everything is collapsing under me little by little!'' (Arrabal, *Theatre III*, pp. 121–22).
Thus the theme of dreams triggers metaphysical quests in Carroll's and Arrabal's
work: appearance and reality, possible and impossible, and self-identity. Their
writings, to some extent elaborate on Breton's question, "Can't dreams also be
applied to the solution of the fundamental questions of life?"[12]

Eager to convey the role of chance in human life and artistic creation, Carroll
and Arrabal find the dream to be the best stylistic as well as philosophic answer
to the problem of mimesis. Arrabal uses dreams as a game that allows him to
discover the laws which govern chance. For him, dreaming is the only form that
reveals to the questing individual the path to knowledge. Carroll also searched
for an ideal means to depict the important roles of nonsense and chance in human
existence. Since his dreams recollected in the waking state took on these aspects
for him, he chose the dream as the form by which to express his insights. *Alice
in Wonderland, Through the Looking Glass*, and *Sylvie and Bruno* are all oneiric
visions. In the preface to *Sylvie and Bruno*, Carroll describes the spontaneous
genesis of his literary works: "As the years went on, I jotted down, at odd
moments, all sorts of odd ideas and fragments of dialogue . . . they also had a
way of occurring *à propos* of nothing—specimens of that hopelessly illogical
phenomenon, 'an effect without a cause' . . . such again have been passages
which have occurred in dreams, and which I cannot trace to any antecedent
cause whatever.''[13] Perplexed by the problem of uniting these absurd snatches
of thought into a story line, Carroll, like Arrabal, turned to the dream as the
structural form in which apparently disconnected ideas could flow one after the
other, linked by grammar, the only element reflecting the reality of the waking
state. The effect of such texts upon most readers echoes Alice's reaction after
listening to the recitation of "Jabberwocky": "Somehow it seems to fill my
head with ideas—only I don't exactly know what they are" (Carroll, *Alice*,
p. 197). Carroll and Arrabal use the dream as the stylistic device which most
faithfully conveys their vision; namely, that of a chaotic reality.

Let us examine the use of language and logic inside the dream form. Usually
it is agreed that language is a means for communicating shared perceptions.
However, in Carroll's and Arrabal's Wonderlands, it no longer has that function.
It is rather a personal idiom. Humpty Dumpty clarifies the enigma of Wonderland
vocabulary as follows: "When I use a word, it means just what I choose it to
mean—neither more nor less" (Carroll, *Alice*, p. 197). This characteristic of
oneiric language, which does not have the goal of communicating with others,
is an obvious criticism of the conventional use of language in society. In this
regard, the pitiful outcasts in Arrabal's *The Tricycle* try to hide their insignificance
through a personal language. The woman Mita suggests that Climando tell the
police a story about a horse that fell in love with a telescope thinking it was a
lamb, an anecdote that she finds irresistible. Climando objects, however, saying,
"They won't like that story either, they'll say they don't understand and then
they'll want to burn me alive" (Arrabal, *Plays*, p. 101). In this same work, the

police officers also speak a version of jabberwocky jargon. This unusual personalized language, a feature of dreams and the fruit of chance, is suitable for challenging the threat of the conventional world where everything must be precise at the expense of truth and beauty. In dreams language, like those who speak it, is freed from constraint.

Thus, although objects have names, their character and function are not fixed. For example, the pigeon calls Alice a snake because she eats eggs. Like other Carrollian characters, it uses an idiosyncratic language in which nouns no longer delineate reality. The pigeon asks Alice, "What does it matter to me whether you're a little girl or a serpent?" (Carroll, *Alice*, p. 76). This same confusion exists in Arrabal's theatrical universe. Micaela, the lascivious heroine of *The Labyrinth*, tries to explain the discrepancy between language and the reality it describes by stating that her father, who calls her an innocent child, has a scale of values that is different from that of others (Arrabal, *Plays*, pp. 38–39). Because of this flexibility, language is always ironic. When the judge in the same play exclaims, "Can dead men walk?" to trap Etienne in his lie, it is an indictment because the word "dead" no longer has its normal meaning (Arrabal, *Plays*, p. 63). So victim becomes executioner; the innocent, the guilty; and sexual lasciviousness, innocence. The couple Arlys and Sylda, whose names indicate antithetical personalities, are two sides of one coin. Dream labels are intentionally equivocal. At times they represent no more than personal labels in a world where everything takes place backwards, where "one's memory works both ways," as the White Queen says (Carroll, *Alice*, p. 247).

To emphasize the oneiric character of language in Carroll's and Arrabal's writings, one also must mention the incantatory power of nouns. This is to say that, at times, words bring about events rather than describe them. When the Duchess's baby grunts like a pig, Alice says, "If you're going to turn into a pig, my dear, I'll have nothing more to do with you" (Carroll, *Alice*, p. 87). Her use of the word "pig" completes the transformation; it is a pig that she is rocking in her arms. In the same way, when Alice thinks the White Queen's voice sounds like a sheep's, the Queen becomes a sheep (Carroll, *Alice*, p. 252). This magical process exists in Arrabal's work also. Kardo and Maldéric pretend to be blind, wearing dark glasses and carrying canes. When they say in jest that they are blind, they are left with bloody, empty eye sockets. Words become the magic potion of fairy tales. The pre-existing forms of words constitute rituals; therefore, Tweedledum and Tweedledee fight for a rattle because the poem says so, and Kardo and Maldéric play chess not by choice but because it was written. In these authors' universes, there is a predestination brought about by language.

Just as everyday language differs from that of dreams, logic in Wonderland takes on new functions. The characters use a dialectic which is directed toward a synthesis, one which is more outlandish than the original oppositions that it seeks to resolve. For example, in *The Tricycle* Climando overwhelms the old man by the following conclusion: "Soldiers who haven't got hair on their legs aren't soldiers. They're soldieresses. And as there aren't any soldieresses, what you're saying isn't true" (Arrabal, *Plays*, p. 82). Obviously this is not the type of logic that seeks to resolve the normal problems of existence. Dream logic is an infantile and idiosyncratic one that obviates objections. Thus, when Climando talks about escaping from prison, it is "logical" for him to cry out, "I've got very long legs, I could run" (Arrabal, *Plays*, p. 101). More importantly, what prevents normal reasoning is the fact that the data never remain the same. The Cheshire Cat uses a logic that disconcerts poor Alice, who asks him for directions:

> "That depends a good deal on where you want to get to," said the Cat.
> "I don't much care where—" said Alice.
> "Then it doesn't matter which way you go."
> "So long as I get somewhere."
> "Oh, you're sure to do that, if you only walk long enough."
>
> (Carroll, *Alice*, p. 88).

Like Climando, the cat knows what it wants to do; for example, to define the word "mad." So it chooses the terms of its proof to accomplish its goal rather than subscribing to rhetorical integrity: "To begin with, a dog's not mad. You grant that? Well, then you see a dog growls when it's angry and wags its tail when it's pleased. Now I growl when I'm pleased and wag my tail when I'm angry. Therefore, I'm mad" (Carroll, *Alice*, p. 89). In dreams logic no longer serves to limit reality but rather to create a universe where everything is possible. In his essay "L'Homme panique," Arrabal uses the word "panic" to describe this sort of lifestyle governed by confusion, humor, terror, chance, and euphoria.[14]

The inhabitants of this universe unquestioningly accept the phenomena surrounding them. They need no a priori definitions. If what is, is confusion, they conform to it. Thus, while Alice finds the Cheshire Cat totally bizarre, the Duchess treats it as a perfectly mundane occurrence. Alice cannot avoid applying everyday logic and facts to Wonderland. Instead of accepting it, Alice murmurs "Curiouser and curiouser" when what happens does not correspond to what she expects. Yet, to survive, it is up to her to adapt to the chaos. As the Caterpillar says, "You'll get used to it in time" (Carroll, *Alice*, p. 72). Giafar in *The Song of Barabbas* and Etienne in *The Labyrinth* are tormented by this same matter-of-fact attitude on the part of those who dwell in these strange regions. Kardo and Maldéric bite Giafar when he refuses to accept the fact that Sylda alone can free them. Later, when Sylda makes her fingernails grow on command, Giafar wants to explain this anomaly as magic tricks because he does not have the necessary faith in the possibilities of dream reality. When the backs of Maldéric and Kardo show no sign of blood after a lashing, Giafar, like Etienne, collapses because effects do not correspond to causes. Etienne in *The Labyrinth* is berated by Justin and the Judge when he accuses them of doing everything in their own way. His refusal to share their faith in dream-reality, which they call the meticulous organization, condemns him.

Etienne is a victim of dream logic, which seeks to destroy the logic of the waking mind. In the waking state, one is dealing with an inexorable progression from cause to effect, but dreams disappoint the mind which has rational expectations. Carroll, constantly interested in the oneiric state, commented in his diary, 9 February 1856: "When we are dreaming and, as often happens, we have a dim consciousness of the fact and try to wake, do we not say and do things which in waking life would be insane? May we not then sometimes define insanity as an inability to distinguish which is the waking and which the sleeping life? We often dream without the least suspicion of unreality."[15] Normal characters who enter Carroll's and Arrabal's universes witness the toppling of the entire framework of their sane judgment. Giafar cannot imagine that the attic in which he finds himself is not an attic, or that it is hanging suspended in a void rather than high above the earth. He persists in trying to explain the absence of the earth by his former logic, saying, "There must be a fog. That's why I don't see anything" (Arrabal, *Theatre III*, p. 109). However, as the spectator knows, Giafar is actually dealing with Arrabal's version of the possible. Similarly, when Alice criticizes the Mad Hatter for his peculiar references to time, which she knows as an impersonal system divided into years, months, days, hours, minutes, he refutes her by saying, "If you knew time as well as I do, you wouldn't talk about wasting it. It's Him" (Carroll, *Alice*, p. 97). The dwellers in Wonderland have to destroy logic, which in their context can only be an aberration. They can discredit the interloper's thought by a process of *reductio ad absurdum*, simply reciting the givens of their world, a world that does not obey any a priori principle.

Since dreams have no boundaries, anything which chance can produce is found in them. However, there are three themes which reappear in most of Carroll's and Arrabal's dreams or nightmares: namely, games, cruelty, and trials. For each author, games represent the perfect incarnation of both possibility and chance. In fact, for Arrabal, they go beyond representation. In his preliminary note to his book on Bobby Fischer and the game of chess, Arrabal cites an exchange between the grand masters Spassky and Fischer which conveys the importance he, too, accords this game. To Spassky's statement, "Chess is like life," Fischer replied, "Chess is life."[16] Games are the philosopher's stone of dreams, because the expert player dominates and controls the others, who become his pawns. Thus Cavanosa proposes to play chess when he wants a sure method to humiliate the lover in *The Grand Ceremonial*. Game-playing is an ideal fantasy device for taking revenge on society, which thinks it knows the rules but refuses to allow for the element of chance. As Sylda in *The Song of Barabbas* says, "No, no, not may the better man win, but may he win who controls chance the best" (Arrabal, *Theatre III*, p. 21). Games abound in Arrabal's plays: chess, roulette, the lay of Aristotle, puzzles—they appear as so many symbols of reality. Arrabal prides himself on being the only man in the world who knows how to illumine the unforeseeable, the future, tomorrow.[17] He, like Destiny, draws up the rules of a Universe-Game freed from the constraint of logic. Fascinated by puns, there is no doubt that he takes literally the Old French term "jeu" and the English word "play." More than ritual, his theater is a series of games, of childhood play in its apotheosis. As he explains, "I write my plays, as one orders each step of a ceremony, with the precision of a chessplayer."[18] In this master game conformists lose. They and society default since they know neither the rules nor the extent of the game.

Carroll, too, was fascinated by games, using chess as the formal frame for *Through the Looking Glass*. The entire story is nothing more than a chess problem in which the White pawn, Alice, is to win the game in eleven moves. The animated chess pieces of this fantasy are the counterparts of the playing cards in *Adventures in Wonderland*. The rules of the game permit characters to disappear and reappear, move and behave in ways which seem unpredictable to the uninitiated. Similarly the duplication of characters (two kings, two queens, two bishops, etc.) stresses the binary aspects of reality as perceived by the author. It also demonstrates what Arrabal's theater dramatizes; namely, that ideas and characters are interchangeable. This use of games as a literary framework, like the chess game in Rabelais's *Gargantua and Pantagruel* (Bk. 5, Chs. 24 and 25), also serves to reveal the derisive character of human life. Men are not autonomous beings, they are helpless pawns. Alice's changes in size and her rapid travels correspond to the buffets which Arrabal's characters receive at the hands of society.

In contrast with normal society, which considers cruelty and death distasteful and disquieting subjects, the world of dreams, like that of children, is candid. Dreams contain none of the hypocrisy and artificial etiquette found in waking society. In them, the mind can indulge with impunity in any outrage, without fear of condemnation or punishment, since, after all, it is always going to wake up. Thus, cruelty and death lose some of their sting. The cyclical character of Arrabal's plays, which constitutes another similarity to dreams, seems to indicate that death, like everything else, is only a passing state. Death fascinates Arrabal. In fact, he exclaims, "What astounds me is that Religion, Death and the Mother are not constant themes in everybody's writings."[19] Cruelty has the same cosmic dimension in his works. In Arrabal's binary and antithetical analysis of reality, love and hate, tenderness and cruelty, life and death, are strangely mixed and equivalent, as in a dream. Yet in the diegetic reality he creates, this dichotomy is not presented as incongruous. In *The Two Executioners*, for example, the mother denounces her husband and enjoys augmenting his agony until he dies. Death, like the skull which monks kept in their cells, is a constant presence in such plays as *Fando and Lis*, *The Condemned Man's Bicycle*, and *Ceremony for a Murdered Black*. The flux of oneiric experience dissipates ambiguous emotions aroused by thoughts of death. Like laughter, dreams provide a means for relieving and releasing the tension experienced by the psyche. Mita, Apal, and Climando decide to kill the man with money, reasoning that "he's sure to want to commit suicide" (Arrabal, *Plays*, p. 83). In dreams, the adult can revert fully and revel in childish cruelty and the suffering of others. Moral imperatives are abolished or eliminated. Thus, Kardo, Maldéric and the father snicker at

Giafar's agony as they torture him. In Arrabal's panic philosophy, cruelty and death are an integral part of the "fiesta" of the game of life.

Similarly, Carroll's works contain numerous comical references to death and cruelty. For example, while falling down the rabbit hole, Alice murmurs, " 'Why, I wouldn't say anything about it, even if I fell off the top of the house!' (Which was very likely true)" (Carroll, *Alice*, p. 27). When she explains to Humpty Dumpty that one cannot avoid getting old, he comments, "One can't, perhaps, but two can. With proper assistance, you might have left off at seven" (Carroll, *Alice*, p. 266). In Wonderland, as in dreams, all instincts are liberated. Carroll and Arrabal take advantage of oneiric license to shock conventional readers or spectators, to remind them that there is a sordid side to every aspect of life. Their characters are impolite, ask disturbing questions, and joke about the most terrifying subjects.

Finally, since both authors are profoundly alienated by traditional society and want to prove that its laws have no value when they are applied to the chaos of life, they utilize the courtroom as the perfect locale for the demonstration of its absurdity. The tribunal should be a place where logic and justice prevail. Society teaches that certain rules and protocol guide trials and that the bench requires evidence before condemning an individual. Not so in Arrabal's *The Labyrinth*, where the disoriented protagonist, Etienne, faces a hostile judge who strips away his remaining illusions. When Etienne tries to defend himself against the false charge of murder, the last remnant of waking logic is destroyed. While munching a sandwich and sipping wine, the judge, totally uninterested in the testimony, announces with his mouth full that "There is not the slightest doubt of the accused's guilt" (Arrabal, *Plays*, p. 65). In the oneiric trial, the necessity for evidence disappears. Similarly, in the trial which concludes *Alice in Wonderland*, the objections of the Jack of Hearts, who is accused of stealing some tarts, fall on deaf ears:

"Please, your majesty," said the Knave, "I didn't write it, and they can't prove that I did: There's no name signed at the end." "If you didn't sign it," said the King, "that only makes the matter worse. You must have meant some mischief, or else you'd have signed your name like an honest man." "That proves his guilt, of course," said the Queen, "so off with . . . " (Carroll, *Alice*, p. 157)

The norm of the dream is confusion, and the destruction of the trial process constitutes the final step in the creation of chaos. Anyone who does not accept the erratic rule of chance is guilty of contempt of court. Laws of cause and effect do not pertain. Whereas society claims to judge crimes with the intent of improving the criminal by punishment, oneiric logic strips away the pretext of the trial. In real life, Alice accepted her punishment because she had done the things she was punished for. In her opinion her guilt made all the difference, but the Queen sees it differently, saying, "But if you hadn't done them . . . that would have been better still, better, and better, and better! " (Carroll, *Alice*, p. 248).

Like Kafka, Carroll and Arrabal want to show man as defenseless because he deludes himself as to the nature of reality and therefore fails to understand his state.

By examining the philosophical and stylistic affinities linking Carroll and Arrabal, one is better able to appreciate the extent of the contemporary author's statements of indebtedness cited earlier. Both writers formulate avant-garde narratives which convey their profound discontent with daily reality by creating images of modern society that mirror its irrationality. Their childish characters share the use of poetic language to achieve liberation from banality. They take revenge on society by constructing new realms where confusion reigns, panic universes where everything is possible. Carroll and Arrabal are two lost children who find fulfillment in dreams, two wanderers in Wonderland.

NOTES

1. Alain Schifres, *Entretiens avec Arrabal* (Paris: Editions Pierre Belfond, 1969), p. 35; my translation.

2. Irmgard Anderson, "From Tweedledum and Tweedledee to Zapo and Zépo," *Romance Notes* 15, no. 2 (Winter 1973), 217–20; Alain Schifres, *Entretiens*, pp. 31, 35, 65, 72, 99; Peter Podol, *Fernando Arrabal* (Boston: Twayne, 1978), pp. 113–16; Thomas Donahue, *The Theater of Fernando Arrabal: A Garden of Earthly Delights* (New York: New York University Press, 1980), pp. 129, 131.

3. See Podol, *Fernando Arrabal*, pp. 58–60.

4. José Monléon, *Fernando Arrabal, Colección de Teatro* (Madrid: Taurus Edicions, S.A., 1965), p. 31.

5. Donahue, *Theater*, p. 29.

6. André Breton *Manifestes du Surréalisme* (Paris: Editions Gallimard, 1965), p. 22.

7. Fernando Arrabal, *Plays, Volume 2*, trans. Barbara Wright (London: Calder and Boyard, 1967); individual plays are identified and cited hereafter in the text.

8. Lewis Carroll (Charles Lutwidge Dodgson), *The Annotated Alice*, ed. Martin Gardner (New York: Clarkson N. Potter, 1960), p. 33; hereafter cited in the text.

9. Fernando Arrabal, *Theatre III* (Paris: R. Julliard, 1965); individual plays (my translations) are identified and cited hereafter in the text.

10. Lewis Carroll, *The Complete Works of Lewis Carroll* (New York: Random House, 1936), p. 296.

11. Schifres, *Entretiens*, p. 10; my translation.

12. Breton, *Manifestes*, pp. 21–22; my translation.

13. Carroll, *Complete Works*, p. 277.

14. Fernando Arrabal, *Le Panique* (Paris: Union Générale d'éditions, 1973), pp. 37–53.

15. *The Diaries of Lewis Carroll*, ed. Roger Lancelyn Green (New York: Oxford, 1957), I, 76.

16. Fernando Arrabal, *Sur Fischer: Initiation aux echecs* (Paris: Editions du Rocher, 1974), p. 10; my translation.

17. Monléon, *Fernando Arrabal*, p. 34.

18. Alain Schifres, "Arrabal, le Theatre Panique," *Realities* 252 (January 1967), p. 55; my translation.

19. Fernando Arrabal, "Arrabal: Auto-Interview," *The Drama Review* 13, no. 1 (Fall 1968), 75.

Mark Twain as Fantasist

William Coyle

By tradition every canonization has a devil's advocate, every hero has a heckler, and every banquet has a Banquo. Such is my role in a discussion of Mark Twain and fantasy as I contend that although during his last years Twain sought in fantasy a refuge from despair, the results were seldom, if ever, wholly successful.

A broad definition of fantasy as whatever is extravagantly fanciful would include Tom Sawyer's dreams of returning as a successful pirate or Huck Finn's incremental prevarication to Jo Wilks, and here Twain's success is beyond question. A more meaningful definition would limit fantasy to the creation of an alternative world involving distortion or reversal of such conventional expectations as chronology, identity, physical appearance, and causation. The fantasy world exists in a penumbra of wonder, and tension is generated by the juxtaposition of appearance with the reader's preconceptions of reality.

Four recurring motifs in the fiction of Twain's last twenty years are characteristic of fantasy. As several biographers have demonstrated, during his last years Twain was obsessed with the dualistic notion of a dream-self and a waking-self. Several of the abortive pieces written during this period involve dreams, usually nightmarish visions of disaster. Another device in both his realistic and his fantastic fiction is the extraordinary alien, the stranger with knowledge and skills superior to the community, which rejects him and resists his efforts to expose or reform it. Almost every piece of Twain's late fiction contains such a character, from Hank Morgan and the anonymous man that corrupted Hadleyburg to Pudd'nhead Wilson and Satan. The failure of such characters to effect any amelioration of human nature or of society reflects Twain's cynicism in his final phase. The alien visitor, of course, is a stock character in science fantasy. Another fantastic device is time-travel, as illustrated by Hank Morgan's transit from Bridgeport to Camelot or by Satan's montage of world history from Cain's murder of Abel to modern warfare. Also, like Swift, Twain was intrigued by minification.

In *The Great Dark* (1898), the Superintendent of Dreams conducts the main character on a nightmare voyage within a drop of water. The reduction of human beings to minuscule form usually served to satirize human vanity.

Despite Twain's use of such devices, I believe that for several reasons his genius was not compatible with the fantastic mode. First, his temperament was too volatile to focus on one concept throughout a work; his imagination could create a fairyland but could not remain within its bounds. Second, his urge to satirize whatever caught his attention at the moment, whether relevant or not, was irrepressible. Even when Mark Twain saluted what he found admirable, his thumb invariably edged toward his nose. Third, in his later work, perhaps because of his disillusionment with "the damned human race," he devoted less creative energy to portrayal of credible characters and more to the construction of complicated, often incredible plot machinery. Finally, his imagination was irremovably anchored in memories of Hannibal and in his earlier representations of that world. The vitality of his childhood recollections is shown in the thumbnail sketches of 168 villagers that he wrote from memory in 1897 and by the freshness of his descriptions of his boyhood in his autobiography. When he created a fantastic setting, echoes of Hannibal kept creeping in.

One apparent exception to my thesis is *A Connecticut Yankee in King Arthur's Court*, and the popular appeal of its basic concept (in the novel, three film versions, two musical comedies, and even a Disney cartoon) makes it ridiculous to call the work a failure. However, as fantasy it is vitiated by the diffusion of its satire and by the clumsy device of introducing the story as the journal of the "curious stranger." Quibbles over genre are fruitless, but I would classify *A Connecticut Yankee* as burlesque history.

Twain's most successful fantasy is *The Mysterious Stranger*; but since he began four versions (two of them laid in Hannibal) without completing any of them and the standard version was cobbled together by Albert Bigelow Paine and Frederick A. Duneka, it cannot be considered an unqualified success. Even here there are echoes of Hannibal. Eseldorf is a sleepy village on a bluff overlooking a majestic river. Like Tom Sawyer's gang, the boys have adventures on the river, smoke pipes (doubtful in Austria of 1590), and listen to ghost stories told by Felix Brandt, a medieval equivalent of Jim. The boys' filching a gold piece to confuse Father Peter's count is a replay of Huck's action when the King and Duke are counting money at the Wilks home. Theodore Fischer's remark that "we were not over-much pestered with schooling"[1] certainly sounds Huck Finnish.

Nevertheless, *Stranger* contains flashes of magic, particularly in the first appearance of Satan. The boys respond eagerly to the enchantment of his presence: "He made us drunk with the joy of being with him, and of looking into the heaven of his eyes, and of feeling the ecstasy that thrilled along our veins from the touch of his hand."[2] He reads the boys' thoughts and fulfills their unexpressed desires, creates birds and a miniature squirrel out of clay, plays enchanting music on a strange instrument, and describes far-off solar systems inhabited by an immortal race. He fashions a castle, stocks it with finger-size people, and then casually crushes it. When he leaves, he thins away like a soap bubble: "He sprang—touched the grass—bounded—floated along—touched again—and so on, and presently exploded—puff! and in his place was vacancy."[3] Despite its factitious composition, echoes of the "matter of Hannibal," and some extraneous satire, *The Mysterious Stranger* seems Mark Twain's most successful fantasy.

Twain's difficulties in composing fantasy can be assessed in one of the numerous pieces he began but left incomplete during his last years, *Three Thousand Years among the Microbes*. He worked on the story between 20 May and 23 June, 1905, at Dublin, New Hampshire, where he had settled after spending the winter in New York. Most critics have made only passing reference to it, although Paine published a portion of the manuscript in his biography. The complete text was published for the first time in the California edition.[4] Sholem J. Kahn describes it as "a beautiful potpourri of real significance,"[5] and Richard Boyd Hauck calls it "Twain's last perfectly balanced effort at serious humor."[6] In *Mark Twain's Last Years as a Writer*, a generally favorable discussion of this phase of his career, William R. Macnaughton calls *Microbes* "unequivocally inferior" but also describes it as "the cheerful work of a man enjoying his imaginings."[7] The cheerful aspect of the story is its animism; all creatures from atom to Adam have souls and live forever through endless permutations in form.

The narrator, a scientist who graduated from Yale in 1853, has been changed into a cholera germ by a magician who was trying to change him into a bird. Twain originally intended Mary Baker Eddy to be responsible for the transformation but apparently found it difficult to account for her involvement.

Mark Twain owned a fine English microscope and spent hours observing a drop of rainwater or blood and fantasizing on the miniature worlds reflected in his lens.[8] Such a session may have supplied the original idea for *Microbes*, which he recorded in August of 1884: "I think we are only the microscopic trichina concealed in the blood of some vast creature's veins, and it is that vast creature whom God concerns Himself about and not us."[9] He later described a similar notion in *Following the Equator*: "In Sydney I had a large dream. . . . I dreamed that the visible universe is the physical person of God; that the vast worlds that we see twinkling millions of miles apart in the fields of space are the blood-corpuscles in His veins; and that we and the other creatures are the microbes that charge with multitudinous life the corpuscles."[10]

As a cholera germ the narrator lives within the body of a drunken tramp named Blitzkowski, who resembles Pap Finn:

He tramps in the summer and sleeps in the fields; in the winter he passes the hat in cities, and sleeps in the jails when the gutter is too cold; he was sober once, but does not remember when it was; he never shaves, never washes, never combs his tangled fringe of hair; he is wonderfully ragged, incredibly dirty; he is malicious, malignant, vengeful, treacherous, he was born a thief, and will die one; he is unspeakably profane, his body is a sewer, a reek of decay, a charnel house, and contains swarming nations of all the different kinds of germ-vermin that have been invented for the contentment of man. (Twain, *Microbes*, p. 436).

How a germ can be aware of such external matters is unclear. Blitzkowski, of course, is a metaphor for the world as Twain saw it in dark moments; other germs regard Blitzkowski as "their globe, lord of their universe, its jewel, its marvel, its miracle, its masterpiece" (p. 436).

The planet of Blitzkowski is divided into 1000 republics and 30,000 monarchies, each jealous and suspicious of the others. The oldest royal dynasty is the Pus family, which has produced 110,000 kings, all named Henry. The largest republic is Getrichquick, located in the richest region, the stomach. Getrichquick recently has annexed some remote islands inhabited by small, dark microbes; the narrator's sarcastic term for such imperialistic expansion is "Benevolent Assimilation."

The narrator is a full-fledged microbe, "the germiest of the germy" (p. 435), but he has retained his human life-span, human perception of time, and memories of his former life; thus, like Hank Morgan in Camelot, he views his new world from a double perspective. The 3,000 years in the title represents about three earthly weeks. In microbic time, by the way, this essay will take two years to read. He complains that he has forgotten the human multiplication tables beyond 4 times 9 is 42 (p. 451)—a rather feeble echo of some of Huck Finn's remarks on mathematics. He also lapses into the kind of mock history Twain had used many times before; he recalls when George Washington went north to take command of the Hessians and the end of the American Revolution when Sir John Franklin and his brother Benjamin persuaded the Diet of Worms to establish a new Year One (p. 467). Despite his jumbled memories he is completing a history of the world.

The name Twain gave his narrator is Bkshp, a shortened form of Blankenship, the family name of the original of Huck Finn. One of his friends is a yellow fever germ named Bblbgrwx, pronounced Benjamin Franklin. Only aristocrats are entitled to vowels. Midway through the story, however, the narrator's friends nickname him Huck from his earthly middle name, Huxley. His other friends have jaw-breaking names, which he converts to David Copperfield, Guy Mannering, King Herod, Colonel Mulberry Sellers, and the like. Each is descended from a noble family and has a coat of arms.

The plot appears to consist of a series of spur-of-the-moment improvisations. The narrator lives happily in a "dozing village" (p. 446) inside Blitzkowski, where mighty rivers put the Mississippi to shame. Success as a singer of minstrel show songs and as discoverer of a fossilized flea brings him the kind of public adulation Twain enjoyed during his last years. His attempts to describe the outside world to his friends Lemuel Gulliver and Louis XIV resemble Huck's struggle to enlighten Jim concerning history. In a long episode he listens to his secretary or thought-recorder girl, Catherine of Aragon, a non-stop talker like Sandy in *A Connecticut Yankee*. She has become a Giddyite after reading *Science and*

Wealth. The space devoted to satire of Christian Science, one of Twain's pet peeves at the time, seems disproportionate to its function in the story. The narrator also has a long theological-sociological discussion with a sleeping sickness germ. In the final episode he persuades his friends that they can become wealthy by an expedition to a remote region known as Major Molar, actually one of Blitzkowski's teeth that has a gold filling. The story ends with Huck progressively reducing the amount of treasure he will share with his friends. He finally decides to keep all the gold himself and give them part of the amalgam and all of the cement.

In summary, the story is amusing, but it is clogged with irrelevant satire of the scattershot variety as Twain ridicules whatever pops into his mind: international marriages, Christian Science, French immorality, provincialism, aristocratic pride, greed, anthropomorphic religion, military doctors, imperialism, permissive dictionaries, free silver, and the doctrine of a moral sense—most of which have little or nothing to do with the universe of Blitzkowski.

Although Mark Twain was proud of his productivity in turning out such a quantity of manuscript in five weeks, he never took time to revise or complete it. Cataloguing the deficiencies of this uncompleted fantasy merely to derogate Twain in his old age would serve no useful purpose. In light of his anguish during his last years, he deserved whatever relief its composition afforded him during this brief period, which, by the way, included the first anniversary of his wife's death. It probably meant no more to him than his endless sessions at the billiard table. He had the good sense and good taste to leave it unfinished and certainly did not foresee its later exhumation or autopsies by ghouls like myself. Still, it can serve as a paradigm of his shortcomings as a fantasist.

The range of fantasy is enormous; it is adaptable to satire, farce, Gothic horror, hallucination, political lampoons, outer space and the landscape of the mind, dreams and mental aberration, projections backward or forward in time, philosophical speculation, and so on; but these myriad possibilities cannot be combined in the same work. Despite landmark exceptions like Wordsworth's "Preface" or Poe's "Philosophy of Composition," attempts to stipulate procedures for the conception and creation of any literary form are rather futile and might be termed "the operational fallacy." Nevertheless, it seems safe (and rather obvious) to say that a fantasy to be effective should have an inner consistency. Its creation requires a focused imagination that lives for the time within the world it creates. Successful fantasy is a steady beam of light, not an intermittent flickering. Mark Twain's genius was realistic, his imagination was mercurial; as a result, his experiments in fantasy do not rank with his recreations of the world he knew at firsthand.

NOTES

1. Mark Twain, *The Mysterious Stranger and Other Stories* (New York: New American Library, 1962), p. 162.

2. Ibid., p. 171.

3. Ibid., p. 177.

4. Mark Twain, *Which Was the Dream?*, ed. John Tuckey (Berkeley: University of California Press, 1968); hereafter cited in the text.

5. Sholem J. Kahn, *Mark Twain's Mysterious Stranger* (Columbia: University of Missouri Press, 1978), p. 100.

6. Richard Boyd Hauck, *A Cheerful Nihilism* (Bloomington: Indiana University Press), p. 157.

7. William R. Macnaughton, *Mark Twain's Last Years as a Writer* (Columbia: University of Missouri Press, 1979), p. 225.

8. Justin Kaplan, *Mr. Clemens and Mark Twain* (New York: Simon and Schuster, 1966), p. 259.

9. John Tuckey, "Introduction," in *Which Was the Dream?*, p. 24.

10. Mark Twain, *Following the Equator*, Author's National Edition (New York: Harper, 1897), V, 114.

The Tarot Cards as a Subversive Tool in Italo Calvino

Constance D. Markey

In Italo Calvino's *The Castle of Crossed Destinies*, we encounter a cruelly amusing parody of the traditional theme of the hero's quest. This portrayal cynically juxtaposes the familiar hero's journey and its uplifting moral against the dilemma of modern man's more tenuous life-quest with its dubious options and hints of despair.

Calvino's deliberately dualistic and subversive use of the tarot cards to illustrate his theme is integral to the novel's dialectical approach to the quest or monomyth.[1] For example, structurally in *Castle*, the arrangement of the cards so that the events all form part of a giant interlocking puzzle provides an illusion, if only initially, of wholeness or synthesis.[2] A kind of de Saussurian system or *langue*[3] thus appears to reign as the steps of the traditional journey unfold almost routinely, and by some master plan, in each episode.

On the other hand, once this convenient model, this seeming integrity, has been suggested, the reverse dynamics of the cards come quickly into play. Despite the apparent unanimity of intent of the tarot maze, the individual *novelle* simply do not finally conform to the conventional quest, much less to any definitive reading. As "arbitrary signs"[4] the cards remain subjective in interpretation; hence they defy final meaning. As more and more doubts and contradictions spring up over the liberty[5] or freedom of the cards, among the novel's card-playing protagonists, the story's antithesis quickly begins to emerge. In the confusion, the traditional message of the epic quest is irrevocably lost. The hero will not return triumphant. Instead his voyage soon evolves into a journey "drained of all future" and without any "end" (Calvino, *Castle*, p. 6).

The original deception that *Castle* will be little more than a recapitulation of the conventional hero's journey begins with the novel's opening lines. Here the narrator already implies a traditional message for the novel, placing himself and the other characters immediately within a forest: the conventional setting where many a traditional epic hero, including Dante, has received the call to depart on his quest: "In the midst of a thick forest, there was a castle that gave shelter to all travelers overtaken by night on their journey: lords and ladies, royalty and their retinue, humble wayfarers" (p. 3).

The forest setting thus proves here a useful means to manipulate the reader. Not only does it lend a mysterious aura to the novel, suitable and even necessary to the mystique of the hero's journey, but, by so doing, it provides the reader with a deceptive clue as to how the novel ought to be read. Enhancing this delusion that the story is the familiar quest is the forest's role as a central backdrop or cornice for all the rest of the tales (besides the narrator's) in the novel. Each tale thus takes its point of departure from the forest, implying at once a false sense of thesis to the grouping of *novelle*.

This initial illusion of the traditional hero's redemptive voyage in the novel is then supported, as noted earlier, by the use of the tarot cards. The central narrator himself endorses the false promise of the cards, introducing them with a pretext designed both to beguile the reader as well as to be useful, at least subversively. At the beginning of the novel the storyteller takes care to alert the reader to the uncertainty of his own memory and to apprise us of his chance encounter with some travel-worn "lords and ladies" (p. 3) in a mysterious castle in the forest. Soon after his meeting with the other knights and ladies, he adds a fascinating but disconcerting note, informing us that he and the others have all been rendered mute by the forest crossing. Because all of the travelers feel eager, even compelled, to speak of their fearful journey but cannot do so in words, a unique solution is proposed. Producing a set of ancient tarot cards, the lord of the manor offers them to the assemblage, hoping that with the aid of these magical cards each traveler will be able to find both his story and his fortune.

Like the myth of the quest itself, the divinatory cards possess a long and seductively romantic history whose evocation only reinforces the novel's mystical aura and sense of integrity.[6] More important, as part of a mantic code or magical "sign system," the cards at first seem to represent a means of assimilating the journey's mysteries, of providing the unknown with the structure of what is known.[7] Thus imbued with a sense of cosmological order, the cards appear to provide an initial coherence to the journey which soon proves significant to the subversive irony of the novel.

The peculiar emblematic nature of tarot cards distinguishes them from other more conventional card decks, and not only enhances their dramatic effect but also adds an unmistakable allegorical stamp to *Castle*. Furthermore, the allegory of the cards, by virtue of its popularly comprehensible subtext or coding,[8] once again draws the reader closer to the "keys"[9] of the familiar hero's journey, particularly that of Dante. As we shall see, the tarot cards mirror in many respects the well-known Dantesque predilection for metaphysics.

Certain cards by nature of the characters they depict evoke sentiments and situations that remind one not just of Dante but of other similar ritual journeys.

The card *The Pope* or *Il Papa* always refers to a high priest or church dignitary, and thus certain magical rites are always associated with him in any card reading. More subtle and fascinating is the card known as *The Hanged Man* or *L'appeso*, a card that makes frequent and evocative appearances in *Castle*. It portrays a man with an illuminating halo around his head, but suspended by his ankles. For us this card conjures up a wide range of symbolic inferences, recalling at once life's reversals, notions of sacrifice, as well as the contemplation of heavenly mysteries.[10] Other cards of quite fundamental even primitive values include *Death* or *La Morte* in the form of the grim reaper, the *Moon, Star, Judgment, Justice,* and the *Wheel of Fortune*, a card as important to *Castle* as its concept was originally to Dante in the *Divine Comedy*.

Just the mere listing of the card names, but better still the examination of their faces in the beautiful Visconti deck, used to illustrate many of the stories in *Castle*, evokes an instant response in the reader who already knows by heart many of the symbolic correlations between the cards and various situations or metaphysical states which they are meant to recall. In individual cards like the *Devil* or *Diavolo*, and *Judgment* or *Il Guidizio* shown poised over the open graves, it takes no imagination whatever to discern the moral lesson which the cards were known to have conveyed in the late Middle Ages and Renaissance and which they still popularly portray today.[11]

Beguiled thus by the allegorical implications of the cards, the reader is yet again subliminally misled into associating the narrator's journey in *Castle* with the symbolic mission of traditional heroes. In the tarot maze the narrator tells us he is seeking a system by which he can arrange his life's journey, divine its purpose and its outcome. Inevitably this same naive hope, that a final solution to the novel lies hidden in the cards, also unconsciously lures the reader. With the narrator, then, the reader turns his attention to the tarot maze with all the awe and fascination reserved for a higher mystical power: "There was something else we saw in those tarots, something that no longer allowed us to take our eyes from the gilded pieces of that mosaic" (p. 6).

Ironically, it is also this same vista of cards with its diabolical glitter which at the very same instant plants a vague dread in the reader and narrator that the end of the journey may not be desirable after all, but that it might instead reveal an empty future. This anxiety, of course, as events quickly indicate proves justified. No sooner has the stage been set in the forest and all the clues mentioned above firmly fixed in the reader's mind for the conventional journey than things immediately begin to go awry. Therefore, even as the novel's original "thesis" of the hero's quest continues to be plotted outwardly at the beginning of each episode in the novel, the spirit of the drama actually and perversely pulls away from the original positive message.

The subversion or "antithesis" of the original story in *Castle* emerges early in the muteness shared by the narrator and his fellow travelers. Similar to the forest backdrop already described, the universality of this motif suggests that it cannot be an idly interjected detail in the novel. In point of fact, we know that at a purely technical level, the muteness of the characters in *Castle* is actually a timely pretext for the author's semiotic experiments with the tarot cards as sign systems. Much critical consideration has been given to Calvino's seemingly playful substitution of cards for language.[12] In one earlier story of *Castle*, "The Tale of the Ingrate and His Punishment," for instance, in the light of the protagonist's muteness and in the absence presumably therefore of real words, the reader and the narrator are frequently abandoned to the mercy of the tarot card emblems to interpolate many of the highly equivocal events in the story: "The card that was laid down next, the *Knight of Swords* . . . announced an unforeseen event: either a mounted messenger . . . or the groom himself . . . or perhaps both things at once" (p. 10).

As the ambiguous passage above indicates, despite the tidy interlocking pattern of the stories, the card puzzle in *Castle* has provided only the merest fiction of a synthetic whole or thesis. The reality of the tarot game is instead another matter entirely. For each time a player selects a card, it constitutes another departure in the story. Each time the card is read, as the central narrator slyly informs us, it undergoes "corrections, variants" (p. 97) according to the eye of the beholder (including the eye of the reader, himself an active participant in this perplexing game). These variables in the cards, expressed in the frustrating number of qualifying words such as *or, or else, maybe*, and *perhaps*, continually clutter the text of *Castle* and are meant to illustrate one of de Saussure's most significant linguistic concepts in a nearly pictorial way.[13] Graphically Calvino demonstrates for us through the text that individual signs in any system of communication are not univalent, but rather are liable to any number of subjective interpretations.

Besides illustrating graphically Calvino's own interpretation of de Saussure's concept of the "arbitrary sign," however, the cards as a means of communication in *Castle* also touch on a philosophical issue, a modern scepticism, close to the heart of Calvino's writing. The loss of stable values for the card signs casts a grim shadow over the novel's initial formula journey, continually threatening its verisimilitude by the new doubts which the cards pose. The constant equivocation over the meaning and fabric of events, therefore, posits a deliberate and ironic reversal of the traditional hero's quest. Instead of a predictable ritual journey, the cards as arbitrary signs dramatize a starkly contemporary and haphazard life journey marked by a purposeless sense of freedom.

Thus, a careful examination of the individual voyages of the individual players in *Castle* reveals that, while there are many trials and obstacles as the card stories intersect which may suggest a moment of truth or a turning point to the events, none of these instances actually precipitates a purposeful change in the traveler's destiny or conveys any sense of the moral rebirth implied by the traditional quest. The characters go everywhere but nowhere, their paths and their cards cross, their lives bump up against each other, but all of these experiences prove non-instructive, nonredemptive, and ultimately futile.[14]

The theme of the classical spiritual crossroads of decision, or the *bivium*,[15] is another prominent feature in many of the stories in *Castle*. For example, in "All the Other Tales'' (p. 41) the paths of Helen of Troy, Astolfo, Ulysses, and Paris converge and disrupt one another's course, creating considerable havoc in the tarot game, but, significantly, events are never resolved. The *bivium* theme again dominates the aptly titled ''Three Tales of Madness and Destruction,'' where three doomed travelers litigate pointlessly for possession of the same cards, hopelessly entangled in the card maze on the table: ''In fact, the three who now started quarreling did so with solemn gestures as if declaiming, and while all three pointed to the same card, with their free hand and with evocative grimaces, they exerted themselves to convey that those figures were to be interpreted this way and not that'' (p. 113).

The ensuing disorder of the cards, like the emotional conflict of the characters over them, no longer typifies the methodical wholeness or system of the tarot game as it is illustrated visually in the novel. Neither does it any longer evoke thematically the reassuring steps of the traditional hero's journey. Rather, the sudden confusion, the freedom, or more expressly the ''absurdity'' in the card readings, marks a decisive spiritual breakdown in the novel, one which best illustrates the negative dynamics of Calvino's writing. In the dramatic struggle we observe at last on both a structural and a thematic level the splintering of what once seemed a coherent pattern of events (system) into a volatile mass of indiscriminate phenomena (liberty). From a structural point of view, this moment in *Castle* would encompass the ''auto-destruction'' of the author's initial thesis.[16]

Thematically this conflict over the cards marks an equally negative turn to the novel's dialogue on modern man's quest. Just as the card variables bring chaos to the tarot game, so, too, the irrational absurdity of the drama's events has corrupted the integrity of the novel's portrait of life. The fragile example of the traditional journey with its virtuous deeds and heavenly rewards, as recreated for centuries in the comforting religious and literary tradition of the hero, has lost all meaning for this more cynical modern hero. Contrary to the traditional life portrait, with its precise concept of right and wrong turns and defined goals, the storyteller in *Castle* finds himself with no fixed itinerary whatever. Life's most dependable signposts, truth and reality, are no longer unequivocal. Appearances are deceiving, chaotic. Before him lies a truly contemporary quest, charged not with traditional values, but with controversy and doubt. Yet, just as surely as the right path has been lost to him, the hero's journey in *Castle* will continue. Indeed, there seems no way out of it, since only fate and death can provide a valid end to his labyrinthine wanderings.

NOTES

1. David Adams Leeming, *Mythology: The Voyage of the Hero* (New York: Lippincott, 1973), p. 6, defines the monomyth as a universal story, ''the journey of the hero figure . . . a reflection of our own journey from birth to death.''

2. See the illustration in Italo Calvino, *The Castle of Crossed Destinies*, trans. William Weaver (New York: Harcourt Brace, 1977), p. 40; hereafter cited in the text.

3. See the discussion of *langue* and *parole* or system (*sistema*) and liberty (*liberta*) as Teresa de Lauretis refers to them in "Calvino e la dialettica dei massimi sistemi," *Italica* 53, No. 1 (1976), 57–74. It should be noted that de Lauretis's definition of *parole* or *liberta*, as well as Calvino's, frequently implies a contingent reality (p. 70) and hence is not entirely in accord with Ferdinand de Saussure's definition of the word in *Course in General Linguistics*, trans. Wade Baskins, eds. Charles Bally and Albert Sechehaye (New York: McGraw-Hill, 1966), p. 69.

4. "Arbitrary sign" is a term coined by de Saussure, which implies that the relationship between the name of something and the thing itself is not fixed, not dependent on any inner relationship between them (*Course*, pp. 67–68). Thus naming becomes arbitrary, dependent on the speaker and, more specifically, on his linguistic community (*Course*, p. 69).

5. de Lauretis's definition of *parole*. See note 3.

6. For the history of the tarot cards, see the analysis by Sergio Samek Ludovici in *Tarocchi: Il mazzo Visconteo di Bergamo e New York* (Parma: Franco Maria Ricci editore, 1969); Stewart Cullin, *Chess and Playing Cards* (Washington, D.C.: Government Printing Office, 1898); and Pierre Guiraud, *Semiology*, trans. George Gross (London: Routledge & Kegan Paul, 1971), pp. 59–65.

7. Guiraud, *Semiology*, pp. 59, 61.

8. See Robert Scholes, *Structuralism in Literature* (New Haven: Yale University Press, 1974), pp. 62–69, for a discussion of coding and subtext in card sign systems.

9. Joseph Campbell's word for the steps in the hero's quest in *The Hero with a Thousand Faces* (Cleveland: World Publishing, 1956), p. 275.

10. The description of the cards and their usual symbolism appears in Arthur Edward Waite, *The Pictorial Key to the Tarot* (Blauvelt, N.Y.: Multimedia Publishing, 1974), pp. 88, 116.

11. Ludovici, *Tarocchi*, p. 151.

12. For more background on the use of tarot cards in narrative by Calvino, see Gerard Genot, "Le destin des recits entrecroises," *Critique* 28 (1972), 788–809, and Maria Corti, "Le jeu comme generation du texts: Des tarots au recit," *Semiotica* No. 7 (1973) pp. 33–48.

13. See Calvino's own interesting thoughts on the use of the cards in narrative in his note to *Castle*, pp. 123–39.

14. Comprehensive discussions of the moral, psychological, and religious overtones of the traditional hero's quest are found in Northrop Frye, *Fables of Identity: Studies in Poetic Mythology* (New York: Harbinger Books, 1963); Carl Gustav Jung, *The Collected Works of C. G. Jung*, trans. R. F. C. Hull, eds. Herbert Read, Michael Fordham, and Gerhard Adler, *The Archetypes and the Collective Unconscious* (Princeton: Princeton University Press, 1976); and Mircea Eliade, *The Myth of the Eternal Return*, trans. W. R. Trask (Princeton: Princeton University Press, 1971).

15. For a discussion of the historical background of the *bivium* theme in literature, see Theodore Mommsen, "Petrarch and the Story of the Choice of Hercules," *Journal Warburg & Courtauld Institutes* 16 Nos. 3–4 (1953), 178–92.

16. de Lauretis, "Calvino," p. 65.

V. FANTASY AND CONTEMPORARY CONCERNS

The diversity of fantasy and its adaptability to a wide range of interests, both timely and timeless, is demonstrated in this section by essays relating the fantastic to the archetypal initiation-quest described by Jung (Thompson), to human gullibility (Morse), to the frightening prospect of a mechanized environment (Dunn and Erlich), to world semantics (Sefler), and to human shortsightedness regarding ecology (Elgin). As society itself has grown more fantastic, science fantasy has managed to stay ahead of it and has been particularly effective in portraying nuclear holocaust, a society in steady state controlled by clones and computers, pollution of the environment, overpopulation, and other terrors that haunt the modern psyche.

Jungian Patterns in Ursula K. Le Guin's *The Farthest Shore*

Raymond H. Thompson

In an article entitled "The Child and the Shadow," Ursula K. Le Guin argues that the universal appeal of fantasy stems from the archetypal patterns which are such vital ingredients of the form, imparting to it vitality as well as enduring fascination. She goes on to discuss these patterns in terms of the psychology of Carl Gustav Jung, whom she describes as "the psychologist whose ideas on art are the most meaningful to most artists."[1] Such an approach to fantasy is clearly valuable, but nowhere more so than in dealing with Le Guin's own work in the field, where the Jungian shadow looms very large indeed.

The Jungian depths of the Earthsea trilogy have not escaped notice: Eleanor Cameron, Rollin A. Lasseter, Margaret P. Esmonde, and Edgar C. Bailey, Jr., have all shown the value of a Jungian approach.[2] Their attention, however, has focused on *A Wizard of Earthsea*. This paper will examine instead how Le Guin's self-proclaimed fascination with and perception of Jungian patterns have affected the structure of *The Farthest Shore*, the novel that concludes the trilogy.

In another article, "Dreams Must Explain Themselves," Le Guin tells us that "*The Farthest Shore* is about death. . . . Coming of age again, but in a larger context." She also confesses that "it is a less well built, less sound and complete book than the others . . . [Ged] took over completely in this book."[3] In both *A Wizard of Earthsea* and *The Tombs of Atuan*, Ged's quest follows the basic pattern of the monomyth outlined by Joseph Campbell in *The Hero with a Thousand Faces*. This quest involves the voluntary journey to the Otherworld (the dark sand eventually reached at the edge of the world in the first novel, the Tomb in the second); an encounter with a shadow presence or barrier that guards the passage (first encounter with the Shadow of Gont, the Red Rock door); a combination of testing and assistance by ambivalent powers (the Shadow which functions as both guide and opponent, Arha/Tenar); ultimate triumph represented by illumination and freedom in which the powers become friendly (reconciliation with the Shadow) or by bride-theft and flight, in which they remain hostile (union with Tenar, established by a bond of mutual trust and love and symbolized by the joining of the two halves of The Ring of Erreth-Akbe, followed by escape through the earthquake-shaken Labyrinth); return to freedom leaving the transcendental powers behind (return to Iffish, return to Havnor); bearing the boon that restores the world (acceptance of the Shadow, Tenar, and the Ring). Yet in both books this quest is well integrated with the central subject: in *A Wizard of Earthsea* Ged's quest is the external analogue of his growth to maturity, and it remains firmly subordinated to the focus on the coming-of-age of Tenar in *The Tombs of Atuan*.

In *The Farthest Shore*, however, Ged's quest increasingly dominates the story, so that interest shifts from Arren, his young companion, to the Archmage himself. The first half of the book focuses on Arren's growth and development; he is a youth full of promise but untried, so that he must learn to recognize his own limitations before he can accompany Ged on the final perilous descent into the realm of the dead. The second half of the novel, by contrast, focuses on Ged's confrontation with Cob, the "Lord of the Two Lands,"[4] and once again the journey he undertakes follows the pattern of the monomyth: Ged enters the realm of the dead, whose entrance is guarded by Cob; he penetrates to its very heart, the black hole that sucks the light out of the world; he seals it, then returns to the living world, which has been saved by his deed.

This division of interest can be partially justified, however, by scrutinizing the relationship of the two central characters to the figure of the shadow. In *Aion* Jung notes that what he calls the "shadow" cast by the conscious mind of the individual contains the hidden, repressed, and unfavorable aspects of the personality. The traits of the shadow appear in Cob, whose preoccupation with self would destroy the entire world; this selfishness manifests itself most strikingly in the qualities of vanity, despair, and fear of death: "Very strange was the mixture of despair and vindictiveness, terror and vanity, in his words and voice" (Le Guin, *Shore*, p. 181). However, the shadow only embodies the negative traits that are actually part of one's own personality, as Le Guin reminds us in "The Child and the Shadow": "Unadmitted to consciousness, the shadow is projected outward, onto others. There's nothing wrong with me—it's *them*. I'm not a monster, other people are monsters" (Le Guin, "Child," p. 64). According to Jung in *Aion*, this process offers the most stubborn resistance to moral control, since the projections are not recognized as such; the cause of the problem "appears to lie, beyond all possibility of doubt, in the other person."[5] Like the shadow creature in *A Wizard of Earthsea*, Cob serves to mirror the faults of the hero. In *The Farthest Shore*, Ged's act of vanity lies in his past, during his punishment of Cob for raising the spirits of the dead: "I was possessed by anger and by vanity," he admits to Arren (Le Guin, *Shore*, p. 75). However, when repressed the shadow merely waxes stronger, and so Cob's power expands to threaten the entire world of Earthsea, affecting first the more remote reaches, but inexorably moving closer to Roke itself which, as the center where magic is the subject of disciplined intellectual study, can be equated with the conscious self. For as Jung explains in *Aion*, "One cannot dispose of facts by declaring them unreal. The projection-making factor, for instance, has undeniable reality. Anyone who insists on denying it becomes identical with it, which is not only dubious in itself but a positive danger to the well-being of the individual."[6] Nevertheless, though he has not left pride entirely behind him, Ged has grown in wisdom since his rebuke to Cob, as can be seen during his rescue of Arren from the slave-traders, for he refuses to punish them. Moreover, though we can perceive the traces of Ged's pride, we can discern little of either despair or fear of death in the Archmage; nor does the author choose to recall events from his youth which might have helped. Instead she provides Ged with a young companion who functions as his alter ego.

At the outset of the story Ged is reminded, "You have always gone alone. Why, now, companioned? " He responds, "I have never needed help before. ...And I have found a fit companion" (Le Guin, *Shore*, p. 25). What Arren has to offer are love and devotion to duty, which mirror Ged's own great virtues, but they must be tempered by stern tests before they can be put to the ultimate trial. In the course of these tests, Arren succumbs not only to vanity, but, even more obviously, to despair and the fear of death, the traits possessed by the shadow of selfishness. Initially Arren's pride is but a spur to his sense of responsibility. When asked if he takes pride in his lineage, Arren wins Ged's approval by responding, "Yes, I take pride in it—because it makes me a prince; it is a responsibility, a thing that must be lived up to" (Le Guin, *Shore*, p. 28). However, his pride rebels when he is made to feel useless to Ged's quest: "He was merely dragged along on it, useless as a child. But he was not a child" (Le Guin, *Shore*, p. 93). And when Ged lies grievously wounded in the boat, he gives way to the inactivity of despair and the fear of death: "I was afraid of death. ... I could think of nothing, except that there was—there was a way of not dying for me, if I could find it. ... And I did nothing, nothing, but try to hide from the horror of dying" (Le Guin, *Shore*, p. 120). Typically, Arren projects the selfish traits of pride and despair on another, namely Ged, whom he blames for bringing about this situation: "In his pride, his overweening pride as Archmage, he feared lest they might gain [eternal life] . . . he would die himself, to prevent them from eternal life" (Le Guin, *Shore*, pp. 101–02). Yet even in this darkest moment commitment remains. Though parched with thirst, the youth saves what water remains in the boat for Ged, never even contemplating taking any for himself, and his first thought after rescue by the raft-folk is for his companion. Consequently, he is able to recognize and to confess his fault, thus earning the right to accompany the Archmage on the most perilous stage of their journey: "He had learned his own weakness, also, and by it had learned to measure his strength; and he knew that he was strong. But what use was strength, if he had no gift, nothing to offer, still, to his lord but his service and his steady love?" (Le Guin, *Shore*, p. 139).

Nevertheless, Arren, the alter ego, has been valuable for his weakness as well as his strength, for it has served as a link to the shadow. As Ged points out to his young companion, the Lord of the Two Lands speaks "in your own voice" (Le Guin, *Shore*, p. 137). The traits of the shadow lie within us. To confront them we must approach our weakness: "You are my guide—the child I sent before me into the dark. It is your fear I follow" (Le Guin, *Shore*, p. 122). However, the guide for the next stage of the journey is the dragon Orm Embar, the traditional animal messenger. In "The Phenomenology of the Spirit in Fairy Tales," Jung identifies the animal as one form of the Spirit archetype, which also appears as the Wise Old Man. As such it shares "on the one hand in the daemonically superhuman and on the other in the bestially subhuman."[7] Both aspects exist in the dragons of Earthsea, which are treacherous and greedy yet possessed of an age-old wisdom and power. In "The Child and the Shadow," Le Guin observes, "It is the animal within us, the primitive, the dark brother, the shadow soul, who is the guide" (Le Guin, "Child," p. 67), and Ged and Arren rejoice that he has come: "This time we will not go astray, I think" (Le Guin, *Shore*, p. 132). Orm Embar does indeed lead them to their quarry and in his role as the animal helper intervenes to save Ged, albeit at the cost of his own life. He is not the first animal to save Ged's life: when he lies spirit-lost in *A Wizard of Earthsea*, Ged is recalled to consciousness by his little otak acting with instinctive wisdom. The otak, too, is slain by the shadow, for though guides may assist along the way, the final confrontation must take place between ego and shadow alone, as Le Guin reminds us in "The Child and the Shadow": "When you have followed animal instincts far enough, then they must be sacrificed so that the true self, the whole person, may step forth from the body of the animal, reborn" (Le Guin, "Child," p. 57).

Orm Embar's sacrifice defeats the shadow power that guards the entrance to the kingdom of the dead, and so Ged and Arren, ego and alter ego, venture down to the heart of this land for their final confrontation with the shadow. The links between all three are reinforced when they meet at the Dry River: "Arren thought, with a little dread but not much, 'We have come too far.' . . . Speaking his thought, Ged said, 'We have come too far to turn back.' . . . A voice in the darkness said, 'You have come too far.' " (Le Guin, *Shore*, p. 176). Arren's answer provides the clue to the final confrontation. Orm Embar has shown the way: to conquer the crippling shadow of selfishness one must be willing to make the ultimate sacrifice of one's own life. And this is what Ged does. To close the black hole that is sucking all the light out of the world, he expends all his power and vitality until there remains "no more light in Ged's yew staff, or in his face. . . . 'It is done,' he said. 'It is all gone' " (Le Guin, *Shore*, p. 185), words that echo those of Christ when he sacrificed himself on the Cross. At the black hole Arren proves himself by rejecting Cob's offer of immortality, and now, despite his own exhaustion, he helps the Archmage return to the world, even crawling "back to the dark" (Le Guin, *Shore*, p. 187) to drag his companion to safety with the last of his strength. This self-sacrifice reflects Ged's own. Nevertheless, Ged's return is more spiritual than real. The deed done, Ged slips out of sight, borne off by Kalessin, the oldest dragon, perhaps to attend Arren's coronation before sailing on a final journey westward over the sea, perhaps to wander in the solitude and silence of the forests of the mountain, where "He rules a greater kingdom" (Le Guin, *Shore*, p. 197).

Ged's death is necessary. In the first place, only by actually undergoing willingly the experience of death can the fear of it be finally overcome. Thus alone can the shadow's power be broken. Yet the shadow's power is both a part of Ged's wizardry and a vital ingredient in the essential tension between light and dark that creates the Balance. Consequently, when Ged releases Cob's anguished spirit into death, he himself must follow if the "Equilibrium of things" (Le Guin, *Shore*, p. 36) is to be preserved. When the Archmage seals the black hole with the words "Be thou made whole" (Le Guin, *Shore*, p. 184), he heals not only a divided and chaotic world but also his own fragmented personality. Ged and Cob must fade in order that Arren can be reborn as Lebannen, the young King of All the Isles. Cob remains among the shadows of the dead, but Ged must return to the surface, for he, like Erreth-Akbe, "is the earth and sunlight, the leaves of trees, the eagle's flight. He is alive. And all who ever died, live" (Le Guin, *Shore*, p. 180).

Yet the pattern of Ged and Arren as ego and alter ego confronting Cob and shadow is not the only one in the novel, and herein lies a structural problem. While Arren serves as Ged's alter ego, Ged's function in relation to Arren is that of the Wise Old Man, who, as Jung points out in "Phenomenology," "represents knowledge, reflection, insight, wisdom, cleverness, and intuition on the one hand, and on the other, moral qualities such as good will and readiness to help, which makes his 'spiritual' character sufficiently plain . . . what is more, he even tests the moral qualities of others and makes his gifts dependent on this test."[8] Arren's experiences in the first part of the book constitute just such a test of moral qualities, necessary before he can win the gift of self-knowledge which Ged possesses. Yet just as all archetypes have a positive side, they also have a negative side, such as that embodied in "the wicked magician who, from sheer egoism, does evil for evil's sake,"[9] and this role is assigned to Cob. To develop the personality, one must listen to the voice of wisdom (Ged's influence) but avoid being possessed by it to the point where one takes on delusions of grandeur (Cob's influence). As a result, it is necessary for Arren to accept Ged's guidance yet preserve and develop his own judgment if he is to achieve kingship. As in the story of King Arthur and Merlin, the sage must depart so that the hero can reach maturity. This pattern, too, requires Ged's death. From the point of view of structure, the problem is that Le Guin has not completely integrated the two patterns of Ged and Arren as ego and alter ego confronting Cob as Shadow on one hand, on the other of Arren as ego developing his personality under the combined guidance and threat of the positive and negative sides of the Wise Old Man or Spirit archetype (Ged and Cob). Yet it is essential for several important reasons that Le Guin initiate Arren's journey through life before Ged's draws to a close.

First, as Ged explains, "In life is death. In death is rebirth. What then is life without death?" (Le Guin, *Shore*, p. 136). To coin an image suggested by the title, as one wave breaks on the farthest shore and recedes, so another rises to take its place. This philosophical need to initiate the new cycle before the old one completes its turn requires a rising young hero coming into his powers, as well as an aging champion expending his in one last titanic struggle.

The struggle to the death that imposes the need for a new hero to replace the old one is demanded by developments within this novel and within the Earthsea trilogy as a whole. Each book moves progressively closer to the experience of death. In *A Wizard of Earthsea*, Ged's journey follows the pattern of the monomyth with its descent to the Otherworld, ending on the shores of death's kingdom; in *The Tombs of Atuan*, Ged and Tenar descend into the Tombs wherein lie the bones of the dead; in *The Farthest Shore*, Ged and Arren enter the actual realm of the dead. The deepening levels of the descent are necessitated by the widening awareness of the shadow's range: Ged must deal first with his own personal shadow, then the shadow of another individual, and finally the collective shadow of all mankind.

Moreover, there is another development within the trilogy as a whole that requires the second pattern with Ged as the Wise Old Man, and that is the progression toward a quaternity, identified by Jung as a symbol of wholeness. Jung writes, "The integration of the shadow . . . marks the first stage in the analytic process. . . . The recognition of anima or animus gives rise, in a way, to a triad, one-third of which is transcendent: the masculine subject, the opposing feminine subject, and the transcendent anima. With a woman the situation is reversed. The missing fourth element that would make the triad a quaternity is, in a man, the archetype of the Wise Old Man."[10] Integration of the shadow is accomplished in *A Wizard of Earthsea*; both the male and female triads appear in *The Tombs of Atuan* as Ged-Arha-Tenar and Arha/Tenar-The Nameless Ones-Ged; Ged functions as the Wise Old Man in relation to Arren in *The Farthest Shore*. This steady movement toward unity concludes with the crowning of a king to rule over all the isles.

This approach is not intended to deny that the characters serve other, non-Jungian functions. It would be surprising were a writer of Le Guin's ability to limit herself thus. Like Ahar/Tenar in *The Tombs of Atuan*, Arren provides the story with a point of view that is particularly valuable for younger readers. What I hope I have demonstrated, however, is how an appreciation of the Jungian patterns in Le Guin's work can help us understand the structural problems in *The Farthest Shore*. The concept of linking Arren and Ged as ego and alter ego in the struggle against the shadow is a fine one that promises to integrate Ged into the action, yet keep the focus on the young Arren, whose character is growing and developing toward maturity. Unfortunately, for the reasons outlined, Ged finally does need to depart. Such a hero deserves a fitting exit, and Le Guin certainly rises to the occasion. Just as in *Beowulf* the self-sacrifice of the aged hero-king overshadows the courage and loyalty of young Wiglaf, so inevitably

Ged's last great act of self-sacrifice overshadows the impressive achievement of Arren, who carries him out of death's kingdom to the farthest shore that lies beyond. As pointed out earlier, Le Guin is well aware of the effect caused by her imaginative involvement with Ged, who "took over completely in this book." However, despite its structural flaws, *The Farthest Shore* remains the author's favorite book, and few would choose to see Ged's heroic struggle against Cob and his magnificent flight home on Kalessin, the Eldest Dragon, in any way reduced in the interests of neater structure. The passing of the hero enriches as well as diminishes the world it leaves behind.

NOTES

1. Ursula K. Le Guin, "The Child and the Shadow," *The Language of the Night: Essays on Fantasy and Science Fiction*, ed. Susan Wood (New York: Putnam, 1979), p. 62; hereafter cited in the text.

2. See Eleanor Cameron, "High Fantasy: A Wizard of Earthsea," *Horn Book* 47 (1971), 129–38; Rollin A. Lasseter, "Four Letters about Le Guin," in *Ursula K. Le Guin: Voyager to Inner Lands and to Outer Space*, ed. Joe De Bolt (Port Washington, N.Y.: Kennikat, 1979), pp. 89–111; Margaret P. Esmonde, "The Master Pattern: The Psychological Journey in the Earthsea Trilogy," in *Ursula Le Guin*, eds. Joseph D. Olander, and Martin Harry Greenberg, Writers of the 21st Century Series (New York: Taplinger, 1979), pp. 15–35; Edgar C. Bailey, Jr., "Shadows in Earthsea: Le Guin's Use of a Jungian Archetype," *Extrapolation*, 21 (1980), 254–61.

3. Ursula K. Le Guin, "Dreams Must Explain Themselves," *The Language of the Night: Essays on Fantasy and Science Fiction*, ed. Susan Wood (New York: Putnam, 1979), p. 55.

4. Ursula K. Le Guin, *The Farthest Shore* (New York: Bantam Books, 1975), p. 179; hereafter cited in the text.

5. Carl Gustav Jung, *Aion, The Collected Works of C. G. Jung*, Vol. IX, Part 2, trans. R. F. C. Hull, Bollingen Series XX (New York: Bollingen, 1958), para. 16.

6. Ibid., para. 44.

7. Carl Gustav Jung, "The Phenomenology of the Spirit in Fairy Tales," *The Collected Works of C. G. Jung*, Vol. IX, Part 1, trans. R. F. C. Hull, Bollingen Series XX (New York: Bollingen, 1958), para. 419.

8. Ibid., paras. 406, 410.

9. Ibid., para. 415.

10. Jung, *Aion*, para. 42.

Monkeys, Changelings, and Asses: Audience, Fantasy, and Belief

Donald E. Morse

The recent California "monkey trial" raised issues reminiscent of the more famous Scopes trial in Tennessee earlier in this century. In both cases the plaintiffs were insulted not simply because the theory of evolution linked them to the primates through a common hypothesized ancestor, but also because the defense insisted on treating the story of the primordial parents dwelling in the Garden of Eden *as only a story*, as a myth, as—dare we suggest?—as a fantasy. So these people brought suit to have the schools teach what they profess to believe: that events happened literally as Genesis describes. Thus the Fall took place in an actual Garden locatable on a map at a specific time on a specific date. This audience had no need to suspend its disbelief since the story's events, characters, and setting were for them all literally true.[1]

Meanwhile in Saint Paul, Minnesota, every Saturday night, Garrison Keillor tells tales of Lake Wobegon, Minnesota, "the tiny town that time forgot, that the decades cannot improve; where all the women are strong and all the men are good looking and all the children are above average."[2] His stories evoke the quintessential American small town with its schools, churches, town meetings, and town characters. Most of us recognize ourselves from time to time in his gently satiric, amusing stories and gossip. The town's businesses "sponsor" the program along with National Public Radio, Cargill, the National Endowment for the Arts, and Powdermilk Biscuits. On a given Saturday night we might hear an ad for Bertha's Kitty Boutique, "Don't forget your cat at Christmas"; Ralph's Pretty Good Grocery, "If you can't find it at Ralph's, you can probably get along without it"; the Chatterbox Cafe, "Where the food is just like home"; and Jack's Auto Repair and Haberdashery, "All tracks lead to Jack's." (Jack also originated the famous Head Stop Program for the overeducated.) However, the most famous sponsor is the most famous product of Lake Wobegon: Powdermilk Biscuits that "come in the big blue box with the picture of the biscuit on the cover or in brown paper bags with the grease stains on the side that indicate freshness.'' They have the special virtue of ''helping shy persons get up and do what needs to be done.'' Powdermilk Biscuits, so the story goes, are made from whole wheat flour by Norwegian bachelor farmers—not because they are some kind of health nuts, but because some years ago a piece of equipment broke and they can't refine the flour as much as they might like. (These same bachelor farmers once earned a place in labor history by threatening to strike if their wages were not reduced since they felt they were overpaid.) The distribution of Powdermilk Biscuits is somewhat limited because Einer, who delivers them to grocery stores from the company's '53 Ford panel truck, refuses to stay away from Lake Wobegon overnight. Still, listeners write in occasionally complaining that their local supermarket does not stock them! (How Dean Swift must be smiling over that.)

Keillor uses the town, its businesses and citizens, to expose folly, to undermine pretension, to deflate pride, and to remind us of our human limitations. His stories are ''the art of being real in the unreal . . . and, as such, [are] a wonderful trick way of telling the truth by means of a lie.''[3] Audiences know that Lake Wobegon cannot be located on any map, yet they recognize its reality; not believing in it literally for there is no such place, they may believe in it imaginatively for there are such people.[4]

Between these two extremes of an audience's convinced belief in the literal truth of the fantastic, such as in Eden and the Fall, and an audience's willing belief in the imaginative truth of the fantastic, such as in Lake Wobegon, lies the spectrum of possible relationships between audience, belief, and fantasy. Quite often the same tale at various historical points may evoke different degrees or kinds of belief.[5] The folk belief in the fairy changeling, for example, is well documented in Ireland, Scotland, England, and Wales. One of Yeats's best, most evocative early poems, ''The Stolen Child,'' concludes by picturing the child's loss of the transient, fragile, domestic human world:

> Away with us he's going,
> The solemn-eyed:
> He'll hear no more the lowing
> Of the calves on the warm hillside
> Or the kettle on the hob
> Sing peace into his breast,
> Or see the brown mice bob
> Round and round the oatmeal-chest.
> *For he comes, the human child,*
> *To the waters and the wild*
> *With a faery, hand in hand,*
> *From a world more full of weeping than he can understand.*[6]

There is, however, a gap between the community that guards its newborn children against kidnapping by the fairy folk and the reader of modern poetry who may enjoy the quaintness of Yeats's subject. The community believes in changelings, not as a literary device but as a fact of life. Yet for both the outline of the story remains the same. Briefly, the fairies in need of a servant or a lover steal a newborn human child and substitute one of their own who is ancient, useless, and worn-out. The parents discover the exchange when they observe their baby's wizened appearance, hear its fretful crying, and experience its sudden, inexplicable, willful temper (all three almost certain to occur in a normal child). Such a substitution is more than a cruel jest: it is a tragedy for parents, relatives, and friends. In late nineteenth- and early twentieth-century Ireland when people thought such a substitution had occurred, one remedy was to put the child on a coal shovel and leave it outside the door all night while repeating certain magical charms in hope of inducing the fairies to return the original baby and take back their own. In some places the people believed so strongly in changelings and this remedy that children died of exposure while their parents waited helplessly indoors through the long, cold night. In M. J. Molloy's Irish folk play *Petticoat Loose*, a young mother, convinced by the witch Biddy Tosser that her baby is a changeling, follows this prescription leaving her child outside on a shovel. The local priest characterizes her act as godless, dangerous, and foolish, but so powerful is the hold of superstition over the community that people do not listen to him. Consequently, the witch's power waxes while his wanes.

In contrast to Molloy, who faithfully renders the powerful hold a folk belief or custom may have over a community, Sylvia Townsend Warner, ignoring the issue of power, uses this belief in changelings to create modern, literary tales as part of her collection, *The Kingdoms of Elfin*. All of Warner's stories assume our *un*willing suspension of disbelief in faerie folk. Her sophisticated tales ironically assume that the received folk tradition may be accounted for logically, empirically, and physically. Thus in "The One and the Other," the changeling is a changeling in all the ways previously described in folk tales, where a fairy is substituted for a human baby, as well as in some new ones. If when a human dwells with the fairies he will live far longer than the normal three score years and ten and if he will retain no memory of human life or relationships, then, reasons Warner's tale, he must have been physically changed in some very basic ways. Once he is inside the fairy fort, therefore, the operation is performed that removes all human blood:

Every day a fasting weasel bites the child's neck and drinks its blood for three mintues. The amount of blood drunk by each successive weasel (who is weighed before and after the drinking) is replaced by the same weight of a distillation of dew, soot, and aconite. Though the blood-to-ichor transfer does not cancel human nature (the distillation is only approximate: elfin blood contains several unanalyzable components, one of which is believed to be magnetic air), it gives considerable longevity; up to a hundred and fifty years is the usual span.[7]

The first parenthetical explanation lends a tongue-in-cheek "scientific" precision to this imprecise process as "each successive weasel . . . is weighed before and

after the drinking.'' The second parenthesis contains a pseudo-scientific explanation which helps account for the lack of complete success in modifying human
nature due to the impossibility of completely reproducing elfin blood. The implication remains that if there were better instruments, we might obtain a more
accurate analysis and be able to attempt a closer approximation of elfin blood.

The substituted fairy goes through a more disagreeable process: "Before an
elf-baby is sent into the human world its wings are extirpated and it is dosed
with an elixir of mortality, compounded from the tears and excrement of changelings. Neither process is wholly satisfactory.''[8] The detached observer's tone,
the coldly elevated "extirpated," the medically precise "dosed" and "compounded," but, above all, the carefully detailed explanations help account, in
part, for the comic success of the stories. Clearly Warner, unlike Molloy, does
not accept nor is she interested in the power folk belief may have over people's
lives. Rather she seizes upon the belief for its comic, literary potential. Through
her use of irony and satire she creates more distance between her subject and
its audience of *New Yorker* readers than Molloy did. For Molloy, the power that
the folk belief in changelings had over people individually and communally
created a warning paradigm valid for all audiences, including the urbane one in
Dublin's Abbey Theatre, where the play was first performed: to follow someone
blindly out of ignorance and fear, says the play, is to invite tragedy.

Apuleius's *The Golden Ass* uses the once-powerful gods as the subject of
witty satire as Warner uses fairies while using belief in metamorphosis to create
a warning paradigm similar to Molloy's. Although the gods were never tragic
but always "comic," as Rachel Bespaloff suggests in *On the Iliad*, they once
did embody those forces which people believed animated or controlled the natural
world and human action.[9] As such they had to be propitiated. Diana, goddess
of the moon, for instance, appeared as fiercely virginal and exacted a horrible
revenge on any male, such as the hapless Acteon, who accidentally or purposely
spied on her. Besides commenting on an aspect of male-female relationships,
this myth also suggests that powers operating in and through nature set limits
beyond which human beings pass at their peril. By the second century A.D. when
Apuleius wrote, Diana and the other mythological gods were no longer objects
of belief. (In *The Golden Ass* Diana and Acteon appear only in the background
as lifelike statues whose artistry and history warn Lucius against magic and
metamorphosis.) Other once-powerful goddesses such as Juno and Ceres are
reduced to gossipy, cranky women bored with themselves and bored with life.
In earlier epics and tragedies, rivalry between the gods or goddesses led to the
slaughter of hundreds and the destruction of cities and kingdoms. In Apuleius's
comic fantasy, the gods indulge in petty jealousies and trivial bickering. (Venus's
small-minded jealousy of Psyche is a good example.) Any residual powers they
may have are derived from and are ultimately attributable to Isis, the one true
goddess. She alone is treated reverently and respectfully; she alone has the power
to transform people into something more than mere mortals.[10]

Beginning as a shortsighted, stupid, brash, unthinking, impetuous, unlucky, curious man—in other words, as a true two-legged ass—Lucius, the novel's hero, is transformed into a four-legged ass. After extensive adventures which help him to recognize the folly of his life, Isis intervenes to change him physically back into a human being and spiritually into her priest. Having tasted the gall of this world while "in ass disguise," he repents and leads a new life: "I am grateful now whenever I recall those days: my many adventures in ass-disguise enormously enlarged my experience, even if they have not taught me wisdom."[11] When transformed, he does not return to his former unthinking self but becomes a new person with patience, fortitude, and humility; by Isis's grace, he is in a sense born again and restored to a new and healthy life. Which is more fantastic: Lucius, the curious fool transformed into an ass, or Lucius, the unabashed hedonist transformed into a holy man? (The first physical transformation is the means by which the second physical and spiritual transformation takes place.)

Through comic metamorphosis Apuleius captures his audience's interest in the story and sustains it with satiric social criticism and amusing incidents until he is able to present his religious belief. Since most of us enjoy hearing about the sins of the sinners but may yawn over the holy deeds of the repentant, Apuleius does not indulge himself or tire his audience with many details about Lucius as priest and holy man. Yet his point is clearly made that everything in life happens for the best, if guided by all-powerful Isis, who controls human destiny. Small wonder the Greek pantheon, once dominant and powerful, appears reduced in the novel to a literary convention which becomes an object of ridicule and satire.

Thus Apuleius in *The Golden Ass* uses the fantastic convention of metamorphosis to reveal what he believes is the transcendent truth about human life. Here, too, is a "wonderful trick way of telling the truth by means of a lie"— or at least by means of a literary convention. Like Garrison Keillor, Apuleius invents a fantasy to point to a universal truth about human beings; like M. J. Molloy he offers a fantastic paradigm as warning against human incredulity and greed; and like Sylvia Townsend Warner he uses fantasy, satire, and wit to amuse and win over his audience; and somewhat like the "monkey trial" plaintiffs, he uses "fantasy" to proselytize his audience for the cult in which he believes. Unlike the latter, however, he does not require his audience to believe literally in the physical reality, but only in the spiritual reality of Lucius's transformation. At the beginning of the book, we must suspend our disbelief in metamorphosis for the sake of a good story; in the middle we discover a scathing satire of incredulity and greed; while at the end we are asked to believe imaginatively in the reality of all-powerful Isis.

So here in one book we find illustrated the variety of relationships between audience, belief, and fantasy. Only a literal reading fails with Apuleius, but then he warned us in his "Address to the Reader" that it would.[12] As the famous Old Testament scholar, James Muilenburg once remarked, "If something is only literally true, it is insignificant." Great fantasy leads us beyond the literal and into another world intimately related to this one where we may discover asses who are men in disguise and vice versa, changelings from the Kingdom of Elfin, and biscuits whose magical properties "help shy persons get up and do what needs to be done."

NOTES

1. A similar controversy has arisen over the teaching of the theory of evolution and Creationists' insistence that the "theory [sic] of creation be given equal time" in school curricula. Their position is weak, if not untenable, since there is no "theory" of creation in the commonly accepted sense of a hypothesis to be tested by weighing evidence. Instead, the Creationists offer only a thesis to be believed with no evidence to be examined beyond the sacred text, which cannot be tested.

2. Garrison Keillor, *A Prairie Home Companion*, National Public Radio, Saturday nights, 6:00–8:00. All quotations are taken from 1980–1981 broadcasts.

3. Jean Giraudoux, *Impromptu de Paris*, quoted in John K. Savacool, "Something Else in the Theatre," *Comment* (Williams College literary magazine, n.d.), p. 41.

4. Keillor's explanation for our failure to find Lake Wobegon on current maps of Minnesota goes back to the nineteenth-century surveys of the state. After the various survey teams finished mapping Minnesota, they tried piecing together their sectional maps only to discover that they had too much. The map spilled over into Wisconsin and the Dakotas! Facing up to their dilemma, they solved it by putting a tiny fold in the center of the map, thus bringing the borders into conformity with the other states. Lake Wobegon lies squarely in the center of the fold and therefore does not appear on any twentieth-century map of the state.

5. The story of the Fall, for example, has at various times been read as history, as fiction, as symbol, as prophecy, and as myth.

6. William Butler Yeats, *The Collected Poems* (New York: Macmillan, 1956), p. 19.

7. Sylvia Townsend Warner, *The Kingdoms of Elfin* (New York: Dell Books, 1978), pp. 1–2.

8. Ibid., p. 5.

9. Rachel Bespaloff, *On the Iliad*, trans. Mary McCarthy (New York: Pantheon Books, 1947). See especially "The Comedy of the Gods," pp. 73–79.

10. "Under my protection you will be happy and famous, and when at the destined end of your life you descend to the land of ghosts, there too in the subterrene hemisphere you shall have frequent occasion to adore me. From the Elysian fields you will see me as queen of the profound Stygian realm, shining through the darkness of Acheron with a light as kindly and tender as I show you now. Further, if you are found to deserve my divine protection by careful obedience to the ordinances of my religion and by perfect chastity, you will become aware that I, and I alone, have power to prolong your life beyond the limits appointed by destiny." *The Golden Ass of Apuleius*, trans. Robert Graves (New York: Noonday, 1951), p. 266.

11. Ibid., p. 203.

12. "If you are not put off by the Egyptian story-telling convention which allows humans to be changed into animals and, after various adventures, restored to their proper shapes, you should be amused by this queer novel" (Ibid., p. vii). Clearly Apuleius counts on our willing suspension of disbelief.

Environmental Concerns in Arthur C. Clarke's *The City and the Stars*

Thomas P. Dunn and Richard D. Erlich

What if we could live inside a big machine? A kind of womb-world which would provide all our needs from cradle to grave so that finally we would need neither cradle *nor* grave, no checking account, taco stand, or septic tank? No cars, bars, wars, famine, pestilence—perhaps no death as well? What if? What then!

The dream (or nightmare) of the self-contained, sulf-sufficient mechanized environment has a tradition as venerable in SF as that of the robot, dating as far back as the late 1800s. In his recent book, *The Known and the Unknown*, Gary K. Wolfe includes a literary history of the genesis of the world machine, parsing the threads of its development in Wells, Forster, and Lang.[1] The most vivid image born of these and more recent artists remains Forster's hellish underground "Machine," a single, all-embracing servo-mechanism strangling its inhabitants by filling their every need.[2]

Since these seminal works appeared, similar visions have steadily appeared in novel and film, including the underground society of Ben Bova's *THX–1138*, the high-rise ambiguous dystopia of Robert Silverberg's *The World Inside*, the nightmarish "Sector" of William Hjortsberg's *Gray Matters*, the split-level United States of Paul Fairman's *I, The Machine*, and the porno-cubicles of "Chase World-TT" in Marge Piercy's *Woman on the Edge of Time*.[3] It is obvious from this list, by no means exhaustive, that the icon of the machine environment has fascinated people in countries where SF is widely read.[4]

These mechanical environments, moreover, are consistently—and not surprisingly—dystopian, their inhabitants suffering one or more losses to the substance of their humanity.[5] Without physical activity, the residents of Forster's machine world atrophy and come to resemble slugs, not people. Without a need to learn the past, the people supported by Fairman's Machine come in time to lose all knowledge of the past, even knowledge of the technology that built the Machine in the first place. The slaves in Bova's underground and in Piercy's

Chase World-TT live a grim Orwellian existence as the trade-off for the security provided by their mechanized habitats. The ''cerebromorphs'' of Hjortsberg's ''Sector'' and the people of Silverberg's Urbmon 116 have lost all purpose and direction beyond ''climbing'' in their machine bureaucracies, their *literal* human filing cabinets.

The womb-machine world, then, serves as the testing ground for an important and extensive set of thought experiments exploring the definition of the word ''human.''[6]

Against this backdrop of confinement and decay, the total environment of Diaspar in Arthur C. Clarke's *The City and the Stars* appears at first blush to be perfection, a welcome relief from the unrelieved horror of the rest of the subgenre.[7] It is an image, secularized, of nothing less than the New Jerusalem:

And I saw a new heaven and a new earth: for the first heaven and the first earth were passed away; and there was no more sea.

And I, John, saw the holy city, new Jerusalem, coming down from God out of heaven, prepared as a bride adorned for her husband.

And I heard a great voice out of heaven saying, Behold, the tabernacle of God *is* with men, and he will dwell with them, and they shall be his people, and God himself shall be with them, *and be* their God.

And God shall wipe away all tears from their eyes, and there shall be no more death, neither sorrow, nor crying, neither shall there be any more pain: for the former things are passed away.

And he carried me away in the spirit to a great and high mountain, and shewed me that great city, the holy Jerusalem, descending out of heaven from God.

Having the glory of God: and her light *was* like unto a stone most precious, even like a jasper stone, clear as crystal;

And had a wall great and high *and* had twelve gates, and at the gates twelve angels, and names written thereon, which are *the names* of the twelve tribes of the children of Israel:

And he shewed me a pure river of water of life, clear as crystal, proceeding out of the throne of God and of the Lamb.

(Rev. 21:1–4, 10–12; 22:1)

That quotation is from the vision of the apocalypse in the Revelation of John, and it is clear that new Jerusalem has much to be said for it as an environment. There is no sea, but that is appropriate for so *orderly* a city-world: the sea is a symbol for Chaos and the Great Mother and for the dissolution of forms, and so the sea does not belong in the ultimate, masculine cosmos of the holy city. Similarly, there is no place for darkness and Old Night in the realm of the God of Light. These are minor problems, though, more than made up for by the advantages of living in a city with no pain, no mourning, no death; a perfectly square city, built of jasper and gold, with a light ''like unto a stone most precious'' and twelve glorious gates, always open (Rev. 21:11, 18, 21, 25). Plus, of course, the eternal presence of God and the Lamb for the residents to contemplate.

However, what if we, perhaps, change the square to a circle? What if we banish God and the Lamb and shut the gates? Would the eternal city still be a good place for human habitation?

In *The City and the Stars*, Clarke asks us to consider such questions. Indeed, he insists that we compare his city to the new Jerusalem. The opening sentence of the novel tells us that his city is "like a glowing jewel." Immediately thereafter, we learn that the city challenges eternity—literally—in a world on which "the oceans . . . had passed away." An unchanging city of constant daylight, Diaspar—named, perhaps, for the mineral diaspore, with, again perhaps, an ironic allusion to "diaspora" (p. 7). Later we learn that the city has a river circling inside it and, unknown to the inhabitants, twelve main tunnels leading into it (p. 61). Most important, it is a city without birth and without death, without disease, without "mourning and crying and pain."

No God, though, in Diaspar and no Lamb—or nonhuman animals of any sort. Diaspar is the work of human beings, begun some one hundred million years into our future and lasting essentially unchanged for one *billion* years. If such a city seems magical to us, we need only note Clarke's Third Law: "Any sufficiently advanced technology is indistinguishable from magic"—and humankind has had quite enough time to get its technology "sufficiently advanced."[8] In the world of *City*, we humans—our distant descendants and the ancestors of the novel's characters—have subdued the earth and established dominion over it and (for a long while) over all of nature in our section of the galaxy (see Gen. 1:28–31, P-Code). Again, though, would Clarke's city be a good environment for humans?

If you are a literary critic or a science fiction fan, you will tell us "No." From a literary point of view, there had to be a wily serpent somewhere in Eden to get the plot going, and there must be some problems in Diaspar. From a more specifically science fictional point of view, there is clearly a problem in Diaspar: stasis.

What bothers Clarke about the city is not the courageous blasphemy of building new Jerusalem on our own. There was nothing courageous about our building Diaspar; on the contrary, building the eternal city was an act of cowardice: the final act of Man's retreat from the stars, our sealing ourselves off in a comfortable, but futile, womb-world (pp. 26, 35–36). There was also nothing blasphemous in the act. Blasphemy requires religion, if not a god, and Clarke explicitly banishes organized religion and religious fanaticism to the distant past (see especially pp. 46, 99–102). If there was something blasphemous in the building of Diaspar, it was building the city instead of joining the migration of the rest of the old Galactic Empire in quest of the mystery, "something—very strange and very great . . . at the other end of space itself" (p. 181). The God of Revelation is not to be found in Diaspar because he is not to be found in Clarke's universe; gods there may be, as we know from Clarke's *Childhood's End* and *2001*, but not that one. Diaspar does get a Lamb, though, of sorts: Vanamonde, the child-like, pure mentality that at the end of days will fight it out with the Mad Mind released by the death of the Black Sun (pp. 190–91).[9]

No, it's not theological blasphemy that bothers Clarke, nor even the ecological heresy, so to speak, of trying to control Nature. What bothers Clarke about Diaspar does have a religious character, however, as well as profound "ecological" significance: Diaspar is unbalanced. In Western terms, the city is in the tradition of the P-Code version of creation in Genesis, without the balancing version of the J-Code. That is, Diaspar is built by men who are bent upon the domination and subjugation of the Earth (Gen. 1:28–30) and who have forgotten that they were created from the dust of the Earth and were put into a Garden "to dress it and to keep it" (Gen. 2:7–9, 15). In Eastern terms, Diaspar is all Yang and no Yin: for all the sexual equality the Narrator tells us about, Clarke shows us a male-dominated culture in Diaspar, an overly mechanized culture, with "an excess of light" (to use Ursula K. Le Guin's phrase from *The Left Hand of Darkness*). Diaspar's "sin" is not the banishment of God but the victory over the natural cycle of birth and death (see p. 188). Its "sin" is the billion-year suspension of effective action and significant free will—even significant consciousness—through an excess of control and planning. Pushed to extremes, opposites conjoin, and it is both esthetically decorous (a familiar irony) and psychologically appropriate that the ultimately "Yangish" city should become the ultimate threat of the feminine principle of Yin: the Great Mother in her most dangerous incarnation—the Terrible Mother disguised as the Nurturing Mother, the tender trap of an eternal womb.

Diaspar needs balance. Its Yang needs a Yin: the City must be balanced by the Garden, and, since Clarke wanted something of a comedy in *City*, not a somber dystopia, Diaspar gets what it needs. Clarke's little prologue to *City* turns out to have been a bit misleading when it told us that there were no more mountains on Earth and implied that all that remained on Earth were Diaspar and desert. There are still some mountains on Earth and even a river and woods, and among them is Lys, a little Garden-world of villages.

The people of Lys accept the cycle of life and death and have retained biological childbirth, with its necessary corollaries of aging and death. They grow much of their own food, although they know how to synthesize it. They have domestic animals and even pets, and they use only appropriate technology. They have retained and perfected mental telepathy, and the ruler that we see in Lys—although "ruler" is too strong a word—is a woman. Uniting Lys and Diaspar is the first and most crucial achievement of the hero of *City*, the Unique, Alvin.[10]

Alvin's job is the standard one for culture heroes and heroes in general: bringing change. Like most heroes, he does this by going through barriers and, as Gary K. Wolfe notes, penetrating those barriers with the immediate goal of making the unknown known.[11] Like a good comic hero, Alvin furthers the integration of human society by bringing together two different cultures of humankind. A new and better world coalesces around Alvin by the end of *City*, but Clarke (somewhat surprisingly) does not push this novel into full romantic comedy and refuses at the end to marry off his hero. Instead, Clarke sticks to a kind of sober Romance, and he leaves Alvin a bit older and much wiser at the end of the novel but still somewhat unfulfilled.

There is a kind of organic decorum in Clarke's decision because he insists on Alvin's being not only a youth of twenty but also a child. Jeserac, Alvin's tutor, tells him that as a Unique he is "the first child to be born on earth"—at least in Diaspar, as we later learn—"for at least ten million years" (p. 17). The omniscient narrator tells us that Jeserac's opinion of Alvin becomes even more emphatic on this point: Alvin, to Jeserac, is an eternal boy who will "never grow up," a child who sees the universe as an intriguing and entertaining toy (p. 134). In two ways, Jeserac is entirely correct. By the standards of Diaspar— where a person lives some thousand years in each of his bodies—of course, Alvin at twenty is still a child. More importantly, Alvin is undoubtedly a manifestation of the archetypal Child, the symbol of rebirth, of Change, of hope for the future; but Jeserac is also profoundly wrong. In remaining in the womb-world of Diaspar and the garden-world of Lys, it is the people of the Earth who are childish. In this regard, it is the forever incomplete explorer in Alvin who is the adult, opening the universe again for his fellow humans and leading them, as if they were children, into a larger world (pp. 174–75; see also pp. 130–31).

This is a paradox Clarke insists on. Explicitly compared with Homer's Odysseus (p. 110) and, perhaps, implicitly compared with Tennyson's Ulysses (p. 144), Alvin spends most of the novel looking like not only the Child but the Eternal Boy, the inveterate quester. This aspect of Alvin is necessary, for Alvin must go to the stars.

Even balanced together, Clarke holds, the City and the Garden are not sufficient environments for adult human beings; we need also the stars. We need to leave our playpen, leave Mother Earth, and make our world the galaxy—and beyond— if we are to fulfill our destiny of full, adult humanity. Alvin returns the stars to the people of Earth. More important, however, in his quest for the stars, he discovers the key to the true past of Earth—and the key to his own nature and destiny. Or the key discovers him, since the "key" is Vanamonde, the pure mentality, who seeks out Alvin's rocketship as part of Vanamonde's own quest for his origins.

Having fulfilled these heroic functions, Alvin does something that seems at first out of character: at the end of the novel he takes, with Hilvar and Jeserac, one last trip in his rocket and then sends it off on its own, under the control of a wondrous robot, to seek out the people of the old Galactic Empire on *their* quest for that "something" at the other end of space. Alvin henceforth will stay on Earth, at home. "True journey is return," as Ursula K. Le Guin puts it; or "There's no place like home," as Dorothy says in *The Wizard of Oz*. Like Homer's Odysseus, but without a Penelope, Alvin returns to stay.

Why, though? Aside from its completing a traditional pattern, why have Alvin settle down? In the recent *Star Trek* movie, Admiral Kirk ends his adventure with *V'ger* only to order his helmsman to take the *Enterprise* "thataway"—

somewhere out there in space. What works for Kirk would have worked for Alvin. Why multiply character reversals and have Alvin stay on Earth?

We have two suggestions. One has to do with the environmental theme in *City*, and the other, in good quest fashion, will return us to our opening quotation from Revelation.

In his longest journey, the trip with Hilvar to the Seven Suns, Alvin recapitulates an important motif in *City*: that of boundaries and frontiers (often with barriers) versus center, hearts. Alvin's trip to the Seven Suns is a trip to the frontier, as far from Earth as he goes in the novel. However, it is also a trip to a center, the heart of the galaxy and of the old Galactic Empire. There he finds *"the planets of eternal light"* (p. 150) and the greatest achievement of the science, art, and technology of the Galactic Empire: a whole sun-system, with planets, created by intelligence. He also finds a planet with no sea, "as dry as Earth" (p. 150), a totally sterile planet of huge buildings. His next stop is a planet that must have started out as some sort of super-park but has degenerated into a jungle: "an unweeded garden / That grows to seed. Things rank and gross in nature / Possess it merely" (*Hamlet*, I.ii.135–37).

Both frontiers and centers are places where heroes learn things, and there is a lesson for Alvin at the Seven Suns. *This*, Clarke seems to say, is what would become of Diaspar and Lys without conscious intervention by intelligence. Alvin always has been intelligent, and as a hero he has had his consciousness raised; he now has some dues to pay, and his duty demands that he remain on Earth. Fortunately for him, Alvin is the hero of an upbeat novel, so his duty also goes along with one of his major desires since he had visited Lys: to combine "love and desire" in fertile sexual union and father a child (p. 188).

There is much else for Alvin to do on Earth if he is to fulfill the traditional duties of the Hero and free the waters and bring fertility to his world. Alvin believes "that Diaspar must escape from the prison of the Memory Banks"— the mechanism of immortality—"and restore again the cycle of life and death" (p. 188), and Hilvar assures him that this can be done. Moreover, Jeserac has come to hope "that Alvin was right in dreaming that all this"—their world— "could be changed. The power and the knowledge still existed—it needed only the will to turn back the centuries and make the oceans roll again. The water was still there, deep down in the hidden places of the Earth; or if necessary, transmutation plants could be built to make it" (p. 189).

In *City*, Man has created the new Jerusalem, "and there was no longer any sea." What Man can do, though, Clarke says, he can undo. He can unmake Diaspar and return to Earth the oceans—the great symbol of change and renewal. He can restore the balance.

In the last two paragraphs of the novel proper, before an italicized comment by the Narrator, Alvin and his friends are up in his rocketship, above the Earth, standing "between two ages" (p. 189). They look down on the Pole of the rotating Earth and "see at one instant both sunrise and sunset on opposite sides of the world. The symbolism was so perfect, and so striking, that they were to remember this moment all of their lives'' (p. 191).

Sunrise, sunset; light and dark; Earth and the stars; life and death; Diaspar and Lys; the City and the Garden—the balance has been restored, and there is hope that Earth will become an environment fit for adult human habitation.

NOTES

1. Gary K. Wolfe, *The Known and the Unknown: The Iconography of Science Fiction* (Kent: Kent State University Press, 1979) Chapter 4, "The Icon of the City," pp. 94–105; see as well the analysis of H. G. Wells's influence on E. M. Forster by Mark Hillegas in *The Future as Nightmare: H. G. Wells and the Anti-Utopians* (New York: Oxford University Press, 1967). See also Eric S. Rabkin, *Arthur C. Clarke*, Starmont Reader's Guide series, No. 1 (West Linn, Ore.: Starmont House, 1979).

2. E. M. Forster, "The Machine Stops," written in 1909, is available in numerous reprints, including *The Science Fiction Hall of Fame*, ed. Ben Bova (New York: Avon, 1974), IIA, 248–79.

3. Ben Bova, *THX–1138* (New York: Paperback Library, 1971), based on the film by George Lucas; Robert Silverberg, *The World Inside* (Garden City, N.Y.: Doubleday, 1971); William Hjortsberg, *Gray Matters* (New York: Simon & Schuster, 1971); Paul Fairman, *I, The Machine* (New York: Lodestone, 1968); and Marge Piercy, *Woman on the Edge of Time* (New York: Fawcett, 1976). We have edited a volume of essays on the subject of world machines, entitled *Clockwork Worlds: Mechanized Environments in SF* (Westport, Conn.: Greenwood Press, 1983). This volume includes an extensive bibliography of the subject.

4. It is interesting to note that there is even a children's literature version of Forster's "The Machine Stops." We are indebted to Margaret P. Esmonde of Villanova University for bringing to our attention Suzanne Martel's *The City Underground*, illus. Don Sibley, trans. Norah Smaridge (New York: Viking, 1964). The building of Arcosanti by dreamer-architect Paolo Soleri gives the study of such SF environments as Diaspar a profound relevance outside literary criticism per se by providing a "real world" parallel for fictional city-worlds. We may expect, it is clear, a fruitful dialogue between science fiction readers and those engaged in building the real future; such a dialogue already exists with respect to robots (Isaac Asimov and General Motors), nuclear power (*The China Syndrome* and Three-Mile Island), and space exploration (the *Enterprise* and the *Columbia*). Far more important than the question of whether science fiction is entering the mainstream is the fact that SF is rapidly establishing itself as the record of dreams and hallucinations which technological man has had and *will need* as he rides Alvin Toffler's roller coaster of change.

Since this essay was written, Larry Niven and Jerry Pournelle have published *Oath of Fealty* (New York: Simon & Schuster, 1981), a novel featuring "The Arcology of Todos santos," a fictional extrapolation of Soleri's arcosanti. The dialogue we expected is going on and, as a dialogue must, is going in both directions. Niven and Pournelle's novel also points at a real-world phenomenon frequently dealt with in dystopian fiction: the bureaucratization of modern life.

The closed, mechanical world has obvious affinities with both the spaceship and the computer tyranny, as Gary K. Wolfe points out in *The Known and the Unknown* (see note 1 above), p. 109, and especially with the "generation ship" elaborating on both. Here the classic SF story on this theme is Robert Heinlein's "Universe" (*Astrology*, May 1941; reprint ed. New York: Dell Books, 1951), while a recent variation which develops as well the brain-computer-master is Kevin O'Donnell, Jr.'s, *Mayflies* (New York: Berkley, 1979). One such generation ship—actually a cluster of ships containing the remnant of humankind and bearing notable similarity to Diaspar in its beauty, variety, and permanence—is found in Norman Spinrad's novella *Riding the Torch* in *Threads of Time*, ed. Robert Silverberg (New York: Thomas Nelson, 1974).

5. In the last decade, studies of machine environments in SF have begun to appear in journals and books. In addition to those mentioned in note 1 above, we wish to mention two: Ed Gallagher, "From Folded Hands to Clenched Fists: Kesey and Science Fiction," in *Perspectives on a Cuckoo's Nest: A Special Symposium Issue on Ken Kesey, Lex et Scientia* 13, Nos. 1–2 (January, June 1977), 46–50, wherein he argues that the world view of Kesey's novel is "the world machine, the cybernetic model, a world whose total service homogenizes humanity," and discusses that world view as it appears in over a dozen SF works; and Carolyn Rhodes, "Tyranny by Computer: Automated Data Processing and Oppressive Government in Science Fiction," in *Many Futures, Many Worlds*, ed. Thomas D. Clareson (Kent: Kent State University Press, 1977), pp. 66–93. Rhodes's essay is a comprehensive study of computer tyrannies with especially good treatment of Kurt Vonnegut's *Player Piano* and Kendall Foster Crossen's *Year of Consent*. Our studies of machine environments include Richard D. Erlich, "Trapped in the Bureaucratic Pinball Machine: A Vision of Dystopia in the 20th Century," in *Selected Proceedings of the SFRA 1978 Convention*, ed. Thomas J. Remington (Cedar Falls: University of North Iowa Press, 1979), pp. 30–44; and Thomas P. Dunn, "E. M. Forster's 'The Machine Stops,' " in *Survey of Science Fiction*, ed. Frank W. Magill (Englewood Cliffs, N.J.: Salem Press, 1979); and Thomas P. Dunn and Richard D. Erlich, "The Mechanical Hive: Urbmon 116 as the Villain-Hero of Silverberg's *The World Inside*," in *Extrapolation* 21 (Winter 1980), 338–47. See also John Huntington, "From Man to Overmind: Arthur C. Clarke's Myth of Progress," in *Arthur C. Clarke*, eds. Joseph D. Olander and Martin H. Greenberg (New York: Taplinger, 1977), especially pp. 213–16 and 218.

6. In *The Known and the Unknown* (see note 1 above), Gary K. Wolfe points out that cities like Forster's Machine and Clarke's Diaspar are "at once tombs of a dying technological culture and potential wombs that preserve the race for its eventual rebirth into the universe" (p. 109).

7. Arthur C. Clarke, *The City and the Stars* (New York: New American Library, 1957); hereafter cited in the text. The novel is for Clarke the very antithesis of casual hackwork. Rather it distills and amplifies material in his very first novel, *Against the Fall of Night* (begun in 1937 and "after four or five drafts" completed in 1946 and published in 1953). *City*, Clarke tells us, gives his readers his "last word on the immortal city of Diaspar" (preface to *City*, p. 5). It seems that, as scholars, we may look to *City* with the confidence that it contains ideas and images carefully considered by one of the greatest dreamer-poets in the field.

8. Arthur C. Clarke, "Technology and the Future," reprinted as ch. 14 of *Report from Planet Three* (New York: New American Library, 1972), p. 130.

9. If the rather stupid Vanamonde seems odd as a Lamb figure, it is because we have forgotten the nature of sheep. Erasmus's *Folly* reminds us that "Such as are destined to eternal life are called sheep, than which creature there is nothing more foolish. . . . And

yet Christ professes to be the shepherd of this flock and is himself delighted with the name of a lamb; according to Saint John, 'Behold the Lamb of God!' Of which there is much mention in the Revelation. And what does all this drive at, but that all mankind are fools—nay, even the very best?'' Desiderius Erasmus, *The Praise of Folly*, trans. John Wilson (1668; reprint ed., Ann Arbor: University of Michigan Press, 1958), p. 139.

10. In *The Cybernetic Imagination in Science Fiction* (Cambridge: MIT Press, 1980), Patricia Warrick notes correctly that the conflict mode of plot is a constant in those SF societies controlled by a computer. See ch. 6, ''The Closed System Model,'' pp. 130–60, especially p. 144. It is noteworthy that Clarke transcends this simple formula in *City*: instead of simply smashing the ''machine'' (or Diaspar), Alvin goes through a series of discoveries, building ''more stately mansions'' for his soul and for the souls of his people.

11. Wolfe, *The Known and the Unknown* (see note 1 above), p. 110.

Science, Science Fiction, and Possible World Semantics

George F. Sefler

> I see a picture; it represents an old man walking up a steep path leaning
> on a stick. —How? Might it not have looked just the same if he had been
> sliding downhill in the position? Perhaps a Martian would describe the
> picture so.
>
> Ludwig Wittgenstein, *Philosophical Investigations*[1]

The Martian civilization was long dead. All that remained was the rubble from
prefabricated huts and sheds. The last Martian died 500 centuries ago; a whole
race died leaving no clue to understanding its civilization. There must be something, somewhere, to give a hint of their culture.

This is the science fiction setting for H. Beam Piper's "Omnilingual." The
story describes the plight of Dr. Martha Dane, a member of an archaelogical
team sent to Mars to explore a lost civilization. In an attempt to decipher the
extinct Martian language, she examined among other things pictures and captions, restored pages of books, and inscriptions. Nothing really provided a break-
through in translation until the archaeological team discovered what seemed to
have been a university. Within no time Dr. Dane was able to read the Martian
science books. In disbelief one of her colleagues queried, "But how can you
be so sure that those words really mean things like hydrogen and helium and
boron and oxygen? How do you know that their table of elements was anything
like ours?"[2]

In amazement others responded: "That isn't just the Martian table of elements.
It's the only one there is. . . . Look, hydrogen has one proton and one electron.
If it had more of either, it wouldn't be hydrogen, it'd be something else. And
the same with all the rest of the elements. And hydrogen on Mars is the same
as hydrogen on Terra, or on Alpha Centauri, or in the next galaxy."[3] "Physical
science expresses universal facts, necessarily it is a universal language."[4]

Although this conclusion is reached in a work of science fiction, it is not unheard-of among certain contemporary philosophers. This notion of the universality of science is, in fact, highly characteristic of the work of both Hilary Putnam and Saul Kripke. From Kripke's perspective, Piper's science fiction work is simply portraying the elements of the periodic table as rigid designators; these elements are transterrestrial, and in all possible worlds, including the Martian, they refer to the same objects. It is questionable whether in Kripke's mind Piper's Martians in fact present us with a possible world different from our actual terrestrial existence. What is clear is that, like Piper, Kripke views the elements of science as designating rigidly:

We identify water originally by its characteristic feel, appearance, and perhaps taste. . . . If there were a substance, even actually, which had a completely different atomic structure from that of water, but resembles water in these respects, would we say that water wasn't H_2O? I think not. We would say instead that just as there is a fool's gold, there could be a fool's water.[5]

Hilary Putnam takes a similar position. Using the framework of science fiction and possible worlds, Putnam develops the notion of "Twin Earth." Here everything is fairly much like our earth. "In fact," Putnam states, "apart from the differences we shall specify in our science fiction examples, the reader may suppose that Twin Earth is *exactly* like Earth. He may even suppose that he has a *Doppelgänger*—an identical copy on Twin Earth."[6] One difference on Twin Earth, however, is that the liquid called "water" is not H_2O but a different liquid, which Putnam designates XYZ. It is undistinguishable from water under normal conditions. Lakes and oceans on Twin Earth contain XYZ, not H_2O, and precipitation on Twin Earth is XYZ, not H_2O.[7] Is water the same on Twin Earth as on our planet? Putnam says no:

Note that there is no problem about the extension of the term "water": the word simply has two different meanings (as we say); in the sense in which it is used on Twin Earth, the sense of water$_{TE}$, what *we* call "water" simply isn't water, while in the sense in which it is used on Earth, the sense of water$_E$, what the Twin Earthians call "water" simply isn't water. The extension of "water" in the sense of water$_E$ is the set of all wholes consisting of H_2O molecules or something like that; the extension of water in the sense of water$_{TE}$ is the set of all wholes consisting of XYZ molecules, or something like that.[8]

Putnam develops his position even more forcefully. He maintains that even prior to present-day development of atomic theory, the two kinds of things were not equal: "the extension of the term 'water' was just as much H_2O on Earth in 1750 as in 1950; and the extension of the term 'water' was just as much XYZ on Twin Earth in 1750 as in 1950."[9] Putnam's views are quite similar to Kripke's. Both look on the language of science as rigidly designating at both the atomic and the compound levels. As Putnam states, "If we extend this notion of rigidity to substance names, then we may express Kripke's theory and mine by saying that the term 'water' is rigid.''[10]

It is this sense of scientific rigidity that I wish to discuss and ultimately to question. The philosophical presupposition here is that scientific language about the world must mean the same in all possible worlds. This is predicated on the assumption that the world, the cosmos, is intelligible in itself, independent of any language. Consequently, scientific language and also empirical language are purely passive; they mirror the articulated character inherent in things. Scientific language reflects the structures already present in things. Facts of the world constitute the ultimate independent foundation of empirical and scientific language and of truth itself. W. V. Quine sums up this philosophical position by stating that "empirical meaning is what remains when . . . we peel away the verbiage. It is what the sentences of one language and their firm translations in a completely alien language have in common.''[11]

This view, I maintain, is suspect. There is no absolute gulf between the empirical and the conceptual. The issue is not whether there exists some external physical world but whether this world comes linguistically prearticulated. Both scientific and empirical language are in some ways constructions of, shapings of, the stuff of experience according to certain human structures. Perceptions are more than passive observations, and empirical language is more than mirroring, reporting statements. The world does not provide an independent foundation to either language or experience; it is not independently intelligible. Descriptive propositions are not absolutely distinct from non-descriptive ones, and factual statements do not reveal something about the structures through which these propositions organize and describe the world.

In the antiquated view that the universe came prepackaged in thing-like categories, language's prime concern was to record such demarcations; a globally alternative language system was an impossibility. Yet if we accept the above notions, this view becomes questionable; following from the Sapir-Whorf hypothesis, indications are that languages carve up the world in different ways. Thus, the ultimate and indisputable truth of scientific language is called into question.

At this point in the argument, Kripke would probably interject that "the way the reference of a term is fixed should not be regarded as a synonym for the term.''[12] Kripke maintains that although descriptions may be contingent or culture-bound, the meaning of a term is not equivalent with this description. The real meaning of a name is the thing to which it refers as determined by an empirical designation. Accordingly, Putnam states: "The rigidity of the term 'water' follows from the fact that when I give the 'ostentive definition': '*This* (liquid) is water,' I intend (2') and not (1'). We may also say, following Kripke, that when I give the ostensive definition '*this* (liquid) is water,' the demonstrative 'this' is *rigid*.''[13]

Kripke's and Putnam's positions, then, depend on the assumption that scientific knowledge is reducible to certain empirical observations. This seems questionable. It is a strange use of language to intend "*This* is H_2O" as an initial referential statement identifying atomic structure. Admittedly, scientific knowledge is related to certain empirical observations. However, what is empirically observable is different from the chemical constitution of things. A substance's constitution as H_2O can never be given directly in terms of observational statements. What is observable is *different* from the chemical properties of the substance. Yet such properties would have to be observable if elements and compounds are scientifically rigid designations. If elements and compounds represented proper names, they would have to be directly designated. In effect, Kripke and Putnam are arguing for a type of fundamental realism in science.

Contrarily, the point to be made is that the elements of the periodic table in chemistry are not different individual things but different combinations of things. They are not elemental but composites of different subatomic particles. Elements are complex rather than simple. They have the form of propositions, not names. If this is the case, then the elements on the periodic table are not rigid designators; they are definite descriptions. When I talk of hydrogen, I am speaking of a certain subatomic structure, a composite notion in chemical notation. The periodic table is not an aggregate of discrete designators but a classification of interrelated components. The language of science is systematic; the universe, an atom, a molecule, an organism—all represent systems.

Dmitri Mendeleyev's discovery of the periodic behavior among elements not only explained the simple relationships among known elements but also predicted the existence of still-to-be-discovered elements. Mendeleyev's system left room for undiscovered elements. This systematic and predictive character indicates that elements (and by extension compounds) are functioning not as designating names but as a system of definite descriptions. Each element of the cosmos is interwoven with all other elements.

Contrarily, Kripke and Putnam function under the assumption of the discreteness and unqualified fixity of elements. By Kripke's definition, a rigid designator is a word used the same in *all* possible worlds. A rigid designator is a word for which there is no *possibility* of use in differing ways. But what word could possibly satisfy this criterion? The open-ended character of language is such that no restrictions of this kind exist unconditionally. At best, we can legislate or prescribe such a restricted use, but this is not what Kripke is saying. He suggests that there exists an a priori or a logical restriction; whereas, I maintain that it would be pragmatic.

One can see the attractiveness of Kripke's rigid designators. The assumption is that rigid designators insure an interlanguage bridge for translation. They supply that common basis, those invariant terms in the light of which Piper's science fiction translation is justified. Helium is helium; oxygen is oxygen. These words designate rigidly. On the other hand, if words were given meaning relative to their own language systems, Kripke or Putnam might say that there would then be no check-factor to distinguish a correct from an incorrect translation. Yet this conclusion is suspect. What allowed for the alleged translation in the science fiction example was not the rigid designation of the elements but the systematic inner relations among those elements relative to the periodic table. It was this systematic structure which was translatable by Dane. The translation was not of the isolated elements in the system but of the system's own structures. The translations of helium and oxygen were done on at least the subliminal, intuitive assumption that the systematic character of the Martian periodic table is the same as ours.

The language of science is systematic and open-ended in the sense that it has a predictive quality and can incorporate newfound data. A rigid designator, on the other hand, is closed, or fixed, in scope; it prescribes an absolute usage of language, apart from any contextual background. Putnam and Kripke assert a direct correspondence between words in different frameworks, irrespective of their contexts. This leads to insurmountable difficulties. Words receive their meanings from an overall framework. To speak of a word's meaning presupposes that the word has been incorporated into a system, fitting together with other words. It is from this context that the word derives meaning.

Although I am not arguing that rigid designators cannot exist, I am saying that the periodic table in science and chemical formulas for compounds are not directly referential and cannot be determined by ostensible definitions. That these elements are identified by descriptions would seem to indicate that—while elements may not be synonymous with these descriptions—our *knowledge* of the elements is not in terms of rigid designators. Note how this changes the argument from a metaphysical base to an epistemological one. Or, more properly, it shows the interrelations of the two kinds of questions. Epistemology provides those conditions in terms of which empirical facts or the facts of science are revealed. This is the connection between epistemology and the world. Often we assume that there is an absolute gulf between the two. The facts of science are purported to unfold as self-standing, structured complexes. On the contrary, human channels of empirical knowledge—the senses—form a regulatory framework for science. Scientific statements are not given to be true a priori. Their truth is given through an epistemological framework in terms of which statements assume meaning. Moreover, these assumptions of frameworks assume heightened meanings once one talks about Martians and possible other worlds.

In an intriguing article, Neal Grossman argues that our justificational observation-statements of science may need justification themselves in a encounter with extraterrestrial beings who sense differently from us.[14] His position relates to Martians, whose light sensitivity is such that the shortest wavelength of light detectable by the Martian retina is longer than the longest wavelength of light detectable by the human retina. There is no overlap of detectability. Thus, for the Martian the statement "Object X is infra-red" is an observation-statement, but for the Earthling it is not. For the Earthling, on the other hand, the statement "Object Y is blue" is an observation-statement, but for the Martian it is not. "Object X is infra-red in color" is a theoretical construct for the Martian. Or, in Kripke's or Putnam's terms, certain observational statements or ostensible definitions which rigidly fix scientific statements for Earthlings can conceivably be definite descriptions for aliens. This possibility creates a problem. If the language of science is universal, if the atomic constitutions of elements and compounds are rigid designators for all possible worlds, then such constitution would have to be directly verifiable, not only by humans but also by aliens. Clearly, this is not necessarily the case in all possible worlds. Putnam's Twin Earth has doppelgängers. What if the aliens' sensory apparatus was quite different from ours? The rigid designators would not be rigid for the aliens.

On 3 March 1972, the *Pioneer 10* spacecraft was launched. It was the first man-made object to leave the solar system, and it carried from Earth a message for any alien to comprehend. Among other things, this message included the proton and electron spins of a neutral hydrogen atom. The reasoning which led to the contents of this message, according to Carl Sagan, is that "it is written in the only language we share with the recipients: Science. . . . The message will be based upon commonalities between the transmitting and receiving civilizations . . . what we truly share in common—the universe around us, science and mathematics."[15]

Certainly, Dr. Dane's translation of the Martian language was based on a commonality between our earthly civilization and the extinct Martian civilization, but the source of this commonality is not necessarily any alleged rigid designators of science. What is common is the act of communication and the logical framework in terms of which the communication occurs. Even for scientific or empirical knowledge to be possible, there must be a presupposed logical framework. A description of the world is not given as true a priori; rather, logically speaking, there are needed principles in terms of which statements assume meaning. It is the possibility of sharing these principles which creates the common basis for extraterrestrial communication.

NOTES

1. Ludwig Wittgenstein, *Philosophical Investigations* (New York: Macmillan, 1958), p. 139.

2. H. Beam Piper, "Omnilingual," in *Mars, We Love You*, eds. Jane Hipolito and Willis E. McNelly (New York: Pyramid Books, 1971), p. 257.

3. Ibid., pp. 257–58.

4. Ibid., p. 259.

5. Saul A. Kripke, "Naming and Necessity," in *Semantics of Natural Language*, eds. D. Davidson and G. Harmon (Dordrecht: D. Reidel, 1972), p. 323.

6. Hilary Putnam, "Meaning and Reference," *Journal of Philosophy* 70 (8 November 1973), 700–01.

7. Ibid., p. 701.

8. Ibid.

9. Ibid., p. 702.

10. Ibid., p. 707.

11. W. V. Quine, *Words and Objects* (Cambridge: MIT Press, 1960), p. 70.

12. Kripke, "Naming," p. 328.

13. Putnam, "Meaning," p. 707.

14. Neal Grossman, "Empiricism and the Possibility of Encountering Intelligent Beings with Different Sense-structures," *Journal of Philosophy* 71 (19 December 1974), 815–21.

15. Carl Sagan, *Cosmic Connection* (New York: Doubleday, 1973), pp. 217–18.

The Comedy of Fantasy: An Ecological Perspective of Joy Chant's *Red Moon and Black Mountain*

Don D. Elgin

It is common, when talking of fantasy, to relate it to the pastoral, the tragic, the chivalric, or the epic tradition. It is equally common to talk about the attitudes toward nature in works of fantasy and about the environmental perspectives of science fiction. What is not common, however, is to suggest that these approaches miss a central philosophical position which has been primarily responsible for the emergence of the contemporary fantasy novel as one of the few ways out of the dead end to which the stream of consciousness/experimental/existential novel has led serious fiction. That philosophical position is readily apparent in the works of most twentieth-century fantasy writers but is particularly well handled in Joy Chant's *Red Moon and Black Mountain*.[1] I shall use it as an example of the way literary comedy and natural ecology have been combined to produce a literature and an ethic which offer both the contemporary novel and its principal subject, man, a hope of surviving.

The ecological perspective insists on our rejection of two ideas particularly dear to Western culture: (1) that the function of art is to remind man of his nobility and spirituality by pointing out the distinctions between him and the rest of the universe and (2) that the philosophy and implications of tragedy represent the highest goals toward which man can strive.

Traditional views of esthetics have insisted that art ennobles man by lifting him to a contemplation of his nobility and spirituality while contemplation of nature debases man by focusing attention on his mortality and bestiality. The contemplation to which man is traditionally raised is of a world or system which is made more comprehensible through simplification. The pastoral, for example, ennobles man by restoring to him the sense of simplicity and control lost in the wilderness of the city. As Juvenal points out in the "Third Satire":

> Live there, fond of your hoe, an independent producer,
> Willing and able to feed a hundred good vegetarians.

Isn't it something, to feel, wherever you are, how far off,
You are a monarch? At least, lord of a single lizard.[2]

Comparable simplification occurs in tragedy (Edmund follows natural laws and becomes a beast; Lear first violates and then follows the laws of the great chain of being and ultimately becomes noble); epic (Achilles determines and thus simplifies his existence by his decision to seek the glory of the heroic code); chivalric romance (Gawain gains moral superiority over the temptations of nature and evil by learning to fulfill completely the traditions of chivalry); and allegory (Everyman rejects the confusing and conflicting claims of the world by seeing all its members reduced to either/or choices that lead to damnation or to salvation). Thus, if nature is portrayed at all, it is nature domesticated, simplified, and idealized; and more often than not, man is portrayed as achieving greatness only by rising above even this simplified nature.

What these traditional views of esthetics have ignored, however, is the basic similarity between the apprehension of beauty in biology and in art, a similarity that springs from integration, from an acknowledgment of the complexity of the process by which individual elements interact to produce a whole. This similarity has been noted by such diverse scholars as Paul Weiss, neurobiologist at Rockefeller University, and Suzanne Langer, philosopher and esthetician; but it is perhaps most specifically expressed by Joseph Meeker in his *Comedy of Survival*:

Works of art are gratifying because they offer an integrative experience, bringing highly diversified elements together in a balanced whole. A great work of art resembles an ecosystem in that it conveys a unitive experience. It is not important that each element be pleasing in itself, but it is essential that the relationship established among elements be true and consistent within the system as a whole. Literature includes much pain and degradation, and music incorporates dissonance within the beauty of the whole. It is necessary that works of art include a full range of pleasant and unpleasant experiences in order to be esthetically satisfying. The ultimate success of a work of art depends upon the finished artistic system as a whole and the fidelity of that system to a complex integrity which includes all creative and destructive forces in balanced equilibrium.[3]

What Meeker is suggesting, of course, is that ecological esthetics points to the union, not the separation, of man and nature; that ecological esthetics points man, not toward the supposed simplicity of the cave, farm, or meadow but toward the more complex system represented by the climax ecosystem; that ecological esthetics demonstrates a holistic approach in which the existence of the whole depends on the functioning of all the parts to achieve an overall effect. Thus Dante's *Divine Comedy* is not a simple presentation of medieval theology and politics. Rather, it is a work which demonstrates that the difference between Hell and Heaven is between those who insist on their own wishes above all other things (resulting in physical chaos, environmental pollution, and moral degradation) and those who see themselves operating as essential parts of an incredibly complex system of order (with its physical radiance, its environmental harmony, and its moral exaltation).

Western man has never accepted this ecological view, however, for two very simple reasons. First, man has preferred the simplicity of his constructed systems to the infinite complexity of the climax ecosystem. Second, the scholar, the writer, or the critic has recognized that taking an ecological point of view means dealing with something infinitely more complex than abstract theories about art and life. He cannot ignore the politics, the economics, the science, the religion, the language, the medicine, or any of the hundreds of other things necessary to bring even a simple poem to fruition. He must attempt to see the whole, and the enormity of the task frightens him so much that he is swept back to his broom closets, to those fragments of knowledge that he finds so comforting precisely because they have simplified his world to the point of absurdity. What he fails to see is that such simplification is ultimately more absurd than anything he has ever feared, for that simplicity can lead to his extinction.

The second idea that an ecological perspective must reject is the tragic concept. At least since the time of the Greeks, man has seen himself as superior to nature and has made certain assumptions to bolster that position. He has assumed (1) that nature is made for mankind, (2) that human morality transcends natural limits, and (3) that the individual human personality is supremely important. Battling with powers greater than himself, the tragic hero strives to affirm his mastery even in the face of his own destruction. Oedipus, Faust, Heathcliff, Dona Perfecta, and Dr. Rieux are examples of the continuity of this attitude. The tragic hero discovers the truth and, often by his death, forces other men to recognize it as well. He is not part of the system, nor will he adapt to it. Rather, he will force the system to change to suit his own view. Failing that, he will die nobly and magnificently.

However, there has always been another view of man and how he should act, a view that springs from his conviction that he is a part of the system and that, unless the system exists, he has little chance of doing so himself. This view is, of course, the comic one. Comedy's only concern is to affirm man's capacity for survival and to celebrate the continuity of life itself. It typically shows neither discovery of a new truth nor permanent conquest over an evil force. Instead of demanding a choice between alternatives, it assumes that, since choice is likely to be error, survival is likely to depend on finding accommodation that will permit all parties to endure. Meeker defines this perspective particularly well:

To people disposed in favor of heroism and idealistic ethics, comedy may seem trivial in its insistence that the commonplace is worth maintaining. The comic point of view is that man's high moral ideals and glorified heroic poses are largely based upon fantasy and are likely to lead to misery or death for those who hold them. In the world as revealed by comedy, the important thing is to live and to encourage life, even though it is probably meaningless to do so.[4]

Comedy, unlike tragedy, insists that man is part of nature physically, morally, and intellectually and that he must adapt himself to the complex natural system. Thus, it is very like the process of evolution, in which various species opportunistically explore their environment in an attempt to maintain their existence by adaptation and accommodation. It is also like the productive and stable climax ecosystem, which encourages maximum diversity, minimizes destructive aggression, and seeks to establish equilibrium among its participants. As such, it puts man in a tradition which is not so "noble" as that of tragedy, but which may be more realistic and humane. It sees man as often foolish, bungling, lecherous, smelly, and pretentious, but it also sees him as compassionate. It regards abstractions and absolutes as nonsensical or nonexistent, but also reaffirms man's ancient ties to the physical world and all its processes.

Joy Chant's *Red Moon and Black Mountain* is not a work in the tragic, chivalric mode, though like *The Lord of the Rings* it is often seen in that light. It is, instead, squarely in the comic and ecologic tradition. The attitude toward nature rejects the oversimplified pastoral, edenic approach in favor of one that emphasizes multiplicity, diversity, and complexity. Moreover, the work insists that man affects his environment positively or negatively by his attempt to integrate himself with nature or to stand superior to it. Thus, nature is never seen as a mere symbol of man's spiritual state but as an actual environment which man affects by his actions. Finally, this work clearly presents a holistic approach to art which emphasizes the existence of a whole system rather than that of the individual. Beauty, pain, degradation, and joy are all present, but what is most present is the insistence that life is possible, not because of the abstraction of heaven but because of the experiences of earth. It is this affirmation of life and of the possibility of joy which makes this work a perfect example of literary ecology as well as making its endurance as a literary classic a certainty.

In *Red Moon and Black Mountain*, there are two seemingly opposed views of nature and man's relation to it. One tradition is represented by the Hurnei, the wanderers of the Northern Plains. The other is represented by the Vanderei, wielders of the Star Magic.

The Hurnei clearly represent a relationship with nature different from the pastoral tradition. We do not have happy sheep gamboling in the fields while happy shepherds sing plaintive love songs to pure and simple shepherdesses in the warm sunshine. What we have instead are hunters whose existence depends on their ability to find game, kill what is needed, and use the results of their kill to fortify themselves against environmental conditions that are sometimes harsh and sometimes kind. It is not a simple world in which man rules over his environment, but an infinitely complex one to which he must adapt if he is to survive. His religion, his social structure, and his ethical system are based on accommodating himself to the environment.

This identification of the Hurnei with nature is apparent from Chant's description of the dance shortly after Oliver's appearance in Kedrinh:

And the voices of the men were the dark sea; while the voices of the girls were the flying white foam; or the vast dark plain, and the silver light that ran over it; or the wind-brought rumour of thunder, and the shimmering levin-light. And the drums rumbled and throbbed and passed into the ground; and the sound became the very heartbeats of the Earth herself, beating up through their feet into their blood, into their brains, into their very bones. (p. 28)

Nature here is not a metaphor for man; rather, man is one of the many parts of the natural world which are blended into a complex whole. Nor is it a simple world; rather, it consists of diverse, contradictory elements through which man's body as well as his spirit becomes tied to the *things* of the earth in all their light and dark aspects.

Further evidence of the identification with nature is the relationship between the Hurnei and the animals. The Hurnei are hunters, but they understand fully that wanton destruction is wrong, not because of a moral creed but because it would destroy the system by which they live. This point is clearly made early in the novel when Hran is punished for killing animals he did not need:

He had twice killed a doe in fawn, twice animals less than a year old, and had even killed more than he could carry back, and left the others on the plain to rot. The chieftain repeated to him the law of laws which he had broken: "Accursed be the man who kills without need"—and cried that because of him the whole tribe might have been put under a curse. He had sinned against the tribe; he had sinned against the laws of Mor'anh; he had sinned against Kem'nanh. Had he any excuse? (p. 69)

When Hran can offer no excuse, he is cast out of the tribe in a ceremony marked by sorrow and by grim necessity. As each member of the tribe observes his departure, Chant remarks, "He would not die; but a man who was cast out of the tribe was cast out of life" (p. 70). Oliver, the young man magically transported to Vanderei, suddenly realizes the meaning of what had previously been little more than a game to him:

Alone, he thought; out-cast. He looked at the spear-heads glowing red in the fire. In this vast land what was one man? Where was he without his tribe about him?

He felt like a child who has played long in the sunlight at a cave's mouth, and suddenly hears from within it a bear's snarling. I never saw the harsh side before, he thought. Now the game is over. Now they have done treating me gently. (p. 70)

Two other minor but significant facts reinforce the identification the Hurnei feel with their environment. In the first place, the tribe wanders at the urgings of Dhalev, the King, not at its own whim. That would not be unusual except that Dhalev is not a human king at all but the mighty stallion who rules the horse herd of the Hurnei, and his moves are based on the weather and the availability of grass and water rather than on abstractions of either culture or convenience. In the second place, the social structure of the Hurnei is based on the demands made by the environment. As Oliver notes several times, the girls are "tomboyish hoydens," but seemingly at a moment's notice they can become women who pack the home, move with the caravan, and keep the young out of harm's way: "He understood how the girls who were at the moment riding their ponies with the men could turn almost overnight from the wild, headstrong tomboys they were to the silent, unobtrusive women—as soon as they were tied to a wagon" (pp. 67–68). Thus, the Hurnei accommodate their life-style and their social structure not to an abstract creed or dogma but to the exigencies of their environment, an environment that is complex, beautiful, harsh, and demanding by turns.

Perhaps the most important indication of the relation between man and nature in this novel is the Hurnei religion. Now religion is seldom found even in serious comedy, for comedy eschews abstractions. Nor is it traditionally associated with ecology, which is more concerned with processes than with theology. It is, however, an integral part of the system here. Although there are references to a kind of supreme deity who rules over the world of Vanderei, that is not the god with which the Hurnei are concerned. Marenkalion may shield Oliver after his defeat of Fendarl, but it is Vir'Vachal, the author of the earth magic, who is worshiped and whose demands must be met by Oliver and by the tribe. Chant describes her as she first appears to Nicholas:

She too was sturdily built, square and strong, with a broad, rather sullen, peasant face and weather-beaten skin. . . . Her eyes passed over the travellers, and Nicholas shuddered. He could not see their colour, but she [sic] felt their fierceness. A slow, deep savagery moved in them, and as she rode heat rippled from her. Not warmth-heat. She was coarse, she was primitive, she was frightening—and yet she was beautiful. She was beautiful in a way he had never dreamed of, did not understand, yet seemed to remember. And looking at her, everything that he had ever called beautiful faded, paled, seemed but husks beside her, and the very thought "beauty" reshaped in the mind until it fitted her; for it had been made of her, and for her, and now all at once it seemed a richer, brighter, more terrible thing. (pp. 131–32)

All the elements of the primitive earth goddess are here, but Vir'Vachal goes beyond that stereotype. Her appeal is instinctual and passionate, and she becomes the force that must be accommodated if the Hurnei are to continue their existence or if Oliver is to complete his task and return to his world. Thus she becomes a symbol of nature itself, nature that abhors the unnecessary death of men or animals. Drawn by the scent of blood to the battlefield, she brings the life of flowering plants to cover the dead, but "it was not for the slain that she mourned; but for the injured earth itself" (p. 230). When Kiron, the King of Vanderei, draws back his lip in disdain, the Earth Priestess angrily points out his folly:

"Oh, you northerners, you lords of men, with your talk of right and wrong! You put on scorn like a robe and curl your lip because in our worship blood is shed. Yet in one night you will spill more blood than we in a thousand years, and no god has demanded this offering! Yes, Vir'Vachal is drawn by the scent of death, and you do not like it. But where she found death, she had left life; and you—what did you do, King Kiron?'' (p. 231)

This statement carries us far beyond Vir'Vachal and the world of *Red Moon and Black Mountain*, for it is a clear rejection of the tragic, heroic code represented by the Star Warriors of Vanderei; it is even a rejection of the battle that has just been fought and an indication of its total futility. It is a negative statement about the kinds of abstractions for which battles are usually fought; it contrasts with the positive affirmation of life that is the goal of comedy and ecology. This is the goal to which Oliver is led in the dramatic conclusion of the Vir'Vachal segment.

Following the battle and Oliver's return to the Northern Plains, he finds that he has become a spiritual outcast. Even worse, he must find his own way home, a way which is tied to the dark passion of Vir'Vachal, who must be bound and must live under the earth rather than over it if people or animals are to live. Blood is all that will bind her, and to save the lives of his fellows, Oliver offers himself. Three things are significant here. First, Oliver is not the tragic hero failing because of a conflict with forces to which he must prove himself morally superior. If hero at all, he is the culture hero who understands that the survival of the system is more important than the survival of the individual within it. Second, Oliver and the Hurnei do not defeat nature or assume mastery over her. Rather they accommodate themselves to the needs of a system that must live in a complex balance in which Vir'Vachal provides life and growth rather than the unbridled sexual passion which would destroy both man and animal. What they are doing, then, is not conquering, reforming, or changing their world; they are simply restoring the norm that abstractions had disturbed, and that is precisely the process followed in literary comedy as well as in climax ecosystems. Finally, Oliver's choice is not made to attain a moral superiority for himself, nor is it one he makes with joy. Rather he makes it to save the lives of the young men, particularly Mnorh, who are his friends. He also makes it because he sees in it the way home which the gods have told him he must find for himself. An outcast in Vanderei, he must return to and become part of the system of his own world, for it is clear that the outcast cannot survive with even a minimal amount of freedom or happiness. However, Oliver still greatly fears the choice he has to make. With an animal's instinctual fear of its own death, Oliver first hopes his offer will not be accepted, then exists at times ''dizzy with fear.'' And yet it is worth noting that during the five days preceding the offering Oliver again felt at one with the tribe. He was no longer the outcast, for ''someone had to go, and he could not stay'' (p. 252). Thus the offering is finally made out of a sense of responsibility to the tribe, out of a logic that pointed out that he could not stay with the tribe, and out of the practical necessity of taking the only way home he could find. Oliver is, then, not a tragic hero, for what he affirms is life rather than abstractions. When he thinks, "But 'life' was such a huge word. It meant everything" (p. 254), he is perfectly in the line of comic tradition as well as ecologic, and it is perfectly appropriate that he finds a god who fits what he has learned and demonstrated: "He was filled with delight and wonder at this strange new form of Godhead, a divinity undreamed of, a god without majesty, a god of harmony without law, with such vitality" (p. 267). It is equally important that Oliver gain from the god a renewed appreciation of life and that he recognize that innocence has been replaced by an experience that he cannot or will not put aside.

Oliver's story with the Hurnei is, however, only half of the novel's plot. The other half—the one to which most critics refer when they classify the novel in the tragic, chivalric, epic tradition—relates the adventures of Nicholas and Penny with the wielders of the Star Magic. However, it is clear that the Star Warriors are not a natural part of their world, that their battles are necessary because they have set up an abstraction against which one of their members has revolted, and that their stay is likely to be short-lived when compared to those forces which integrate with rather than divorce themselves from nature.

The Star Warriors, children of a god, possess all the traditional characteristics of chivalric, tragic, epic heroes. Nicholas and Penny recognize that the first person they see in this new world is a princess: "A Princess led them. So tall she was, so beautiful, proud, and gay, she could have been nothing else. Her hair was very long and black as jet, blowing out behind her; her face was pearl-pale, and her lovely laughing mouth the color of amber. They saw no jewels, only a plain cloak wrapped around her; but her royalty needed no trappings" (p. 12). Later we learn that the High Lords chose the Star Warriors "to guide and to rule them [men] and to bear the brunt of the battle that was to be waged" (pp. 142–43). Kiron has "a stern and royal face," the face of a king carved in alabaster: handsome, dignified, and still," and "His eyes were clear green, reserved and even a little sad, with the loneliness of kings" (p. 166).

Thus, they are stereotypes but with one difference: their rule and their power are limited. They are limited first by the fact that they cannot participate in the common elements of humanity. As Princess In'serinna tells Penny: "You see, feeling cold is a matter of contrast, of being warm within and cold without, of being accustomed to warmth. But everything has its price; and the price of Star Magic is this, that we forsake warmth forever. All warmth" (p. 53). Their second limitation is that their battle against Fendarl, even if it is won, will be at best a temporary victory. As Kiron tells Oliver, "And there lies our sorrow. It is certain grief if we lose; but not certain joy if we win. For if Fendarl has the victory we are lost; but if he falls we do but live to fight again" (p. 190). When this "temporary" victory is seen in light of the fact that the Star Warriors cannot bring life to be as Vir'Vachal can, the transitory nature of this tradition is clearly highlighted.

The end result of these two limitations is that the Star Magic and the Star Warriors will pass away, leaving nothing permanently changed. The lasting effects will be wrought by Princess In'serinna, who gives up the Magic for warmth, for love, and for life, and by the Iranani, who will endure past all others in the Great Council: "We of Iranani, we have no magic and no strength of arms to offer, but we are *his* enemies. And if it comforts you I think he may find our power, the power of life and laughter, the hardest in the end to overthrow; too quick to catch, too frail to bind. We cannot destroy him, if you fail; but we can outlive him" (p. 175).

In short, the Star Warriors and Fendarl are abstractions. They divorce themselves from nature with a predictable effect—the destruction of each other and of the environment. The pollution of nature comes from both sides, the good as well as the evil, for if Kunil-Bannoth has brought about the bleakness of stone and weather on the Black Mountain, Kiron and his forces are equally responsible for the deaths, which only Vir'Vachal can mend. Significantly, however, no such pollution is associated with the Hurnei or their god.

All real hope in the novel springs from those elements that reflect the comic sense of multiplicity, accommodation, and diversity. From the forest wanderer who troubled Nicholas because he "looked fiercely mortal—even earthy" to the ageless forests of Nelimhon, it is clear that the tragic abstractions are to be avoided, regardless of how attractive they may be. Men must acknowledge their ties to the animal world and follow the instincts which come from that heritage. Oliver does so with regard to the battle, and it is only by doing so that he is able to kill Fendarl and survive. Even at that, however, he acknowledges that there is no real victory: "But he could remember only the death wail of a man in great terror, a man whom he had killed; and killed in the end not out of justice or necessity, but in the rage and hatred of his heart" (p. 225). The intra-specific ethic against killing one's own kind thus operates to indicate what abstractions bring men to: destruction of the physical environment, needless slaughter of other creatures, and separation from the system of which one must be a part.

I have suggested that the tragic perspective has led to an environmental crisis of monumental proportions and that our continued embrace of that perspective offers us only the promise of our imminent demise, a demise that will be all the more amazing since we will never understand why it has come about. Also, I have suggested that the tradition of literary comedy, embracing and affirming life in all its diversity, offers a mode of behavior and a relationship to nature which makes possible man's participation in his environment rather than his segregation from it. Further, I have suggested that the major importance of the development of the fantasy novel in the twentieth century lies in its affirmation of this comic, ecologic point of view. The fantasy novel offers twentieth-century literature and twentieth-century man a way out, a way out of death and into life. The only question is whether, in our vanity and pride, we can accept our demotion from being totally superior to being an essential part of a complex whole. Fantasy writers like Joy Chant, J. R. R. Tolkien, C. S. Lewis, Harlan Ellison, and others have shown clearly the image of man acting as a part of his environment, as a partner in a complex system where man's responsibility becomes to adapt himself to the exigencies of the world. That may mean a different kind of morality, and it may mean a different perception of the kind of life a man must lead, but it may also mean man's ethical integration into a world from which he has been too long estranged.

NOTES

1. Joy Chant, *Red Moon and Black Mountain* (New York: Ballantine Books, 1971); hereafter cited in the text.

2. Juvenal, *Satires of Juvenal*, trans. Rolfe Humphries (Bloomington: Indiana University Press, 1958), p. 42.

3. Joseph Meeker, *The Comedy of Survival: Studies in Literary Ecology* (New York: Scribner, 1974), p. 130.

4. Ibid., p. 26.

Bibliography

Secondary sources (historical, biographical, critical, etc.) cited in the essays are listed below. Works cited in two or more essays are listed first in a "General" category; others are listed under the title of the essay in which they are cited. In a few instances, the listing has been updated by the addition of significant books and articles published since the essays were written.

GENERAL

Campbell, Joseph. *The Hero with a Thousand Faces*. Cleveland: World Publishing, 1956.
Hillegas, Mark. *The Future as Nightmare: H. G. Wells and the Anti-Utopians*. New York: Oxford University Press, 1967.
Irwin, W. R. *The Game of the Impossible: A Rhetoric of Fantasy*. Urbana: University of Illinois Press, 1976.
Penzoldt, Peter. *The Supernatural in Fiction*. New York: Humanities Press, 1965.
Rabkin, Eric S. *The Fantastic in Literature*. Princeton: Princeton University Press, 1976.
Rogers, Robert. *A Psychoanalytic Study of the Double in Literature*. Detroit: Wayne State University Press, 1970.
Todorov, Tzvetan. *Introduction à la littérature fantastique*. Paris: Le Seuill, 1970. *The Fantastic: A Structural Approach to a Literary Genre*. Trans. Richard Howard. Cleveland: Case-Western Reserve University Press, 1973; Ithaca: Cornell University Press, 1975.
Tymms, Ralph. *Doubles in Literary Psychology*. Cambridge, Eng.: Bowes & Bowes, 1949.

ALICE PARKER, "RENÉE VIVIEN IN THE NIGHT GARDEN OF THE SPIRIT"

Bonnet, Marie-Jo. *Un Choix sans équivoque. Recherches historiques sur relations amoureuses entre les femmes, XVIe-XXe siècle*. Paris: Denoël, 1981.

Cixous, Hélène. *La Venue à l'écriture*. Paris: Union Generale d'Editions, 1977.

———. "The Laugh of the Medusa." *Signs* 1 (1976), 875–93.

Lorenz, Paul. *Sappho 1900: Renée Vivien*. Paris: Julliard, 1977.

Marks, Elaine. "Lesbian Intertextuality." In *Homosexualities and French Literature*, George Stambolian and Elaine Marks, eds. Ithaca: Cornell University Press, 1979, pp. 353–77.

———. "Women and Literature in France." *Signs* 3 (Summer 1978), pp. 832–42.

The Prism of Sex: Essays in the Sociology of Knowledge, Julia A. Sherman and Evelyn Tordon Beck, eds. Madison: University of Wisconsin Press, 1979.

Wickes, George. *The Amazon of Letters*. New York: Popular Library, 1978.

RUTH B. ANTOSH, "MICHEL TREMBLAY AND THE FANTASTIC OF VIOLENCE"

Ripley, John. "From Alienation to Transcendence." *Canadian Literature* 85 (1980), 44–59.

ROBERT A. COLLINS, "SWANN ON SWANN: THE CONSCIOUS USES OF FANTASY"

Collins, Robert A. *Thomas Burnett Swann: A Brief Critical Biography*. Boca Raton: Florida Atlantic University Foundation, 1979.

———. "Thomas Burnett Swann: A Retrospective." *Fantasy Newsletter* 57 (March 1983), 6–9; (April 1983), 18–20.

Page, Jerry. "Thomas Burnett Swann." *Lore* (February 1966), pp. 1–4.

Schlobin, Roger C. "Thomas Burnett Swann's Nixies: Pain and Pleasure." *Extrapolation* 24 (Spring 1983), 5–12.

JANET PÉREZ, "THE FANTASTIC IN TWO RECENT WORKS OF GONZALO TORRENTE BALLESTER"

Amis, Kingsley. *New Maps of Hell: A Survey of Science Fiction*. New York: Harcourt Brace, 1960.

Díaz (Pérez), Janet W. "Literary Theory, Satire, and Burlesque in Torrente's *Fragmentos de Apocalipsis*." *Proceedings, Pacific Northwest Conference on Foreign Languages* 30 (1979), 149–52.

Lértora, Juan Carlos. "Fragmentos de Apocalipsis y la novela polifónica." *Revista Canadiense de Estudios Hispanicos* 4 (1980), 199–205.

Pérez, Janet. *Gonzalo Torrente Ballester*. Boston: G. K. Hall, 1984.

ROSEMARY JACKSON, "NARCISSISM AND BEYOND: A PSYCHOANALYTIC READING OF *FRANKENSTEIN* AND FANTASIES OF THE DOUBLE"

Bakhtin, Mikhail. *Problems of Dostoevsky's Poetics*, trans. R. W. Rostel. Ann Arbor: Ardis, 1973.

Bersani, Leo. *A Future for Astyanax: Character and Desire in Literature*. Boston: Little, Brown, 1976.

Burniston, Steve. "Lacan's Theory of the Constitution of the Subject in Language," in *On Ideology*. London: Hutchinson, 1978.

Coleman, Stanley M. "The Phantom Double." *British Journal of Medical Psychology* 14 (1934), 254–73.

Devine, George, and U. C. Knoepflmacher, eds. *The Endurance of Frankenstein: Essays on Mary Shelley's Novel*. Berkeley: University of California Press, 1979.

Downey, J. E. "Literary Self-Projection." *Psychological Review* 29 (1912), 299–311.

Jackson, Rosemary. *Fantasy: The Literature of Subversion*. London: Methuen, 1981.

Keppler, C. F. *The Literature of the Second Self*. Tucson: University of Arizona Press, 1969.

Kiely, Robert. *The Romantic Novel in England*. Cambridge: Harvard University Press, 1972.

Kristeva, Julia. *Desire in Language: A Semiotic Approach to Literature and Art*. Oxford: Oxford University Press, 1980.

Lacan, Jacques. *Écrits: A Selection*, trans. Alan Sheridan. London: Tavistock, 1977.

———. *The Language of the Self*, trans. Anthony Wilden. Baltimore: Johns Hopkins University Press, 1968.

Laplanche, J., and J. B. Pontalis. *The Language of Psychoanalysis*, trans. Donald Nicholson-Smith. London: Hogarth Press, 1973.

Massey, Irving. "Singles and Doubles: Frankenstein," in *The Gaping Pig: Literature and Metamorphosis*. Berkeley: University of California Press, 1976.

Miyoshi, Masao. *The Divided Self: A Perspective on the Literature of the Victorians*. New York: New York University Press, 1969.

Prickett, Stephen. *Victorian Fantasy*. Hassocks, Sussex: Harvester Press, 1979.

Punter, David. *The Literature of Terror: A History of Gothic Fiction from 1765 to the Present Day*. London: Longman, 1980.

Rank, Otto. *The Double: A Psychoanalytic Study*, trans. Harry Tucker, Jr. Chapel Hill: University of North Carolina Press, 1971.

Rubinstein, March A. " 'My Accursed Origin': The Search for the Mother in *Frankenstein*." *Studies in Romanticism* 15 (1976), 165–94.

Standard Edition of Complete Psychological Works of Sigmund Freud. 24 vols., ed. James Strachey. London: Macmillan, 1953.

Vinge, Louise. *The Narcissus Theme in Western European Literature up to the Early Nineteenth Century*. Lund: Gleerup, 1967.

Wain, Marianne. "The Double in Romantic Narrative: A Preliminary Study." *Germanic Review* 36 (1961), 257–68.

LEE B. JENNINGS, "MEYRINK'S *DER GOLEM*: THE SELF AS THE OTHER"

Franke, Eduard. *Gustav Meyrink: Werk und Wirkung*. Büdingen-Gettenbach: Avalun, 1957.

Jansen, Bella, "Über den Okkultismus in Gustav Meyrinks Roman *Der Golem*." *Neophilologus* 7 (1922), 19–23.

Jung, C. G. *Psychologie und Alchemie*. Zürich: Rascher, 1952.

Metzner, Ralph. *Maps of Consciousness*. New York: Collier, 1971.

Schödel, Siegfried. "Über Gustav Meyrink und die phantastische Literatur." *Studien zur Trivialliteratur*, ed. Heinz Otto Burger. Frankfurt: Klostermann, 1968.

Schwarz, Theodor. "Die Bedeutung des Phantastisch-Mystischen bei Gustav Meyrink." *Weimarer Beitrage* 12 (1966), 716–19.

Sperber, Hans. *Motiv und Wort: Studien zur Literatur- und Sprachpsychologie*. Leipzig: Reisland, 1918.

Strelka, Joseph. *Auf der Such nach dem verlorenen Selbst*. Bern: Francke, 1977.

KAREN SCHAAFSMA, "WONDROUS VISION: TRANSFORMATION OF THE HERO IN FANTASY THROUGH ENCOUNTER WITH THE OTHER"

Boyer, Robert H., and Kenneth J. Zahorski. "Science Fiction and Fantasy Literature: Classification through Juxtaposition."*Wisconsin English Journal* 28 (1976), 2–8.

Frye, Northrop. *Anatomy of Criticism*. Princeton: Princeton University Press, 1957.

Manlove, Colin. *Modern Fantasy: Five Studies*. Cambridge: Cambridge University Press, 1975.

Otto, Rudolf. *The Idea of the Holy*. 1923; reprint ed. New York: Oxford University Press, 1958.

Tolkien and the Critics, eds. N. D. Isaacs and R. A. Zimbardo. South Bend: Notre Dame University Press, 1968.

RONALD FOUST, "RITE OF PASSAGE: THE VAMPIRE TALE AS COSMOGONIC MYTH"

Barclay, Glen St. John. *Anatomy of Horror: The Masters of Occult Fiction*. London: Weidenfeld and Nicolson, 1978.

Binderman, Charles S. "Vampurella: Darwin and Count Dracula." *Massachusetts Review* 21 (1980), 411–28.

Carlson, M. M. "What Stoker Saw: An Introduction to the History of the Literary Vampire." *Folklore Forum* 10 (Fall 1977), 26–32.

Eliade, Mircea. *The Sacred and the Profane: The Nature of Religion*, trans. Willard S. Trask. New York: Harper and Row, 1961.

Foust, Ronald. "Monstrous Image: Theory of Fantasy Antagonists." *Genre* 13 (1980), 441–53.

Hennelly, Mark M., Jr. "Dracula: The Gnostic Quest and Victorian Wasteland." *English Literature in Transition* 20 (1977), 13–26.

Hogarth, Peter, and Val Clery. *Dragons*. New York: Viking, 1979.

Hume, Robert D. "Gothic versus Romantic: A Revaluation of the Gothic Novel." *PMLA* 84 (1969), 282–90.

Neumann, Erich. *The Origins and History of Consciousness*, trans. R. F. C. Hull. Princeton: Princeton University Press, 1970.

Newman, Paul. *The Hill of the Dragon*. Totowa, N.J.: Rowman & Littlefield, 1979.

The Portable Jung, trans. R. F. C. Hull. New York: Viking, 1970.

Praz, Mario. *The Romantic Agony*, trans. Angus Davidson. London: Oxford University Press, 1933.
Varma, Devendra. *The Gothic Flame*. New York: Russell and Russell, 1957.

MICHAEL BUDD, R. STEPHEN CRAIG, AND CLAY STEINMAN, *"FANTASY ISLAND*: THE DIALECTIC OF NARCISSISM"

Bordwell, David, and Kristin Thompson. *Film Art: An Introduction*. Reading, Mass.: Addison-Wesley, 1979.
Lasch, Christopher. *The Culture of Narcissism*. New York: Warner Books, 1979.
Williams, Raymond. *Television: Technology and Cultural Form*. New York: Schocken Books, 1974.

J. P. TELOTTE, "CHILDREN OF HORROR: THE FILMS OF VAL LEWTON"

Freud, Sigmund. *Beyond the Pleasure Principle*, trans. James Strachey. New York: Liveright, 1961.
Lubbock, Percy, ed. *The Letters of Henry James*. New York: Scribner, 1920.
Siegel, Joel. *Val Lewton: The Reality of Terror*. New York: Viking, 1973.
Telotte, J. P. "A Photogenic Horror: Lewton Does Robert Louis Stevenson," *Literature/Film Quarterly* 10 (1982), 25–37.

JAMES WHITLARK, "SUPERHEROES AS DREAM DOUBLES"

Crawford, Hubert H. *Crawford's Encyclopedia of Comic Books*. Middle Village, N.Y.: Jonathan David, 1978.
Crawley, A. E. "Doubles." *Encyclopedia of Religion and Ethics*. New York: Scribner, 1951. III, 858.
Feiffer, Jules. *The Great Comic Book Heroes*. New York: Dial Press, 1965.
Gilbert, Calire. *Nerval's Double: A Structural Study*. Romance Monograph Series. University: University of Mississippi Press, 1979.
Glut, Donald F. "Frankenstein Meets the Comics," in *The Comic Book*, eds. Don Thompson and Dick Lupoff, Carlstadt, N.J.: Rainbow Books, 1977.
Grimm, Jakob. *Teutonic Mythology*, trans. James Steven Stallybrass. New York: Dover, 1965.
Horn, Maurice. *The World Encyclopedia of Comics*. New York: Chelsea House, 1976.
Kayton, Lawrence. "The Relationship of the Vampire Legend to Schizophrenia." *Journal of Youth and Adolescence* 1 (1972), 303–14.
Lee, Stan. *Origins of Marvel Comics*. New York: Simon & Schuster, 1974.
Thalmann, Marianne. *The Romantic Fairy Tale: Seeds of Surrealism*. Ann Arbor: University of Michigan Press, 1964.
Tonnelat, E. "Teutonic Mythology," in *New Larousse Encyclopedia of Mythology*, trans. Richard Aldington and Delano Ames. Hong Kong: Hamlyn, 1959.

Wackenroder, Wilhelm Heinrich. *Werke und Briefe*. Heidelberg: Lambert Schneider, 1967.

JEAN-PIERRE LALANDE, "ARTAUD'S THEATRE OF CRUELTY AND THE FANTASTIC"

Breton, André. *Manifestes du surréalisme*. Paris: Gallimard, 1967.
Campbell, R. J. "On Saying the Unsayable." *Critical Quarterly* 22 (1980), 69–77.
Costich, Julia F. *Antonin Artaud*. Boston: Twayne, 1978.
Schneider, Marcel. *La Littérature fantastique en France*. Paris: Fayard, 1964.

ROGER C. SCHLOBIN, "THE SURVIVAL OF THE FOOL IN MODERN HEROIC FANTASY"

Danby, John. "The Fool and Handy Dandy," in *Shakespeare: Modern Essays in Criticism*, ed. Leonard F. Dean. New York: Oxford University Press, 1961.
Fingarette, Herbert. *The Self in Transformation: Psychoanalysis, Philosophy, and the Life of the Spirit*. New York: Harper & Row, 1965.
Goldsmith, Robert Hillis. *Wise Fools in Shakespeare*. East Lansing: Michigan State University Press, 1963.
Jung, C. G. *Psychological Types*, trans. H. G. Baynes; rev. R. F. C. Hull. Princeton: Princeton University Press, 1971.
Langer, Susanne K. *Feeling and Form: A Theory of Art*. New York: Scribner, 1953.
Neumann, Erich. *Depth Psychology and a New Ethic*, trans. Eugene Rolfe. New York: Harper & Row, 1973.
Schlobin, Roger C. *The Literature of Fantasy: A Comprehensive, Annotated Bibliography of Modern Fantasy Fiction*. New York: Garland, 1979.
Welsford, Enid. *The Fool: His Social and Literary History*. London: Faber and Faber, 1935.
Willeford, William. *The Fool and His Scepter: A Study in Clowns and Their Audience*. Evanston: Northwestern University Press, 1969.

MICHAEL R. COLLINGS, "THE EPIC OF *DUNE*: EPIC TRADITIONS IN MODERN SCIENCE FICTION"

Aristotle. *On Poetry and Style*, trans. G. M. A. Grube. New York: Liberal Arts Press, 1958.
Candelaria, Frederick H., and William C. Strange, eds. *Perspectives on Epic*. Boston: Allyn and Bacon, 1965.
Foerster, Donald M. *The Fortunes of Epic Poetry: A Study in English and American Criticism*, 1759–1950. Washington, D.C.: Catholic University Press, 1962.
Pearce, Roy Harvey. "Toward an American Epic." *Hudson Review* 12 (1959), 362–67.
Pommer, Henry F. *Milton and Melville*. Pittsburgh: University of Pittsburgh Press, 1950.
Tillyard, E. M. W. *The English Epic and Its Background*. New York: Oxford University Press, 1966.

JAMES L. HODGE, "TOLKIEN'S MYTHOLOGICAL CALENDAR IN *THE HOBBIT*"

Brockhaus' Konversations-Lexicon. Berlin: Brockhaus, 1903. XVI, 720.
De Vries, Jan. *Keltische Religion*, in *Die Religionen der Menschheit*, ed. Christel Schroder. Stuttgart: Kohlhammer, 1961.
Frazer, Sir James George. *The New Golden Bough*, ed. Theodor H. Gaster. Garden City, N.Y.: Doubleday, 1961.
Rees, Alwyn, and Brinley Rees. *Celtic Heritage*. London: Thames and Hudson, 1961.
Squire, Charles. *Celtic Myth and Legend: Poetry and Romance*. Hollywood, Calif.: Newcastle, 1975.
Strom, Ake V., and Haralds Biezais. *Germanische und Baltische Religion* in *Die Religionen der Menschheit*, ed. Christel Schroder. Stuttgart: Kohlhammer, 1975.
Sturluson, Snorri. *Heimskringla*, trans. Samuel Laing. New York: Dutton, 1961.
———. *The Prose Edda*, trans. Jean I. Young. Berkeley: University of California Press, 1954.
Tuchman, Barbara W. *A Distant Mirror*. New York: Knopf, 1978.

DOUGLAS A. BURGER, "THE SHIRE: A TOLKIEN VERSION OF PASTORAL"

Tolkien, J. R. R. *Tree and Leaf*. London: Unwin, 1964.

RICHARD H. ABRAMS, "LEONTES'S ENEMY: MADNESS IN *THE WINTER'S TALE*"

Barber, C. L. *Shakespeare's Festive Comedies*. Princeton: Princeton University Press, 1959.
Barroll, J. Leeds. *Artificial Persons: The Formation of Character in the Tragedies of Shakespeare*. Columbia: University of South Carolina Press, 1974.
Blissett, William. " 'This Wide Gap of Time' ": *The Winter's Tale*." *English Literary Renaissance* 1 (1971), 52–70.
Girard, René. *Deceit, Desire, and the Novel*, trans. Yvonne Freccero. Baltimore: Johns Hopkins Press, 1965.
Levin, Harry. *The Question of Hamlet*. New York: Oxford University Press, 1959.
Lidz, Theodore. *Hamlet's Enemy: Madness and Myth in Hamlet*. New York: Basic Books, 1975.
Neely, Carol Thomas. "*The Winter's Tale*: The Triumph of Speech," *Studies in English Literature* 15 (1975), 321–38.
Siemon, James Edward." 'But It Appears She Lives': Iteration in *The Winter's Tale*." *PMLA* 89 (1974), 10–16.
VanLaan, Thomas F. *Role-Playing in Shakespeare*. Toronto: University of Toronto Press, 1978.

STEVEN M. TAYLOR, "WANDERERS IN WONDERLAND: FANTASY IN THE WORKS OF CARROLL AND ARRABAL"

Anderson, Irmgard. "From Tweedledum and Tweedledee to Zapo and Zépo." *Romance Notes* 15 (1973), 217–20.

Breton, André. *Manifestes du Surréalisme*. Paris: Gallimard, 1965.

Donahue, Thomas. *The Theater of Fernando Arrabal: A Garden of Earthly Delights*. New York: New York University Press, 1980.

Monléon, José. *Fernando Arrabal: Colección de Teatro*. Madrid: Taurus Edicions, 1965.

Podol, Peter. *Fernando Arrabal*. Boston: Twayne, 1978.

Schifres, Alain. "Arrabal: le Théâtre Panique." *Réalités* 252 (January 1967), 55.

———. *Entretiens avec Arrabal*. Paris: Pierre Belfond, 1969.

WILLIAM COYLE, "MARK TWAIN AS FANTASIST"

Hauck, Richard Boyd. *A Cheerful Nihilism*. Bloomington: Indiana University Press, 1971.

Kahn, Sholem J. *Mark Twain's Mysterious Stranger*. Columbia: University of Missouri Press, 1978.

Kaplan, Justin. *Mr. Clemens and Mark Twain*. New York: Simon & Schuster, 1966.

Macnaughton, William R. *Mark Twain's Last Years as a Writer*. Columbia: University of Missouri Press, 1979.

CONSTANCE D. MARKEY, "THE TAROT CARDS AS A SUBVERSIVE TOOL IN ITALO CALVINO"

Cannon, JoAnn. "Literature as Combinatory Game: Italo Calvino's *The Castle of the Crossed Destinies*." *Critique* 21 (1979), 83–91.

Corti, Maria. "Le jeu comme generation du textes: Des tarots au recit." *Semiotica* 7 (1973), 33–48.

Cullin, Stewart. *Chess and Playing Cards*. Washington, D.C.: Government Printing Office, 1898.

Eliade, Mircea. *The Myth of the Eternal Return*, trans. W. R. Trask. Princeton: Princeton University Press, 1971.

Frye, Northrop. *Fables of Identity: Studies in Poetic Mythology*. New York: Harbinger Books, 1963.

Genot, Gerard. "Le destin des recits entrecroises." *Critique* 28 (1972), 788–809.

Guiraud, Pierre. *Semiology*, trans. George Gross. London: Routledge & Kegan Paul, 1971.

Jung, Carl Gustav. *The Collected Works of C. G. Jung*, trans. R. F. C. Hull, eds. Herbert Read, Michael Fordham, and Gerhard Adler. Princeton: Princeton University Press, 1976.

de Lauretis, Teresa. "Calvino e la dialettica dei massimi sistemi." *Italica* 53 (1976), 57–74.

Leeming, David Adams. *Mythology: The Voyage of the Hero*. New York: Lippincott, 1973.

Ludovici, Sergio Samek. *Tarocchi: Il mazzo Visconteo di Bergamo e New York*. Parma: Franco Maria Ricci editore, 1969.

Mommsen, Theodore. "Petrarch and the Story of the Choice of Hercules." *Journal Warburg & Courtauld Institutes* 16 (1953), 178–93.

de Saussure, Ferdinand. *Course in General Linguistics*, trans. Wade Baskins, eds. Charles Bally and Albert Sechehaye. New York: McGraw-Hill, 1966.

Schneider, Marilyn. "Calvino at a Crossroads: *Il castello dei destini incrociati*." *PMLA* 95 (1980), 73–90.

Scholes, Robert. *Structuralism in Literature*. New Haven: Yale University Press, 1974.

Waite, Arthur Edward. *The Pictorial Key to the Tarot*. Blauvelt, N.Y.: Multimedia Publishing Co., 1974.

RAYMOND H. THOMPSON, "JUNGIAN PATTERNS IN URSULA K. LE GUIN'S *THE FARTHEST SHORE*"

Bailey, Edgar C., Jr., "Shadows in Earthsea: Le Guin's Use of a Jungian Archetype." *Extrapolation* 21 (1980), 254–61.

Cameron, Eleanor. "High Fantasy: A Wizard of Earthsea." *Horn Book* 47 (1971), 129–38.

Esmonde, Margaret P. "The Master Pattern: The Psychological Journey in the Earthsea Trilogy," in *Ursula Le Guin*, eds. Joseph D. Olander, and Martin Harry Greenberg. Writers of the 21st Century Series. New York: Taplinger, 1979.

Lasseter, Rollin A. "Four Letters about Le Guin," in *Ursula Le Guin: Voyager to Inner Lands and to Outer Space*. ed. Joe De Bolt. Port Washington, N.Y.: Kennikat, 1979.

DONALD E. MORSE, "MONKEYS, CHANGELINGS, AND ASSES: AUDIENCE, FANTASY, AND BELIEF"

Bespaloff, Rachel. *On the Iliad*, trans. Mary McCarthy. New York: Pantheon Books, 1947.

THOMAS P. DUNN AND RICHARD D. ERLICH, "ENVIRONMENTAL CONCERNS IN ARTHUR C. CLARKE'S *THE CITY AND THE STARS*"

Dunn, Thomas P. "E. M. Forster's 'The Machine Stops,' " in *Survey of Science Fiction*, ed. Frank W. Magill. Englewood Cliffs, N.J.: Salem Press, 1979.

————, and Richard D. Erlich. "The Mechanical Hive: Urbom 116 as the Villain-Hero of Silverberg's *The World Inside*." *Extrapolation* 21 (1980), 338–47.

————.*Clockwork Worlds: Mechanized Environments in SF*. Westport, Conn.: Greenwood Press, 1983.

Erlich, Richard D. "Trapped in the Bureaucratic Pinball Machine: A Vision of Dystopia in the 20th Century," in *Selected Proceedings of the SFRA 1978 Convention*, ed. Thomas J. Remington. Cedar Falls: University of North Iowa Press, 1979.

Gallagher, Edward J. "From Folded Hands to Clenched Fists: Kesey and Science Fiction." *Lex & Scientia* 13 (January–June 1977), 46–50.

Olander, Joseph D., and Martin H. Greenberg, eds. *Arthur C. Clarke*. New York: Taplinger, 1977.

Rabkin, Eric S. *Arthur C. Clarke*, West Linn, Ore.: Starmont House, 1979.
Rhodes, Carolyn. "Tyranny by Computer: Automated Data Processing and Oppressive Government in Science Fiction," in *Many Futures, Many Worlds*, ed. Thomas D. Clareson. Kent: Kent State University Press, 1977.
Warrick, Patricia. *The Cybernetic Imagination in Science Fiction*. Cambridge: MIT Press, 1980.
Wolfe, Gary K. *The Known and the Unknown: The Iconography of Science Fiction*. Kent: Kent State University Press, 1979.

GEORGE F. SEFLER, "SCIENCE, SCIENCE FICTION, AND POSSIBLE WORLD SEMANTICS"

Grossman, Neal. "Empiricism and the Possibility of Encountering Intelligent Beings with Different Sense-Structures." *Journal of Philosophy* 71 (1974), 815–21.
Kripke, Saul A. "Naming and Necessity," in D. Davidson and G. Harmon, eds., *Semantics of Natural Language*. Dordrecht: D. Reidel, 1972.
Putnam, Hilary. "Meaning and Reference." *Journal of Philosophy* 70 (1973), 699–711.
Quine, W. V. *Words and Objects*. Cambridge: MIT Press, 1960.
Sagan, Carl. *Cosmic Connection*. New York: Doubleday, 1973.

DON D. ELGIN, "THE COMEDY OF FANTASY: AN ECOLOGICAL PERSPECTIVE OF JOY CHANT'S *RED MOON AND BLACK MOUNTAIN*"

Meeker, Joseph. *The Comedy of Survival: Studies in Literary Ecology*. New York: Scribner, 1974.

Index

About the Contributors

RICHARD H. ABRAMS is Assistant Professor of English at the University of Southern Maine. He writes on Shakespeare and Dante.

RUTH B. ANTOSH is Assistant Professor of French at Colgate University. She has presented papers on the role of fantasy and dreams in the works of J. K. Huysmans and is now completing a book on Michel Tremblay.

MICHAEL BUDD, R. STEPHEN CRAIG, and CLAY STEINMAN are Associate Professors of Communication at Florida Atlantic University, where they teach courses in film history, film criticism, and broadcasting.

DOUGLAS A. BURGER is Associate Professor of English at the University of Colorado, where he regularly teaches a course in the literature of fantasy. He has presented papers on J. R. R. Tolkien at several professional meetings and has published in *Chaucer Review*.

MICHAEL R. COLLINGS, Associate Professor of English at Pepperdine University, has published *Piers Anthony*, as well as articles on relationships between fantasy and language and on Ursula K. Le Guin, Roger Zelazny, Brian W. Aldiss, and other writers. He is Secretary of the International Association for the Fantastic in the Arts and edits *Thaumaturge* for that group.

ROBERT A. COLLINS, Associate Professor of English at Florida Atlantic University, organized the first three conferences on the Fantastic in the Arts. He is currently editing *Fantasy Review*, for which he received a Balrog award in 1982, and is preparing a full-length critical biography of Thomas B. Swann.

WILLIAM COYLE Is Professor of English at Florida Atlantic University. He has written a variety of critical articles and textbooks and has edited several reference books, including this one.

THOMAS P. DUNN and RICHARD D. ERLICH are Associate Professors of English at Miami University, Ohio. In collaboration and individually, they have published numerous articles on science fiction as it relates to mechanized environments and on Ursula K. Le Guin, Frederik Pohl, C. M. Kornbluth, and other authors. They have edited two collections of scholarly essays for Greenwood Press: *The Mechanical God* and *Clockwork Worlds*.

DON D. ELGIN is Associate Professor of Humanities at the University of Houston-Downtown. His major teaching and research interests are fantasy and its relation to contemporary issues.

RONALD FOUST is Assistant Professor of English at Loyola University of the South, where he teaches courses in fantasy, science fiction, and literary criticism. He has published articles in a number of journals and is currently working on a book-length study of American fantasist Abraham Merritt.

JAMES L. HODGE, Professor of Modern Languages and Chairman of the German Department at Bowdoin College, has published numerous articles on myth, folklore, and fantasy.

ROSEMARY JACKSON, a Senior Lecturer in Literature, Bristol Polytechnic, England, has written reviews and articles on nineteenth-century fantasy and on the relationship of psychoanalysis to literary theory. In 1981 she published *Fantasy: The Literature of Subversion*, and she is presently studying women's writing in relation to language, the unconscious, and spirituality.

LEE B. JENNINGS is Professor of German at the University of Illinois at Chicago. He has published extensively on myth, archetype, and the grotesque in German literature and is presently writing a study of E. T. A. Hoffman and eros.

JEAN-PIERRE LALANDE is Assistant Professor of French and Latin at Moravian College, Bethlehem, Pennsylvania. He is particularly interested in Surrealism and in the use of fantastic devices in the theatre of Sartre, Beckett, and Ionesco.

CONSTANCE D. MARKEY is an Instructor in Italian at Loyola University, Chicago. She has presented papers on Italian literature and on film at a number of professional meetings.

DONALD E. MORSE, Chairman of the Department of Rhetoric, Communications and Journalism, Oakland University, Rochester, Michigan, recently completed a term as President of the College English Association. He has published articles on Joyce, Auden, and Donleavy and on professional issues. He is currently doing research on Irish fantasy.

ALICE PARKER is Assistant Professor of Romance Languages at the University of Alabama. Her major fantasy interests involve mythic systems, goddess worship, mystery religions, and similar subjects as they relate to feminist themes.

JOAN PÉREZ is Professor of Spanish at Texas Tech University and Editor for Spanish, Twayne World Authors Series. Her academic specialty is twentieth-century Spanish literature, especially post-Civil War Castilian and Catalan writers.

KAREN SCHAAFSMA is an Instructor in English and a doctoral candidate at University of California, Davis. In her research she is analyzing the relationship between the hero in fantasy and the supernatural Other.

ROGER C. SCHLOBIN, Associate Professor of English at Purdue University, North Central Campus, is the compiler of *The Literature of Fantasy: A Comprehensive Annotated Bibliography* (1979) and *André Norton: A Primary and Secondary Bibliography* (1980). He is the editor of *The Aesthetics of Fantasy Literature and Art* (1982), the Starmont Reader's Guides to Contemporary Science Fiction and Fantasy Authors (1979—), and the Garland Library of Fantasy Classics (1982). He is a frequent speaker at conferences; has published numerous essays, bibliographies, and reviews; and serves as consultant for a number of publications and other projects.

GEORGE F. SEFLER is Professor of Philosophy and Dean of the School of Humanities, Education and Social Sciences at Purdue University Calumet, Hammond, Indiana. He has published a number of articles on philosophy, language, and science fiction.

STEVEN M. TAYLOR is Assistant Professor of French at Marquette University. He has published several articles on medieval, French literature and nineteenth-century French and Russian literature.

J. P. TELOTTE is Assistant Professor of English at Georgia Institute of Technology, where he teaches courses in film and modern literature. He has published articles on film in a number of journals. His particular interest is horror and fantasy films, and he is completing a book on the subject.

RAYMOND H. THOMPSON, Associate Professor of English at Acadia University, Nova Scotia, teaches medieval literature, fantasy, and science fiction.

His major research interests are the Arthurian legend and the novels of Gordon R. Dickson.

JAMES WHITLARK is Assistant Professor of English at Texas Tech University. He is particularly interested in Oriental occultism and its relation to British and American literature.

DATE DUE

ILL 3/6/89	ILL 12-1-06		
ILL 12/3/89			
FEB 8 1990			
ILL 4/19/92			
SEP 30 1992			
ILL 12/8/93			
ILL 11/17/95			
APR 5 1998			
ILL 5/17/03			
AUG 2 0 2005			
NOV 2 8 2005			
GAYLORD			PRINTED IN U.S.A.